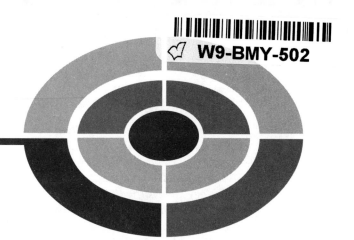

Accounting
Demystified

OTHER BOOKS IN THE DEMYSTIFIED SERIES

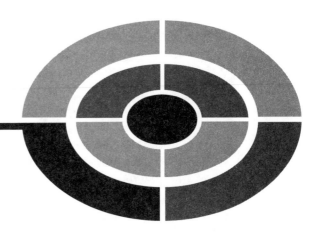

Accounting Demystified

A Self-Teaching Guide

LEITA A. HART, CPA

McGRAW-HILL
New York   Chicago   San Francisco   Lisbon   London
Madrid   Mexico City   Milan   New Delhi   San Juan
Seoul   Singapore   Sydney   Toronto

The McGraw-Hill Companies

4 5 6 7 8 9 0   FGR/FGR   0 9 8 7 6

ISBN 0-07-145083-1

This publication is designed to provide accurate and authoritative information in regard to the subject matter covered. It is sold with the understanding that neither the author nor the publisher is engaged in rendering legal, accounting, or other professional service. If legal advice or other expert assistance is required, the services of a competent professional person should be sought.

> —From a Declaration of Principles jointly adopted by
> Committee of the American Bar Association and a
> Committee of Publishers.

McGraw-Hill books are available at special quantity discounts to use as premiums and sales promotions, or for use in corporate training programs. For more information, please write to the Director of Special Sales, McGraw-Hill Professional, Two Penn Plaza, New York, NY 10121-2298. Or contact your local bookstore.

 This book is printed on recycled, acid-free paper containing a minimum of 50% recycled, de-inked fiber.

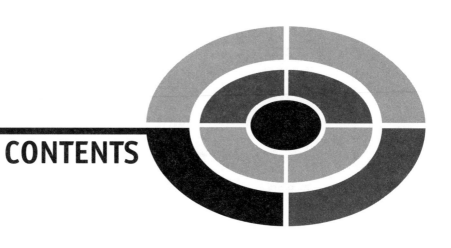

CONTENTS

Contents

Contents

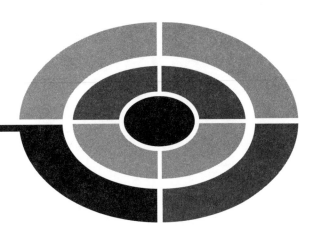

Acknowledgments

My husband told me not to write this book and then went ahead and supported me in my efforts anyway. So for his kindness, patience, and love, I dedicate this book to him. Jeff, you are a wonderful husband and father. You are a giver deluxe, and I am so lucky to be married to you.

I must also thank my baby Grace for arriving on schedule and for arriving healthy. Grace and Sara, you are precious to me.

And thanks to John Woods of CWL Publishing Enterprises, who recruited me to write this book and to Bob Magnan, also of CWL, who edited to help pull the final manuscript together.

And God, thank you for dropping this project in my lap: it is good to know that you are looking out for us.

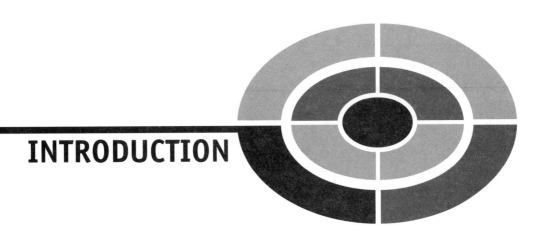

INTRODUCTION

Why Is Accounting Important?

I was out of school and had my CPA (Certified Public Accountant) license for several years before all the debit and credit micro detail the professors stuffed into my brain started to make real sense. And only after teaching the language of accounting and finance to others did it really become clear. An old Japanese proverb instructs, "Those who want to learn must teach." Very true in my case.

When I was asked questions, I was forced to take all my technical, detailed knowledge and distill it so that I could answer the question in an understandable and clear way. And that is what this book is all about—answering your questions in an understandable and clear way.

I don't know why the professors choose to start the first week with a discussion of debits and credits. I have a sneaking suspicion that, at my alma mater at least, it was a way to weed out tentative, unsure students. You had to be pretty darn sure you wanted to be a business major to sit through and memorize all that stuff.

I am not going to put you through that experience. You bought this book hoping I'd make the subject easy, and I am going to do everything I can to make it painless. I find that many learners like to start with the big picture first. Many like to know why they need to know something before they just memorize a bunch of rules. So in Part One, debits and credits are mentioned only once. The emphasis is on grasping the big picture.

In Part Two, I go into more detail. Here we discuss debits and credits and inventory valuation and exciting stuff like that. But I am not going to discuss obscure transactions, such as the repurchase of preferred stock under stock option plans. (It is scary to just write that sentence!) I imagine that would be

more detail than 99 percent of the readers of this book need. If you want that sort of detail, please consult accounting standards (through the Financial Accounting Standards Board and/or the Governmental Accounting Standards Board), an accounting professor, or an advanced accounting text.

In Part Three, I discuss how financial information is used in business and various business information systems. In this section we cover budgeting and cost accounting and how those systems differ from general ledger or financial accounting. I also talk about how governmental and not-for-profit accounting has its own special way of doing things.

And in the last part, we take everything from the first three parts and perform a high-level financial analysis on two competitors and raise some interesting questions about their performance.

So we go from the big picture, to detail, to practical application.

Why Should You Learn This Stuff?

Good question! It might seem easier to just leave all this technical stuff up to someone else so that you can focus on your job. Maybe you are in marketing, sales, product design, administration, quality—anywhere but in the finance and accounting department! You have successfully avoided the topic so far, but it just keeps coming up in meetings and conversations. It is like a nagging grandmother, always there, always hoping you will call.

Not understanding the language of business and leaving money decisions in the hands of accountants are bad ideas for several reasons:

- Accountants don't know your job, the real goings-on of the business, as well as you do. They shouldn't tell you how things should be.
- Accountants might make bad decisions. I don't know how many times I hear managers complain of how they are being victimized by a stringent and unreasonable budget created by the accountant. Big mistake! The accountant shouldn't have created the budget; the manager should have done it.
- You are ultimately responsible for results. When things go well or go badly, it is you that upper management looks to. Accountants don't make sales, do marketing, or design new products; often, all they do is compile and report data. You'd do well to keep informed of what is going on financially so you can answer tough questions or consciously bask in praise.

- You want your career to go somewhere. Maybe you have noticed that the further you move up the chain of command in your organization, the more you hear talk about money. If you can't talk the talk, you won't be promoted to walk the walk.
- Accountants and other financially savvy members of your team might be snowing or manipulating you. You might have a sneaking suspicion that things are going on that you don't know about because you don't know what you don't know. In other words, how can you ask about something you know nothing about? Information is power.
- You would like to stay engaged during management meetings where financial results are discussed. When computer experts talk to me, they can quickly tell that they have surpassed my level of understanding when I start nodding and smiling in a glazed manner. This does nothing to enhance my credibility or stature with that computer expert. Not knowing what is going on in finance can be a detriment to your credibility with upper management. Wouldn't it be nice to be able to participate in a discussion about money?
- Business is about making money. You might think it is about the product or marketing or sales. But it's all about money: The reason that you have a product and market it and sell it is to make money. And accounting is the language of money.
- Accounting really isn't all that hard. It is just a system and a language. Hey, if I can learn it, so can you!

Accounting Is Just a System and a Language

You see, accounting is one of the oldest systems around for tracking data. In business, someone has always wanted to know how much money was made or lost. For centuries, accountants have kindly kept track of the dollars that flow in and out of organizations of all types.

The systems that have been set up to track this information can be—and I emphasize *can* be—difficult to use and interpret. The debit and credit stuff can get pretty confusing. But with a little effort, I know that you will be able to extract some information that will help you make decisions about what to do next in your business.

For example, most accounting systems will spit out data on how much it costs to create a product or provide a service. Now why do we care about this? Because we must price our product or service for more than we spent on it. Selling something for more than you put into it is called a *business*. Selling something for less than you put into it is called a *hobby*!

You might also want to know how well your sales staff is doing at pushing your latest gizmo. Your accounting system should be able to tell you volume of sales per salesperson as well as the customers to whom they are selling the gizmos. This can be very useful data if you want to determine whom to reward and whom to send back to sales school.

Some Accounting Systems Are Real-Time and Very Detailed

Any basic accounting system will tell you simple things like how much cash you took in today and how much you paid out today. Accounting systems track all of the money that goes in and out of the business and categorizes the ins and outs into useful groups so we can judge where the money came from and what it was used for. Bottom line:

All accounting is *a counting*.

But some businesses believe that accounting can and should do more for them. For this extra bit of tracking, for this extra counting effort, if you will, they pay in both time and money.

One *Fortune* 500 Company invested a huge amount of time and effort in creating a daily accounting report that told how many products it was selling, how it was selling the products (by phone, by Internet, in stores), and what kind of profit each product generated. They decided it was worth it for them to get immediate feedback on whether the bells and whistles they were offering their customers were selling. If they weren't selling, they changed offerings immediately. They didn't want to waste a week, a month, or a quarter hawking low-demand goods. The accounting system gave them power to make decisions quickly.

In most decisions in business, an evaluation has to be made as to whether the cost is worth the resulting benefit. The same must be said of accounting. What is the information worth to you?

But before we can even make that decision, you need to know what kind of information a basic accounting system can provide and you need to understand the terminology behind it.

I hate to tell you this, but accountants are not working at changing their tunes—or their terminology—any time soon. Mohammed (that's you) is going to have to go to the mountain (that's accounting terminology, information, and accountants). I am glad you have decided to take this journey with me. I will make the mountains into little, tiny, bumpy hills for you.

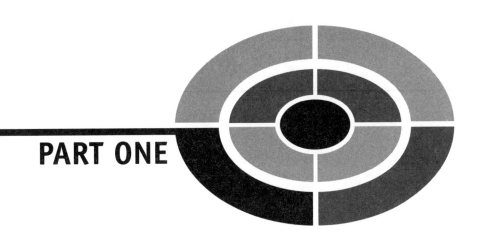

PART ONE

The Big Picture

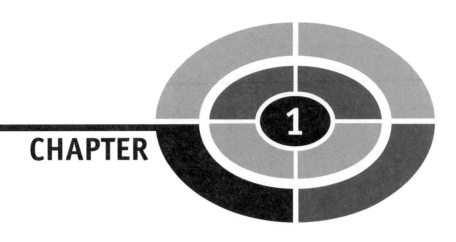

CHAPTER 1

Where Did All This Lingo Come From?

Business is very simple. Money flows into an organization and money flows out. But we in the finance and accounting profession sometimes get a little out of hand giving fancy names to very simple concepts. This fancy lingo can cause more than a little bit of confusion. So it is helpful to envision accounting as a foreign language. Most of the rules and concepts are perfectly intuitive and simple; you just have to know what to call them.

The title of this book, *Accounting Demystified*, is very appropriate. It is definitely attributing too much romance and intrigue to the profession to call it a mystery, but it does probably sell a few more books than the title *Clarifying Accounting Lingo*. (That is why I am writing and someone else is marketing this book!)

What I want to do for you is give you the ability to have an intelligent conversation with an accountant or finance person. I want you to be able to justify your actions in terms that the folks holding the purse strings can understand and appreciate. I want you to be able to go to meetings with your management team and understand what the heck they are talking about. I don't want you to have to nod your head like you understand, when you don't, so I am going to give you the knowledge to ask intelligent questions regarding finance.

What I am not going to do is bore you or muddy the waters with a load of unnecessary detail. You know, I was out of college and already had my CPA certificate before all the detail the accounting professors had me memorize gelled together in my head to form a big picture. I am going to take the opposite approach with you. We are going to start with the big picture and then go into a bit of detail. We are not going to go into super detail. I think it is best to keep it at a high level.

I am not going to tell you how to handle an advance repurchase agreement on stock or how to calculate a bond discount. This is too much detail for 99.99 percent of the population—and probably you. But if you do need this kind of detail, this book will give you the basis to start asking those questions and understanding what the finance person says in response.

As Glinda the Good Witch says in *The Wizard of Oz*, "It is always best to start at the beginning." So let's take a minute to get a sense of how this system we have in place began a long time ago. It actually started in a very romantic and sometimes mysterious and dramatic place, Italy.

The Birth of the Accountant

The system we use today to track money in business was invented in Italy during the Renaissance. An Italian merchant invented it so that he could easily summarize his results at the end of the day. The system had a simple system of checks and balances to make sure that everything he had recorded was done correctly.

The Italian merchant called his system the double-entry accounting system, and it was very simple to understand. Each and every transaction must balance. The "ins" had to equal the "outs." This is the root of debits and credits that we will talk about in more detail in Chapter 6.

For instance, let's say this merchant sold jewelry. When he sold a piece of jewelry, the jewelry went *out* of his business. But, in return, something came *in*—some cash. Through a series of entries into his books, the ins would equal the outs.

With this system, he could make sure that every transaction was recorded completely, because the books had to balance. If the books didn't balance, he knew he had missed something.

This system was also useful in that it posted the information to discrete accounts or categories that could be summarized at the end of the day. He could look at his cash account category and see how much cash he had brought in that day; he could look at his jewelry inventory category to see how much jewelry he had left to sell. All very convenient.

This system was so convenient and useful that he decided to share it with his friends. His friends liked it and, because Italy was a trade center, soon businesses all over the world were using the system. (Don't ask me what they were doing previous to this; I imagine just keeping a list of cash on long sheets of parchment.)

But the folks who were the most excited about this new system were the lenders—the banks and financiers who gave merchants money to expand their businesses. Before this system, they had to rely on subjective information to decide who to loan money to. They made decisions based on family reputation, where they lived, what kind of carriage they drove. Now they could decide based on some real hard data.

The only problem is that everyone's data looked a little different because they all used different rules. They chose how to treat a transaction according to how good it made their books look.

For example, let's say that you are a sales representative for the famous artist Michelangelo. Your job is to find him commissions so that he can concentrate on his art, not on selling. The head of the Medici family, a very influential and wealthy Italian family, has commissioned Michelangelo—through you—to sculpt a replica of David for the foyer of their villa.

When do you record a sale in your books? When you shake hands with the head of the Medici clan and say, "We'll have it to you in three years"? Or when Michelangelo puts chisel to marble? Or when the statue is installed in the villa? Do you record a sale when you bill for the statue or when the Medicis pay in cash?

All of these viewpoints had validity. The lenders didn't like this at all. They desired consistency. They wanted everyone to use the same rules so that the financial statements would be comparable. They wanted to know, when choosing to invest in one of three businesses, which business was actually doing better.

The lenders demanded rules so everyone would be consistent. It was then that accountants were born. Accountants are just the folks who know the rules on how to keep the records consistent. A dark day in the annals of history, I know, but ....

Gaps in GAAP?

Nowadays accounting rules are voluminous. The standards that accountants use to create financial statements are called *generally accepted accounting principles* (GAAP). There is a set of GAAP that applies to most everyone, and then there is GAAP for specific industries. The oil and gas business has different transactions than a software developer, so we have to have different rules for each group.

GAAP is created by a rulemaking body called the Financial Accounting Standards Board (FASB, pronounced faz-bee). Governmental entities, such as cities or counties, have their own rule-setting body called the Governmental Accounting Standards Board (GASB, pronounced gaz-bee).

Unfortunately, GAAP is full of gaps or loopholes. GAAP is designed to make financial statements comparable and consistent. And generally, most transactions are treated conservatively, meaning that transactions are not recorded until we are absolutely sure that the transaction will occur or has actually occurred.

But some organizations take advantage of the gaps in GAAP just to make their financial statements look a little bit better than their competitors' statements. Wealthy folks hire savvy tax accountants to find shelters for their wealth so they don't have to pay so much tax. Corporations hire savvy accountants to enhance their financial results. In essence, the tax accountant is hired to take advantage of the loopholes in the tax code. Well, GAAP is also full of these loopholes. You can't think of everything someone would do.

In the early 2000s, Enron was caught taking advantages of these loopholes to puff up its financial results. Two years after the scandal broke, many members of the Enron executive team were still roaming free. Enron saw a loophole in GAAP and took full advantage of it.

Now, WorldCom was another story. The leaders at WorldCom took a hard-and-fast GAAP rule and broke it outright. They were immediately arrested and jailed.

And now that it appears that the accounting profession did not do a very good job regulating itself with GAAP and licensing efforts, the federal government has stepped in to create even more rules and regulations for the accountant to follow.

Have I turned you off from a career in accounting yet? Wait, there's more! No, actually, I'll stop. It is too depressing to go on.

Another related profession was invented at this time. It is the group that comes in to make sure that you are following GAAP. Right—it's the auditors. Talk about some shakeups in a profession,. but that is another story for another book.

One Huge Database

Now, back to this double-entry accounting system. How many transactions to you think a behemoth organization like IBM has per day? I don't even know, but I know it's plenty—tens of thousands, at least.

All of these transactions are captured in a huge database. Every company has one; it is called the *general ledger*. This general ledger, like any database, has fields of information. And according to how detailed you want to get, it can have dozens of fields of information. Information the general ledger captures includes:

- date of transaction
- amount of transaction
- debit or credit
- account title and code
- budget code
- vendor
- purchase order number
- invoice number
- payment date
- payment method

And the general ledger, just like any database, can be sorted just about any way you want. Accountants will tell you that is not true, because they don't want to generate a bunch of different reports, but they can sort it by date, by amount, by account, by budget code....

So let's pretend that you and I work at IBM. You are a muckety-muck executive manager and I am your accountant. I am not very customer focused: I just enter transactions and tell people "No" all day. So I print out the general ledger for the week on that green-and-white striped general ledger paper with the holes in the side and I load it on a dolly. It is sorted by date entered. How big do you think that stack would be? It could easily take me several dollies to deliver the report to you.

So I walk into your office and dump the report at your feet and say, "Happy decision making!" and walk out. My job is done.

Is this what you want? No, you don't want all this detail; you want a summary.

The Three Key Financial Statements Are Just Summaries

That is all the three key financial statements are—summaries of the general ledger from three different perspectives. They are the summaries that everyone is used to seeing and using. Every publicly traded company in the United States generates these three key financial statements.

The *balance sheet* (Figure 1.1) is the super summary of the general ledger. It is the general ledger rolled up into as few categories as possible.

Balance Sheet	
Assets	**Liabilities**
Cash	Accounts Payable
Investments	Long-Term Debt
Accounts Receivable	
Inventory	**Equity**
Fixed Assets	
Intangibles	Stock
	Retained Earnings

Figure 1.1 Balance sheet model

The balance sheet is called the balance sheet because it has to balance, just like the general ledger does and just like every transaction entered into the general ledger does.

I also call the balance sheet the mother of all financial statements. The other two financial statements are the babies of this mother.

Over the centuries, someone said, "I appreciate your sharing this balance sheet with me, but I could use a little more detail. In particular, I could use a little more detail about how you generated earnings." So we put a little magnifying glass on retained earnings and tracked how earnings were generated with the *earnings statement*.

Some call it the *income statement* (Figure 1.2), some the *profit and loss statement*, the *P&L*, or even the *statement of earnings*. No matter what it is called, it picks out only transactions from the general ledger that contributed to the earnings or the profit that the organization generated. It is the baby of the balance sheet, giving us detail only on earnings.

```
┌─────────────────────────────────────────┐
│           Income Statement              │
│                                         │
│   Sales                                 │
│   Less cost of goods sold               │
│   ─────────────────────────────        │
│   Gross margin                          │
│   Less operating costs                  │
│   ─────────────────────────────        │
│   Operating margin                      │
│   Less taxes, other                     │
│   ─────────────────────────────        │
│   Net income or net profit margin       │
│                                         │
└─────────────────────────────────────────┘
```

Figure 1.2 Income statement model

The third key financial statement was only recently added to the bunch. The FASB started requiring it after our last big nationwide financial crisis, the savings and loan crisis. It, too, is a baby of the balance sheet because it takes one item off the balance sheet and gives us more detail on where it came from. It focuses on cash, my favorite business asset.

The *cash flow statement* is very similar to your bank account statement that you get at home. It tells you how much money you started the month with, how much cash you paid out, how much cash you deposited, and how much cash is left at the end of the month. (See Figure 1.3.)

```
┌─────────────────────────────────────────┐
│         Cash Flow Statement             │
│                                         │
│   Beginning CASH                        │
│   Plus CASH collected                   │
│   Less CASH paid                        │
│   ─────────────────────────────        │
│   Ending CASH                           │
│                                         │
└─────────────────────────────────────────┘
```

Figure 1.3 Cash flow statement model

Cash is the lifeblood of business; without it, you can't pay payroll, pay bills, or buy any inventory to sell.

Each of these financial statements will be described in greater detail in later chapters.

All of the statements put together tell a story about the business—and every story is unique. The income statement for a service business will look entirely different from the income statement for a manufacturing operation. OK, not entirely different, but different enough to make it interesting.

And these three key financial statements contain about 80 percent of the business lingo that finance and accounting folks throw around on a regular basis. So if you get a grip on them, understand what they tell you and don't tell you, and how they are related to each other, you will have mastered a good portion of business speak.

Liquidity, Profitability, Growth, and Financing

Most stories of how well a business is doing focus on four main questions:

- How flexible or liquid is the organization?
- How profitable is the organization?
- What are the growth rate and growth potential of this organization?
- How is the business financed?

Each of these questions—except for the growth question—can be answered by looking at the three key financial statements. Let's first look at the balance sheet and discuss liquidity and financing.

Quiz

1. The double-entry accounting system is thus called because
   - (a) it was invented by an Italian
   - (b) it was invented during the Renaissance
   - (c) you have to enter every transaction two or more times
   - (d) each entry has two sides to it—a debit and a credit

2. GAAP stands for
   - (a) generally accepted auditing practices
   - (b) generally accepted accounting practices
   - (c) generally accepted accounting principles
   - (d) government accepted accounting procedures
   - (e) generally accepted accounting procedures

3. The GASB makes accounting rules for small businesses.
   T or F

4. The database of accounting information is called
   (a) the accounting ledger
   (b) the general ledger
   (c) the transaction database
   (d) the annual financial report

5. The three key financial statements are
   (a) the balance sheet, the statement of activities, and the statement of owners' equity
   (b) the balance sheet, the statement of activities, and the cash flow statement
   (c) the balance sheet, the income statement, and the cash flow statement

6. The three key financial statements are
   (a) unorganized lists of accounting data
   (b) summaries of the general ledger
   (c) too detailed to use

7. The balance sheet
   (a) is the super-summary of the general ledger
   (b) is the mother of all financial statements
   (c) must balance
   (d) all of the above

8. Aliases for the income statement include
   (a) the P&L
   (b) the profit and loss statement
   (c) the statement of earnings
   (d) all of the above

9. The cash flow statement is similar to
   (a) a cash register receipt
   (b) an income statement
   (c) a balance sheet
   (d) a bank account statement

10. The bottom line on the income statement is called
    (a) net income
    (b) net worth
    (c) owners' equity
    (d) net assets

11. Balance sheet components include
    (a) fixed assets, net income, and cash
    (b) fixed assets, cash, and accounts payable
    (c) cash, cost of goods sold, and operating expenses

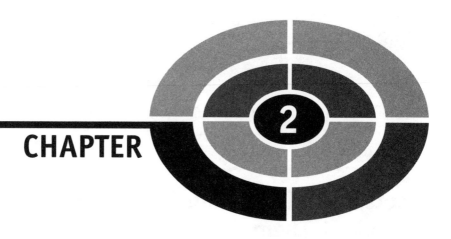

CHAPTER 2

The Balance Sheet— The Mother of All Financial Statements

The balance sheet was probably the very first financial statement ever created. It expresses the relationship that is basic to the double-entry accounting system:

$$Assets = Liabilities + Equity$$

So on one side of the balance sheet, we see the assets. On the other side, we see liabilities and equity.

Assets – Liabilities = Equity
☺   ☹   ☺ or ☹

This relationship among assets, liabilities, and equity actually makes better sense if we view it from another angle.

Assets, Liabilities, and Equity: Another Way to Look at Them

The basic equation of the balance sheet is:

Assets = Liabilities + Equity

A more intuitive way to express this equation is shown in Figure 2.1.

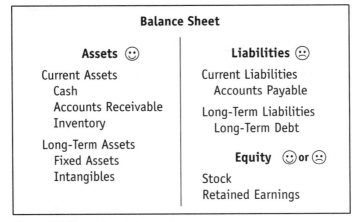

Figure 2.1 Happy face balance sheet

Or, in very simple language:

Happy − Sad = Either Happy or Sad

Assets are happy things that you own.

Liabilities are sad amounts that you owe other people.

Equity is the difference between the two—either a happy or sad remaining balance.

Equity is a concept that many of us are comfortable with because of our homes. We have equity in our homes because the amount that the house is worth is more than the amount we owe on it.

Have you refinanced your house recently? When you did, they asked you for all sorts of information on your financial health and ability to repay the loan. You probably created a personal balance sheet for the lender (Figure 2.2).

The first thing you did was to list all of your assets—all the cool stuff you own that you could sell off for cash if you needed, in order to repay the loan. Your assets would include the house, a car, some investments, your retirement account, a beach house, some jewelry, etc.

Then you had to list all of your liabilities—the amounts you owed on all this stuff. So you had to list your mortgage, your car note, your beach house mortgage, and your credit card debt.

Personal Balance Sheet

Things You Own ☺	**Amounts You Owe Others** ☹
Cash in the bank	Home mortgage
Investments in brokerage account	Car #1 note
Retirement account	Car #2 note
House	Beach house mortgage
Car #1	Boat note
Car #2	Credit card debt
Beach house	
Boat	Happy Reminder ☺
Jewelry	Net Worth
Furnishings, art	

Figure 2.2 Personal balance sheet

The difference between the two—assets and liabilities—is your equity or, in personal terms, net worth. You have heard the term net worth applied to wealthy folks. "Ross Perot has a net worth of $10 billion" or whatever. This does not mean that Ross Perot has $10 billion in a bank account in Switzerland; it means that his stuff is worth $10 billion more than he owes on it. He has equity in his real estate and business holdings.

Businesses are like this, too. They list their assets and then their liabilities. The remainder is the equity that has built up in the company.

By the way, in government, this remainder is called *fund balance*—but more about that in Chapter 12.

Two Mistakes in Reasoning

In teaching this topic, live, I see my participants making two mistakes over and over, so I want to warn you about them. On the right-hand side of our balance sheet are two categories of items—a liability category and an equity category. Equity is not a subset of the liability category; it is an entirely different category unto itself.

The second mistake people make is that they want to link one side of the balance sheet to the other. For instance, they want to say that retained earnings is in cash. Remember that the balance sheet is the super summary of the general ledger. It rolls up the information in the general ledger—thousands, sometimes hundreds of thousands of transactions—and categorizes the data into just a few key accounts. So you can't and shouldn't try to link one side to the other.

Now, How Do We Use the Balance Sheet to Make Decisions?

The balance sheet tells us three crucial stories. First, it tells us who, in essence, owns the business. Second, it tells us how lean and mean the organization is running. And third it tells us how liquid the organization is. Let's cover each of these stories in turn.

THE FIRST QUESTION THE BALANCE SHEET ANSWERS: WHO OWNS THE BUSINESS?

When you first open the doors of your business, you have two places to get money: either by taking out a loan or by selling ownership, or stock, in your business to others or to yourself. Look at the right-hand side of our balance sheet model (Figure 2.3). You will not have any retained earnings or accounts payable on day one because you have not created or sold anything.

So let's first look at debt and stock.

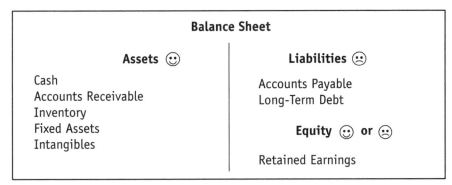

Figure 2.3 Balance sheet model

When You Have Debt, the Lenders Own the Business

Long-term debt is loans that the business took out either to expand or to just plain operate. When you have a loan, in essence, the bank owns your business. Just as when you have a home mortgage, you don't really own your house until you pay the bank the final principal payment.

What do banks expect in return for doing business with you? They expect interest. So doing business with banks costs something. They expect to be paid on a regular basis. You cannot skip payments for a few years at your convenience. If you do that, they will call the loan and come take away the stuff you pledged as collateral.

And if you are what they consider a high-risk loan client, they might require you to do all sorts of things in the loan agreement. Clauses of the loan agreement are called *loan covenants*. Loan covenants are promises that you make to the bank in return for getting the money. The bank doesn't ever give you $10 million and say, "Go have a good time." There is always a catch.

I have seen loan covenants that require the borrower to keep a certain amount of cash in the lending bank at all times. Covenants might require you to keep inventory levels at a certain amount or limit debt with other lenders. If you fall outside of their dictated parameters, you have "busted the covenants" and the bank can call your loan.

If you are super high risk, the loan covenants can require you to replace members of your board of directors with bank officers or require that you report to them on a daily basis the results of your operations. A friend of mine was a CFO for a company that had filed for bankruptcy. The bank decided to loan them more money in hopes that the money they had already invested in the company would not go to waste. My friend had to create the three key financial statements, plus a detail on sales prospects and inventory balances on a daily basis and send it to the bank. The bank also kicked the owners off the board and replaced them with a few business consultants that they believed could turn the company around.

If you take the money, you also take these terms.

When You Have Stock, the Stockholders Own the Business

Now, if you have stockholders as the owners of your company, you worry about a different set of issues. Stockholders expect two types of return on their investment. One is to share in the wealth in the form of dividends. Many companies do not pay dividends. A dividend is usually declared on a quarterly or annual basis and is meant to take the profit that the company made and pay it out in cash to the shareholders. In growth companies, the stockholders prefer that the company, instead of paying them the cash, take the extra profits and plow them back into the company. This will give the investors the second type of return that they are looking for—growth of the value of the stock. If the company plows the profits back in and grows in market share or creates exciting new products, the worth of the stock goes up.

The shareholders have a lot of power. They have the right to vote anytime the articles of incorporation of the business are changed. You can liken the articles of incorporation to the U.S. Constitution. The articles spell out how the business is organized, how many folks are on the board of directors, how often they meet, what the mission of the organization is, if they pay dividends and when, how many shares of stock can be issued, etc.

But even more important is the shareholders' power to choose the leaders of the corporation. They get to choose who sits on the board of directors. The board of directors chooses the executive management, and executive management chooses every other player in the organization. It is not uncommon for the shareholders to get together and vote new directors in, thus influencing the future of the company. So the shareholders are at the top of the food chain.

Corporations, then, end up doing things to please their shareholders that might not be beneficial to the internal operations of the company. I was teaching a Finance for Nonfinancial Managers course at a *Fortune* 500 company a few years ago on the day that the company announced its quarterly results to Wall Street. Unfortunately, the company did not make its projected revenue figures and they expected that their stock price would plummet as a result.

So to prove to Wall Street and the shareholders that they were serious about maintaining profitability, they laid off thousands of people on the same day they announced quarterly results. I was told that the team that had hired me had been eliminated and that I was welcome to finish the day's training, but they weren't sure when they would have me back. (I was back after the next quarter, by the way.)

This move did indeed stabilize the stock price. It only decreased by pennies; the stockholders loved the move. But internally, the *Fortune* 500 company was in turmoil for half a year. Morale went down the toilet. So what looked good from the outside, to investors, might not have been the best move internally.

So to summarize, by financing your organization with stock, you might be taking on an obligation to pay dividends on a regular basis *and* you give up some control of your business, as shareholders are the top of the food chain.

When You Have Retained Earnings, the Business Owns the Business

Now, when you have retained earnings, the company owns the company. Retained earnings are the earnings or profit that the company made that it holds and doesn't pay out as dividends.

What Can You Do with Profits?

When you make a profit, three things can happen to your money. The first is mandatory: you have to pay out a good chunk of your profit in taxes. With the remainder, you can either pay the owners or stockholders dividends or retain it in the company and do with it as you please. The amount that is held is accumulated in the account called *retained earnings*. Many companies do not pay dividends. The shareholders prefer that the earnings be kept to fund growth.

Retained earnings is, in general, the best way to finance your company's operations. Think of it in personal terms. You do not want to take a loan out from your parents or go into major credit card debt to finance your life. We can equate that to long-term debt. You also do not want to sell parts of your body (or your soul to the devil!) to finance operations. You can very loosely equate that to stock or equity financing. You prefer to make your own money and pay your own way. In this way, you are not beholden to anyone. This can be equated to retained earnings.

What Is Venture Capital?

Venture capital is a contribution of money or resources by someone who believes your company will grow and prosper. Venture capital is usually structured in part like debt and in part like stock or equity.

Venture capitalists may expect that you repay their contribution in periodic payments. This is structured like debt and would be accompanied by a corresponding set of debt covenants.

Venture capitalists may also expect to own a piece of your company for the long run. They may expect dividends and the right to vote on important company matters. They may even want to put one of their own people on the board to keep an eye on things. This is structured like equity or stock financing.

Usually, venture capital is a combo financing: a little bit of debt, a little bit of equity. All the terms of the contribution—the interest rate, the dividend rate, and the amount of control the venture capitalist has—are negotiable. But in the quest for additional resources, some companies will agree to almost any terms.

THE SECOND QUESTION THE BALANCE SHEET ANSWERS: HOW LEAN AND MEAN IS THE ORGANIZATION RUNNING?

The best business in the world is one where you put a dime in and get a dollar out. The less we waste our resources, the more return we will generate, and this makes business worthwhile.

One of the most important things to examine to determine if a company is running lean and mean is how it manages working capital.

WHAT IS WORKING CAPITAL?

There is the traditional view of working capital and the innovative view of working capital. Many accountants will tell you that they like to see a large balance in working capital. I will argue that the balance of working capital should be as small as possible. A small working capital balance indicates good management of resources.

The Textbook Definition of Working Capital

The formal, textbook definition of working capital is

working capital = current assets – current liabilities

Now, you ask, what are a *current asset* and a *current liability*?

Generally, we segregate our assets and liabilities into groups: one group is long term and one is current (Figure 2.4).

Balance Sheet

Assets ☺	Liabilities ☹

Current Assets
  Cash
  Accounts Receivable
  Inventory
Long-Term Assets
  Fixed Assets
  Intangibles
	Current Liabilities
	  Accounts Payable
	Long-Term Liabilities
	  Long-Term Debt
	
	Equity ☺ or ☹
	Stock
	Retained Earnings

Figure 2.4 Balance sheet model showing current and long-term assets and liabilities

Long-term assets would include fixed assets. These are things that we are going to hold onto for a while, generally at least a year, such as land, buildings, machinery, and furniture. Long-term liabilities would include a 10-year bank loan.

Current assets and current liabilities, on the other hand, are assets and liabilities that will generate or use cash in the current or near period, within a year. For example, we consider accounts receivable to be a current asset because we believe we will collect on our receivables in a month. We consider accounts payables to be current liabilities because they will use cash in the near period.

Back to our definition of working capital (Figure 2.5):

working capital = current assets – current liabilities

cash,	accounts payable
accounts	
receivable	
inventory	

Figure 2.5 Working capital formula

Let's put cash aside for a minute. Let's talk about the other components of working capital.

Should Accounts Receivable Be Large? Do we want our accounts receivable balance to be large? No, we don't. If it were, that would indicate that our customers are getting to use our products and services without paying for them. They are using our money, and we like to minimize that. We would prefer to be paid up front for our services and products. At the least, we want to be paid as soon as possible after we provide our products and services.

Should Inventory Be Large? Do we want our inventory balances to be large? No. Because that would mean that we have tied up our cash in stuff and if we needed our cash we might not be able to get it quickly. We want to be as liquid as possible.

Should Accounts Payable Be Large? Looking at the other side of the equation, we want to have a relatively large accounts payable balance. This would indicate that we are using other people's money—vendors' money—as much as possible. Isn't that tricky? We want our cash up front, but prefer to pay our vendors later. This allows us to have as much cash on hand at all times as we can.

So given this selfish "I'd rather have the resources than you!" principle and leaving cash out of the equation for a minute, if we have a small accounts receivable balance and a small inventory balance and a large accounts payable balance, we would necessarily have a small working capital balance.

The Real Meaning of Working Capital

Now let's go beyond the textbook definition of working capital to the real meaning. Working capital is the resources you have tied up in your business that are working for you. Working capital is the money you have tied up in your product or service.

Another way to look at it is "How many resources do we have to keep plowed into the business in order to make our product or service?" How much do we have to invest on a regular basis in inventory, how much in payments to vendors and employees, how much in granting our customers credit, and how much in rents, utilities, and other day-to-day necessities?

In the ideal world, this investment of resources is minimal. The best businesses in the world are the businesses where we put a little in and get a whole lot out. Wouldn't it be great if you could just invest 10 cents in a business yet make 5 dollars when you sold your product?

So, now let's consider the cash component. I see cash in two categories: day-to-day cash and rainy-day cash. Rainy-day cash is sort of like your reserve in case of emergency or in case of some cool business opportunity. Some organizations might have millions, even billions, of dollars of rainy day cash. On the balance sheet the cash balance will be enormous. This does not mean they need this much money to operate on a day-to-day basis. The cash they might need working for them every day might be minimal.

So a true calculation of working capital should take out rainy-day cash and look only at the cash needed to operate on a regular basis and the resources tied up in receivables, inventory, and payables. If day-to-day cash needs are minimal, if receivables and inventory are minimal, and if payables are maximized, then working capital will be as small as possible. A small working capital balance is one key indication of a lean, mean operation.

THE THIRD QUESTION THE BALANCE SHEET ANSWERS: HOW LIQUID IS THE ORGANIZATION?

One of the best things to do to understand the financial health of the organization is to see how the balance sheet would shake out if the company liquidated.

Liquidity is one of the more intuitive business terms. Have you ever seen those Oriental rug liquidation sales? What are the company owners trying to do? They are trying to convert all the rugs into cash so that they can buy some new rugs.

When your organization is liquid, it means that that you are like water. Water is flexible and strong. Liquid organizations have assets that can flow wherever they want them to go. Cash—the most liquid asset—can go be used for anything. Other liquid assets can be sold for cash easily and without significant loss in value.

If you have $100,000 in your pocket today, you can do whatever you want: go out on the town and have a rip-roaring time, buy a new car or two, take your friends to a fabulous meal. If the same $100,000 is tied up in your house, enjoy cable—you aren't going anywhere.

Let me give you a story of how illiquidity can hurt a business. When I graduated from the University of Texas in Austin, one of the top employers in Austin was a company called Tracor. Tracor was a defense contractor and I knew many engineers who worked there and were very happy. Tracor had a huge campus with about 10 buildings with underground parking and a snazzy cafeteria. Deer ran through the campus and the test labs were full of fabulous equipment that would make any engineer proud.

Tracor was growing and doing great—until the political environment changed. When the Democrats came into office, spending on weaponry slowed. And Tracor—which had all of its money tied up in those wonderful facilities, expensive engineer salaries, and long-term, slow-paying government contracts—choked. They were illiquid and the layoffs began. Every day my engineer friends would go into work not knowing if they'd still be employed at the end of the day. Now Tracor is gone and other companies occupy their buildings.

Contrast this with the largest employer in Austin now, Dell. Dell is highly liquid. It does not have fancy buildings or equipment. I've never seen a deer on campus, but the cafeterias are nice. Dell, at this moment, has nearly $10 billion in cash. Very little of its resources are tied up in inventory or facilities. When the market turns down, as it does every so often, Dell is able to withstand the downturn because of all this extra cash. They are liquid and can respond to opportunities in the marketplace faster than competitors that do not have that much cash.

A Pretend Liquidation

So let's pretend we are a simple manufacturing operation. But all of a sudden, our owners have decided that they are tired of striving to make shareholders happy and want to start a spiritual retreat center in the mountains of Montana. They plan on liquidating the business and giving all the employees a nice severance package and moving as soon as possible.

So the first thing they do is stop paying utilities and rent. Next they give the employees a severance package and pay off vendors.

Then they start selling all their goodies. What could a manufacturer sell?

- finished inventory
- raw materials inventory
- headquarters building
- cash
- manufacturing building
- manufacturing equipment
- office equipment
- accounts receivable
- investments
- patents or designs
- brand name of the company or product lines

Factoring Accounts Receivable

When you need cash fast, you might consider selling your accounts receivable—the amounts that others owe you. Instead of waiting 30 or more days for your customers to pay you, you can get cash on the receivables right away by selling them to someone else. This is called *factoring,* and the person who buys them is usually a bank or a factoring agent.

The factoring agent gives you 85 cents for each dollar of receivables. You walk away with the cash in hand, and then the factoring agent collects from the customer in a month or two.

The advantage of factoring your accounts receivable is that you don't have to wait to get your cash: you can have it now. The disadvantage is that you have to pay a pretty steep fee for doing so, often around 15 percent. So you get less cash than if you had waited. (Also, the customers are notified that instead of paying you, they will be paying this factoring agent. This might cause them some confusion or concern.)

Let's organize that list of goodies from most liquid to least liquid. Why don't you make up your list first and then check it against what I have below (Figure 2.6)?

Cash — **Most Liquid**
Investments
Accounts Receivable
Raw Materials Inventory
Finished Goods Inventory
Office Equipment
Manufacturing Equipment
Headquarters Building
Manufacturing Building
Bird Bath Designs
Brand Names — **Least Liquid**

Figure 2.6 Scale of liquidity

Why is raw materials inventory before finished goods inventory? Raw materials are more liquid because you can simply send them back to the vendor.

Why is office equipment before manufacturing equipment? Because there are more people in the world who would want to buy your office chair and desk than your custom widget-making machine.

Buildings are near the bottom of the list because they might take months, possibly years to sell, depending on their desirability.

Intellectual property, such as patents and brand names, are even less liquid than buildings, because any number of businesses might move into your building, but only a few people in the world would want to buy the brand name of your product lines—maybe.

So, as we are looking at this list, think of your own organization. Are most of their goodies at the top of this list or at the bottom? If they are at the bottom, your organization might not be very liquid.

Dell is very liquid. It has miniscule amounts tied up in intellectual property or real estate property. Many of its buildings are leased. It has $10 billion in cash, minimizes its receivables by asking its customers to use credit cards, and holds only three days worth of raw and finished good inventory. Its holdings are on the top end of the list.

Why is liquidity important to a company like Dell? Well, if the market changes, if a competitor acts, Dell can easily respond. If all of its resources were tied up in intellectual property or real estate, it would have to let the opportunity pass.

So back to our scenario, liquidating our company. Now that we have paid everyone their severance pay, paid off our vendors, paid our last payments on utilities and rents, and sold off all our goodies, we should have a big pile of cash in our hands.

After Liquidating Our Assets, We Pay Off the Owners

Now it is time to pay off the owners with this money. This is the story that the right side of the balance sheet tells us. It tells us who owns the business. After we have paid off the vendors, our accounts payable, we have three accounts to work with.

So, in paying off the owners, who do you think gets the money first?

The bank. As part of the loan covenants, the bank stipulates that, in case of liquidation, it gets its money first.

Next come the stockholders. Any funds that are left are given to them. If, after the company pays off the bank, only one dollar is left, the shareholders split the dollar and cry about their mediocre return.

The Difference Between Preferred and Common Stock

Preferred stockholders pay a premium for their stock and in return get special privileges. These privileges vary per company, but commonly include more voting rights per share, a higher dividend rate, and first claim on the resources in case of liquidation. Common stockholders get the leftovers, but usually pay a lower price for their stock.

What happens if the company doesn't even have enough cash to pay off the bank? This is called *bankruptcy* or rupturing the bank. In this case, the shareholders or owners of the company get nothing, and it usually means they have to dig into their own pockets to make up the difference to pay the bank. Banks don't often walk away from such a sad situation and passively let the business owners hit the road. They will often pursue the owners for the remainder.

In Texas, we have a law called the Homestead Exemption Act that allows individuals to keep their house and a mule (in modern terms, a car) in case of bankruptcy. The bank can't touch these items. However, it can get to everything else—your coast house, your second car, your savings account, etc. So in the early 1990s, when the economy in Texas was in such bad shape and folks were going bankrupt left and right, those under the counsel of a lawyer went out and bought a Mercedes and the best home they could afford before declaring bankruptcy. That kind of stuff doesn't play as well 15 years later. The banks are serious about getting their money back and are calling for a repeal of this law.

WHERE DO YOU WANT THE BALANCES ON THE BALANCE SHEET TO BE?

Look at the balance sheet model again, at the assets. What kind of balance do you want to see in cash, large or tiny? Large!

What kind of balance do you want to see in receivables, large or tiny? You want this number to be as lean as possible. A disproportionate balance might indicate that the company has a hard time collecting from its customers.

```
┌─────────────────────────────────────────────────────┐
│                    Balance Sheet                      │
│                                                       │
│         Assets          │        Liabilities          │
│                         │                             │
│   Cash                  │   Accounts Payable          │
│   Investments           │   Long-Term Debt            │
│   Accounts Receivable   │                             │
│   Inventory             │        Equity               │
│   Fixed Assets          │                             │
│   Intangibles           │   Stock                     │
│                         │   Retained Earnings         │
│                         │                             │
└─────────────────────────────────────────────────────┘
```

Figure 2.7 Balance sheet model

How about inventory? You prefer that the company have a minimal invest-ment in inventory. If your resources are tied up in inventory, they aren't tied up in cash, which is where we want the majority of our resources, right?

How about equipment and buildings? Again, minimal.

How about intellectual property? Again, minimize if you can. One of the main types of intellectual property is patents. Ideally, you only get patents that will have a value down the line or patents that allow you to protect yourself against

---

Cheap Is Good

Two of my clients in Austin, both high-tech companies, are a study in contrasts.

One is a high-tech telecommunications company. They paid me an enor-mous amount of money to come in and do what I do. I was thrilled with my fee. I was also thrilled with the facility where I taught. It had this white board on a track that I could pull anywhere in the room. It had a fabulous projection sys-tem. Two of the walls were floor-to-ceiling windows that looked out on the beau-tiful Texas Hill Country. I was in trainer heaven.

With the other client, I have a hard time getting a flip chart, much less a pro-jection system or a white board on tracks. The rooms are cramped and noisy because their facilities are cheaply made. And a window? Forget it! The fees I make out there are nothing to write home about.

When the economy took its inevitable periodic nosedive a few years ago, my fancy telecommunications client was hit hard. They were spending too much money on facilities, equipment, and meetings. I haven't worked out there in years and the folks who hired me were laid off. In contrast, my cheap client is still going strong and I do work with them every month. Cheap is good!

I remember reading an interview with the CFO of Southwest Airlines. He was asked why they made it after 9/11 when other airlines were struggling. He said it was because Southwest Airlines always assumes they are in a financial crunch, they are never extravagant, and they always make decisions that are as frugal as possible. Interesting.

---

competitors. Patents are expensive to create because of legal fees and documentation costs and should not be undertaken just for the sake of having them.

An engineering friend of mine works for a company that once was part of Motorola. He was expected to produce two or three patents a year. Motorola divested itself of his division in part because it did not respond quickly enough to market changes and changes in technology. Getting all those patents slowed it down.

Another thing about patents is that they are hard to sell or get value from. Technology changes so rapidly that your patent today might not be worth anything tomorrow. Or there might be only one or two folks who would want to buy your patent, and they might not be interested in buying it when you are looking for that extra cash.

Some industries are going to have heavy balances in some of the less liquid categories and can't help it. For instance, the airlines are going to have huge fixed-asset or equipment balances and can't help it. Department stores might be forced to hold huge inventory balances and can't help it. (I feel it is important to point out here that industry leaders are often the ones to break the mold. Wal-Mart, the leader in retail, has minimized its inventory balances by holding its entire inventory on consignment.)

It is very important to know that you cannot compare balance sheets between industries. You can't compare, for example, an airline's balance sheet with the balance sheet of a department store. The comparison is just not meaningful.

For comparison sake, it is best to stay within the industry. But even that presents challenges, as different businesses within the same industry have different business models. (More about that in the financial analysis section of this book.)

Now look at the other side of the balance sheet. What kind of balance do you want to see in debt? You want it to be reasonable. You don't necessarily want to see zero debt. Debt can be a wonderful tool in many circumstances.

Again, back to your personal life. If you didn't have debt in terms of a home mortgage or a car loan, you couldn't live near enough to your job to get to work on time each morning. To live debt free, you might have to live in the country in a trailer eating beanie-weenies every day—not a pretty picture.

Oftentimes, debt allows a company to expand and take advantage of opportunities it might otherwise have to pass up. So some debt is fine; we just don't want the burden to be too much to handle.

Now, down the balance sheet to equity. The balance for stock is generally fixed at the price that the shareholders paid in for the stock on the first day of the company's inception. Occasionally, the company might issue more stock to finance growth or special projects.

Stock on the Balance Sheet

The value of the stock on the balance sheet does not fluctuate with market price. This is a surprise to many folks I talk to. They expect that the market value of the stock will affect the financial statements. It doesn't. Whatever the company sold the stock for on the first day is the amount that shows up on the books.

Then why do companies care about the stock price? Well, usually, the people who run the company also personally own stock in it. Their personal wealth rises and falls based on the stock price. Also, if the stock price is healthy, the organization might be able to get additional financing—in debt or equity—much more easily than if their stock price was at rock bottom. Good reasons to care!

Ideally, in a highly evolved company, the stock balance would be decreasing over time because the company was buying back its stock. This does several happy things. It increases the value of each remaining share of stock out on the market, because there are fewer shares in fewer hands, and it concentrates control of the company into fewer hands. You end up with fewer people outside the company telling you how to run your business.

Finally, the figure for retained earnings should, of course, be healthy. However, if the company pays dividends, the shareholders might prefer that the company, instead of retaining earnings in the company, distribute the wealth to them. So the ideal balance of retained earnings depends on the philosophy of the organization. They might prefer to share the wealth with the owners by paying dividends rather than keeping it inside the company to grow.

A Quickie Analysis

One of the most useful techniques for analyzing a balance sheet is to create a pie chart of each side. Very simple, very visual, very informative.

What you do is take the left-hand of the balance sheet—the assets—and total all the assets up. Let's say for simplicity's sake that total assets equaled $100 million. Then you total up the liabilities and equity. It better also be $100 million. (If not, your balance sheet does not balance: you did something wrong.)

Now take each asset component and determine how much each one represents in relationship to the total. Let's say cash is $20 million, inventory is $40 million, receivables are $30 million, and fixed assets are $10 million. Now you can create a simple pie chart showing the proportion of each of these items (Figure 2.8).

Looking at the pie chart, does this balance seem reasonable or wise? One key way to determine that is to compare this year's pie chart with pie charts from previous years. Is the pie chart looking better or is the pie chart looking worse? For instance, a decrease in inventory might make us smile. Why? Remember: inventory is not as liquid as cash—and we love cash.

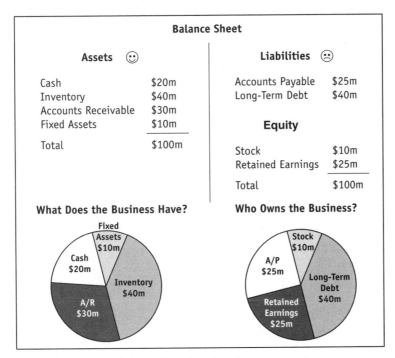

Figure 2.8 Pie chart balance sheet (continued on next page)

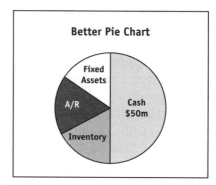

Figure 2.8 Pie chart balance sheet (continued)

On the other side of the balance sheet, we can do the same thing. Let's say that long-term debt is $40 million, accounts payable is $25 million, stock is $10 million, and retained earnings is $25 million. What would a better pie chart look like? Well, we might see a decrease in long-term debt, an increase in retained earnings, and a slight decrease in stock as the company is buying its stock back and retiring it.

In our financial analysis in the final five chapters, we look at a real balance sheet for two corporations.

Quiz

1. Assets =
   (a) liabilities plus cash
   (b) liabilities plus equity
   (c) liabilities plus net income

2. Assets are
   (a) happy things that you own
   (b) sad amounts that you owe other people
   (c) disclosed on the cash flow statement
   (d) highly liquid

3. Equity is a similar concept to
   (a) net working capital
   (b) net income
   (c) net worth

4. The amount a business holds in equity is in cash in its bank account.
   T or F

5. Which of the following is the most liquid asset?
   (a) building
   (b) equipment
   (c) inventory
   (d) cash
   (e) accounts receivable

6. Factoring is when you sell your accounts payable to a third party.
   T or F

7. When an entity does not have enough resources to pay off its lenders or the bank, it
   is called
   (a) liquidation
   (b) bankruptcy
   (c) claim management

8. The value of stock on the balance sheet shifts with the market price of the stock.
   T or F

9. In general, inventory balances should be
   (a) high
   (b) low
   (c) stable

10. In general, accounts receivable balances should be
    (a) high
    (b) low
    (c) stable

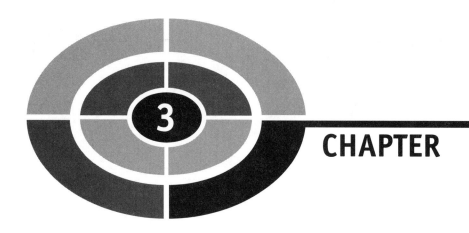

The Income Statement— A Focus on Earnings

The top four concerns of business are liquidity, profitability, growth, and financing. The income statement focuses primarily on profitability and growth.

The income statement has many aliases. Some call it the *P&L*, some the *profit and loss*. Governments are so opposed to the word profit that they call the income statement the *statement of revenues and expenditures*. I have also heard it called the *statement of earnings*.

Memorize This Formula!

What is common to all income statements, no matter what their name, is that they follow a very basic formula.

$$revenues - expenses = profit$$

That makes perfect intuitive sense. Profit is what you have after you subtract expenses from sales revenue. Profit also has aliases. It is called earnings, income, and net income.

The income statement would be so simple if we had only three numbers: revenue, expenses, and profit. But of course, we don't stop there. We want more information. The income statement is broken down into categories and subtotaled several times before we get to the final profit or net income figure. And the subtotals are primarily focused on segregating costs into categories.

To understand the subtotals, we need to first tackle some cost terminology.

Cost Terminology

Accountants are not happy just naming something a "cost." It is useful to us to categorize and subcategorize costs. The two most common ways that we discuss cost center around the way a cost behaves and the way a cost is applied. Let's do the behavior breakdown first.

THE WAY A COST BEHAVES

Costs can behave as variable, semivariable, or fixed.

A *fixed* cost remains the same no matter how many units you produce or how many employees you have. It is stable. If we graphed it over a period of a year, it would look like this:

A good example of a fixed cost is rent. It stays the same no matter what month it is or how many units you produce.

A *variable* cost goes up and down, depending on something else. It might vary with production or number of employees. If we graphed it over a period of a year it might look like this:

A good example of a variable cost is parts. The more products you manufacture, the more parts you need.

A *semivariable* cost is somewhere in between. It might be fixed for a while and then jump, like this:

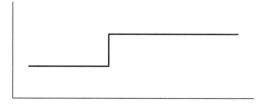

Or it might have a fixed component at its base and then vary on top of the fixed component, like this:

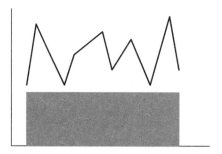

A good example of the first type of semivariable cost would be labor. If you employ six guys, you are at the bottom level. As soon as you hire a new guy, your cost jumps and stays high.

A good example of the bottom graph is electric utilities. You pay a fixed cost just to have the service turned on and then the usage changes month to month— a more variable behavior.

Now, all of this is just shades of gray. A fixed cost—even rent—would look variable if you graphed it over a 10-year period. And if you compress the scale of your graph, a variable cost can look fixed.

So, what should you take away from this? That there is no textbook definition of what qualifies a cost as fixed, variable, or semivariable. When someone starts talking this lingo with you, you need to ask her to clarify what costs she is lumping into what category. Folks have told me that component costs are fixed because they are the same per unit. That is one way of looking at it, but it does not take into account that you use varying amounts every day. So the caveat here is be careful how you use and interpret this terminology. And you thought accounting was exact and precise? Surprise!

THE WAY A COST IS APPLIED

The next way of discussing costs is by how they are applied to a product or service. The cost can be either directly applied to the product or service or indirectly applied.

Direct costs are costs that you can logically and easily trace to the creation of the product. Let's say we are making birdbaths. The cost of the components (the wire and the cement) and the labor to create the birdbaths are direct costs. You can easily determine how much cement and wire go into each birdbath. You can also determine how many labor hours it took to mold and finish the birdbaths. Direct link, direct costs.

Indirect costs are all the other costs incurred in marketing, selling, and designing the product. Here is a partial list of items that might be considered indirect costs:

- marketing
- advertising
- utilities
- rent
- travel
- sales
- legal
- executive
- security
- accounting
- auditing
- packaging design
- product research
- reception

These costs are harder to trace directly to the product. For instance, if you have seven product lines and you asked members of the executive team how they contributed to each product line, you would most likely get a blank stare in return or they would say that they contributed to each product line equally. Of course, this isn't true.

So what we do in accounting to keep it simple is to allocate these indirect costs to the product using what we like to call an *indirect cost allocation* method. Some companies call it a *burden rate*.

We take all of the expenditures for the executive team and put them into what is called an *indirect cost pool* (a fancy way of saying "a lump of costs"). We then come up with a way to easily allocate them to the products or product lines. For instance, we might have allocated the costs based on volume of sales. Whichever product line generated the most sales got the largest chunk of the executive costs.

Is that fair and accurate? No. But is it easy for the accountant and normally how it works.

So if you are a project manager and are trying to sell a particular project, you might hear back from the accounting department that, in addition to the direct costs of your project, such as the new equipment and additional labor, you must also add in a burden rate. They might say, "Yes, we understand that your project will cost the company $460,000, but we also want you to factor in an additional 20 percent to take into account organizational support." That extra 20 percent might push you right over the edge and make your project seem unprofitable.

Know that this burden rate or indirect cost allocation rate is created by the accounting department and is subject to debate and change. The folks at one company I teach for seem to change both the rate and the components of their indirect cost allocation every six months. They keep refining it and adding different components or taking some out.

Something to be aware of here is that you may be able to successfully argue that your particular project should not be weighed down by all the costs the accountants calculated. If you ask the accountants for their allocation methods, you may actually be able to find some costs that should not be attributed to your project.

Now why do we go through all this rigmarole anyway? Why calculate the direct and indirect costs of creating a product or service? Because we want to make sure that we are making a profit on each sale. If we don't know the cost of our products or services, we might very well be selling them for less than it costs us to make them, and that would be bad.

Activity-Based Costing—Cost Accounting on Steroids

Activity-based costing (ABC) takes cost accounting to new levels of detail. The creators of ABC rightly argue that allocating cost based on production volume or dollar sales volume is not accurate or fair. They instead recommend that a detailed study be made of each function in the organization. In this study, all cost categories are scrutinized and their activities documented. The cost is then allocated based on activities, not volume; hence the name *activity-based costing*.

Here is a rather silly example to show you how hard ABC has been for many organizations to implement. Back to our executive team example. The accounting department helps detail the activities of the executive team to better determine how to allocate costs. The executives document that they spent two hours on a conference call with management, two hours lunching with a key client, one hour responding to a request from a stockholder, one hour signing documents, etc. This still might not get us any closer to coming up with a better allocation for the cost of the executive team to the product lines.

Some other costs are a bit easier. Take, for example, the cost of a supervisor in the manufacturing plant. We might have, using simpler cost accounting methods, allocated his time to all product lines based on volume. By studying his activities, we find that he spends more time every day working with a particularly troublesome product and the employees who manufacture it. In this way, we would uncover two pieces of information—one, that this troublesome product is taking up more time than we thought, and therefore might need to be redesigned or even canned, and two, that if we decide to keep manufacturing the product, we might need to charge more for it because as it is we might be selling it at a loss.

Now that we have covered the two main ways that accountants talk about cost—in terms of how cost behaves and the way cost is applied—we can look more closely at the income statement and the way it is broken out.

The Significance of Gross Profit Margin and Operating Profit Margin

Notice that the income statement (Figure 3.1) is subtotaled in two places before we get to the final profit figure.

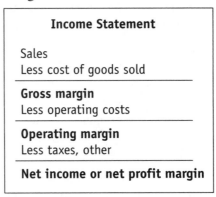

Income Statement

Sales
Less cost of goods sold

Gross margin
Less operating costs

Operating margin
Less taxes, other

Net income or net profit margin

Figure 3.1 Income statement model

The first subtotal is the result of taking sales and subtracting the cost of goods sold. This subtotal is called *gross profit margin*. I have also heard it called a variety of other things, so check out your own company's financials to uncover your company's terminology.

The next subtotal is the result of taking gross margin and subtracting out operating expenses. This is called *operating profit margin*. This margin, too, has aliases, so check your own financials.

Where do you think direct costs go? In cost of goods sold or in operating expenses? Right! In cost of goods sold. So gross profit margin is the result of subtracting the direct costs of creating your product or service from total sales.

Indirect costs go in operating expenses. So operating profit margin is the result of taking both indirect and direct costs out of sale revenue.

This is the line that most of us need to pay attention to and manage—operating profit margin. It is the profit we garner from operating, from the day-to-day creation and sales of our product or service.

The items below this line are generally out of the manager's control—things like taxes and the gain or loss on the sale of a business segment. These are called *nonoperating items* and are classified at the bottom of the statement. We put these at the bottom so we can trend operating profit margin from year to year without any strange, nonrecurring, or unusual jumps.

For instance, I just read a company's financials that revealed a negative operating profit but a positive net income because of a gain on a foreign currency transaction. Will they realize a gain on a foreign currency transaction next year? Who knows? Will they be able to pull their operating profit out of the dumper? We hope so.

The Income Statement Tells a Story about Profitability

Look at the information in Figure 3.2. The very bottom line—the net income—is the same for both years, but something happened in the second year that should raise our concern. The cost of goods, or the direct costs, went up by 10. Thankfully, we were able to cut operating expenses by enough to make up the difference.

Income Statement		
	01	**02**
Sales	100	100
Less Cost of Goods Sold	70	80
Gross Margin	30	20
Less Operating Expenses	20	10
Operating Margin	10	10
Less Taxes/Other	5	5
Net Income or Net Profit Margin	5	5

Figure 3.2 Income statement trended percentage

Now, instead of looking at those figures as dollars, look at them as percentages. It is always good practice to convert dollar figures into percentages. Both dollars and percentages tell a story. While you might be impressed with the sheer dollar size of the net income, you might be missing the story that it is only 2 percent of sales.

THE P&L TELLS US WHAT WE HAVE LEFT

Try this analogy. Turn total revenues into a bar of Ivory Soap and whittle the bar of soap to see how much you have left after you pay all of your expenses. Your expenses whittle away at your revenue. Are you going to be left with a soap ball or with a generous hotel-sized bar of soap? How about a soap flake?

For instance, one high-tech manufacturer I work with has an income statement that breaks out as shown in Figure 3.3.

Dell Inc. Income Statement		
	Dollars	**%**
Revenues	41,444	100%
Cost of Goods	33,892	82%
Gross Margin	7,552	18%
Operating Expenses	4,008	10%
Operating Margin	3,544	9%
Other	899	2%
Net Income	2,645	6%

Figure 3.3 Dell Inc.'s income statement—Fiscal year ending Jan. 30, 2004 (in millions)

So we start out with $41 billion in revenue. That is our total bar of soap. Now we take four-fifths of it to pay for cost of goods (82 percent). Ouch! We now have a hotel-sized bar of soap. We have 18% of our bar of soap left. Next we take out operating expenses. This takes the remaining half and halves it again. Now we have half a hotel-sized bar of soap. After we take out taxes and other unusual stuff, we get to keep 6 percent of our bar of soap—a sliver of a bar of soap. But 6 percent of $41 billion is $2.6 billion—nothing to sneeze at.

EBIT and EBITDA

What are EBIT and EBITDA? These are hip little acronyms that are fun to pronounce. EBIT is pronounced e-bit and EBITDA is pronounced e-bit-dah. (Sounds like we're talking Latin!) EBIT stands for earnings before interest and taxes. EBITDA stands for earnings before interest, taxes, depreciation, and amortization.

These are just two more ways of cutting or subtotaling the income statement, very much like our gross and operating margins. For EBIT, you take the bottom line of earnings—the net income—and add back in interest and taxes.

For EBITDA, you take the net income and add back in interest, taxes, depreciation, and amortization.

EBITDA is a number that many organizations hold their managers to. If the EBITDA number makes targets, the managers are rewarded. This makes more sense than bonusing the managers on bottom-line net income, because bottom-line net income is the result of factoring in a lot of costs that are not under the managers' control. Interest paid on debt is not generally under the control of the front-line managers; they do not make decisions on how the organization is financed. Taxes, depreciation, and amortization are also not under the control of front-line managers.

So there are two more fancy acronyms you can use to impress your boss.

Quiz

1. Governments call the income statement
    (a) the P&L
    (b) the revenue projection(c) the deficit indicator
    (d) the statement of revenues and expenditures

2. The formula of the income statement is
    (a) cash – expenses = profit
    (b) revenues – cost of goods = profit
    (c) revenues – expenses = profit
    (d) cash – cost of goods = profit

3. A variable cost might vary with levels of production.
    T or F

4. A good example of a fixed cost is
    (a) materials cost
    (b) overhead labor costs
    (c) rent
    (d) utilities

5. Which of the following would likely be a direct cost?
   (a) materials
   (b) manufacturing labor
   (c) utilities
   (d) rent
   (e) legal fees
   (f) marketing expenses
   (g) a and b
   (h) a, b, and c
   (i) a, e, and f

6. The technique of distributing indirect costs to different products is often called
   (a) the indirect cost allocation method
   (b) the direct cost distribution technique
   (c) the burden percentage calculation methodology

7. To which margin should managers be held accountable?
   (a) net margin
   (b) gross margin
   (c) operating margin
   (d) profitability margin

8. What sorts of items end up on the bottom of the income statement?
   (a) earnings from foreign currency transactions
   (b) sale of a business segment
   (c) cost of goods sold
   (d) selling, general, and administrative expenses
   (e) c and d
   (f) a and b

9. EBITDA will always be a smaller number than EBIT.
   T or F

10. EBIT stands for
    (a) earnings before investments and taxes
    (b) earnings before interest and taxes
    (c) earnings between interest and taxes

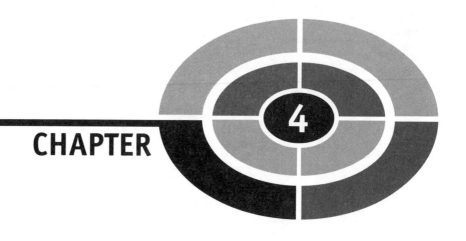

CHAPTER 4

The Cash Flow Statement—Do We Have Enough for Payroll?

The cash flow statement performs very much like your bank account statement at home. It tells you how much cash you had at the beginning of the month and how much cash you had at the end of the month. It summarizes how much cash you collected and how much cash you paid out.

The cash flow statement is often confused with the income statement. Some people figure that the final balance of cash will be the same number as your net income. This is never true when you use the accrual basis of accounting—and you probably do.

```
+-------------------------------------------+
|          Cash Flow Statement              |
|                                           |
|   Beginning CASH                          |
|   Plus CASH collected                     |
|   Less CASH paid                          |
|   _____          |
|                                           |
|   Ending CASH                             |
+-------------------------------------------+
```

Figure 4.1 Cash flow statement model

Cash versus Accrual Method of Accounting

The cash method of accounting is used by very few businesses because it takes such a simple view of transactions. Most of us use the accrual method of accounting.

The cash method of accounting works well if you have a very simple business. Let's take as an example a hot-dog vendor on a college campus. Every weekday morning, the hot-dog vendor wakes up, hitches his hot-dog cart to the back of his truck, and drives over to Sam's Warehouse and buys hot dogs, buns, condiments, and sodas. He pays cash. He drives over to campus and sets up shop. He sells his hot dogs and sodas for cash. At the end of the day, he eats the leftovers. The next morning, he starts all over again.

His business is all about cash. He doesn't owe anyone money and his customers don't owe him any money. There are no receivables and payables. His business is very simple—unlike most businesses.

Most businesses operate with receivables and payables and keep track of their transactions using the accrual method of accounting. The accrual method records everything that happened in the business, whether or not it impacts cash.

You can make a sale and record it on your books, but not collect payment in cash from your customer for 30-plus days. Using the accrual method, you accrue—or record—the income on your income statement. But nothing has happened over on the cash flow statement. What you have just done is create an account receivable.

You can also incur an expense but not pay it in cash. For instance, when I do a training for a university, they are getting the benefit of my services on the day that I do the training, but they won't pay me for a few months. (Universities are notoriously slow to pay their vendors.) So they record an expense on the income statement for my fee and record an account payable. Again, there is no immediate impact on cash.

So, because of timing differences, the final net income—or the bottom line—on the income statement will never be the same as the ending cash balance on the cash flow statement. Under the accrual method, you record things before they impact cash.

A Real-Life Example of How Profit and Cash Differ

An engineer friend of mine once started a business with several of his engineer friends. They made global positioning systems and were geniuses in regard to the product. However, none of them knew how to run a business.

My friend was given the responsibility for keeping the books and records and negotiating contracts. His title was "Engineer in Charge of Finance." (Do you smell trouble here?)

After much suffering, he came to me and confessed that his partners were upset with him and that he was worried that the business was going to fail. He said that his partners expected the net income off the income statement to be in the bank account and they were very disturbed that they had to keep reaching into their own pockets to pay for payroll. Indeed, on the income statement they were very profitable, but they didn't have any cash. They thought that my friend had made a major error in the way he was keeping the books or that he had misplaced huge amounts of cash.

None of them understood the accrual method of accounting and the importance of cash flow.

The company was indeed very profitable because they had landed a juicy contract with the Coast Guard to equip its boats with global positioning systems. So on the income statement, they recorded a $400,000 sale. But does the Coast Guard pay fast? No! And the Coast Guard was paying in little bitty installments. My friend would install a global positioning unit on a boat and eventually bill the Coast Guard. The Coast Guard took several more months to pay. The cash was dripping in, not flowing.

Another mistake my friend made was to allow all of his employees to buy whatever they wanted. He didn't think it was kind to place restrictions on what employees purchased, so he left it up to their discretion to buy what they needed. They had a lovely company boat—to test the global positioning equipment, of course—and art in the boardroom, fancy test equipment, and way, way too much raw materials inventory. And because he wanted to have good credit with all his vendors, he paid every bill that hit his mailbox immediately. Ooh!

So no money was coming in and a whole lot was going out. No wonder he was out of cash.

I introduced him to the cash flow statement and instructed him to watch it over the next few months. I asked him to plot out exactly what money was coming in each day and how much money was going out each day. This way he would know, ahead of time, whether he would have enough money to pay payroll.

At the moment, all of his partners were tapped; they had no more money to contribute into the company. So he did what anyone would do and went to a bank for a loan. Any guesses what the bank told him? They turned him down because he was too much of a risk. Obviously he knew nothing about running a business or cash flow.

Instead the bank offered to factor his accounts receivable. Factoring, as explained in Chapter 2, is selling receivables to the bank or a factoring agent for cash. They pay much less than the receivables are worth, but then they are the ones waiting for payment.

My friend walked away with 87 cents on the dollar for his Coast Guard receivable, in cash, and was happy to have it. The interest rate was steep, but he had the money they needed to stay in business.

Unfortunately, as part of the factoring arrangement, the bank notified the Coast Guard to make future payments on the contract to the bank, not to my friend. This raised a concern with the Coast Guard, who knew that factoring was a high-cost, last-ditch effort to raise capital. They threatened to never do business with my friend again and to rescind their current contract. They didn't want to do business with someone who would not be able to support the product years down the line.

Fortunately, after much negotiating and pleading, my friend was able to save his contract and relationship with the Coast Guard. He watched cash flow like a hawk and eventually sold his business to a competitor for millions of dollars. He is now happily retired and living on the Texas coast fishing.

The morale of this story is that profit and cash are different because of timing. The accrual method of accounting causes transactions to affect profit that won't affect cash for months to come.

Why Was the Cash Flow Statement Added Recently?

The cash flow statement was added to the set of required financial statements because of the savings and loan crisis of the 1980s. The savings and loan banks were recording all these wonderful loans on their income statements and puffing up their bottom-line profits, but were not collecting on these loans or realizing the income in cash. Eventually, their lack of cash took them under.

So the Financial Accounting Standards Board added the cash flow statement so we know whether income was actually ever realized in cash—a very important piece of information in any business.

Unfortunately, the FASB made a big boo-boo (in my opinion) when they finally wrote the rules regarding the cash flow statement. They gave accountants an option on the way they present the cash flow statements—and the accountants almost always opt for the format that is less user-friendly but easier to create.

Accountants can choose between the direct presentation method and the indirect presentation method. The direct presentation method is akin to our simple model shared at the beginning of the chapter. It simply lists the money that came in and the money that went out. This is my favorite method. However, accountants complain that it causes them too much work, so they usually use the indirect method.

The indirect method reconciles net income to cash. So instead of listing how much was collected and how much was paid out, it uses reconciling language—such as net increase in payables and net decrease in inventory. Even accountants have a hard time reading and interpreting the indirect method statement, so if it's Greek to you, don't be too hard on yourself.

Figures 4.2 and 4.3 give examples of the direct and the indirect methods of cash flow statements.

From either of these statements, the user-friendly direct method or the easier-to-create indirect method, you can garner some interesting information about an organization.

The Direct Method Statement of Cash Flows

Cash Flows from operating activities
Inflows
Cash from customers
Outflows
Cash paid to suppliers
Other expenses paid

Cash Flows from investing activities
Purchase of plant

Cash Flows provided by financing activities
Sale of stock

Change in cash

Figure 4.2 Direct cash flow statement

Indirect Method Statement of Cash Flows

Cash Flows from operating activities

Net income
Adjustments to reconcile income
Depreciation
(Increase) Decrease in A/R
(Increase) Decrease in inventory
Increase (Decrease) in A/P

Cash Flows from investing activities
Purchase of plant

Cash Flows provided by financing activities
Sale of stock
Change in cash

Figure 4.3 Indirect cash flow statement

Classifying Cash Flows into Three Categories

What the cash flow statement does that your bank statement doesn't do is categorize the amounts that you collected and the amounts that you paid. Your bank account statement only lists the check numbers and deposit dates; it doesn't tell you what all of those figures were for.

Both the direct and indirect methods divide cash flows into three categories:

- operations
- financing
- investing

Let's talk about each of these in turn.

OPERATING ACTIVITIES

The operations section gives us an idea of how much cash the organization generated in its day-to-day delivery of its products and services. This number can and should be compared with the operating income on the income statement. If operating income and operating cash flow are vastly different, you need to start asking some tough questions. It might mean that the organization is recording sales that will never be collected in cash. Ooh.

Cash *inflows* from operating activities include:

- cash receipts for the sale of goods or services
- cash receipts for the collection or sale of operating receivables (receivables arising from the sale of goods or services)
- cash interest received
- cash dividends received
- other cash receipts not directly identified with financing or investing activities

Cash *outflows* for operating activities include:

- cash payments for trade goods purchased for resale or use in manufacturing
- cash payments for notes to suppliers or trade goods
- cash payments to other suppliers and to employees
- cash paid for taxes, fees, and fines

- interest paid to creditors
- other cash payments not directly identified with financing or investing activities

FINANCING ACTIVITIES

The financing category tells us how much cash was generated by debt or equity financing. Saying it another way, the financing section details the cash flows between the organization and the folks who help finance the organization through debt and equity.

An interesting twist here is that interest used to repay debt is not included in the financing category; it is included in the operating category. Remember: at the very beginning of the book I said that accounting is just a set of rules about how to keep records. Not everything is intuitive or sensible. You are just going to have to accept this one and move on!

Cash *inflows* from financing activities include:

- cash proceeds from the sale of stock
- cash receipts from borrowing
- cash receipts from contributions and investment income that donors restricted for endowments or for buying, improving, or constructing long-term assets

Cash *outflows* from financing activities include:

- cash disbursed to repay principal on long and short-term debt
- cash paid to reacquire common and preferred equity instruments
- dividends paid to common and preferred stockholders

INVESTING ACTIVITIES

The last category is investing. And, as you might expect, this section of the cash flow statement details how much cash the entity made and used in making investments in other entities, such as the purchase of stocks or bonds of another entity. What you might not expect is that this category includes the purchase and sale of productive assets, such as manufacturing equipment. This is, per the profession's view, an investment in the company's future and should not be classified under either operations or financing.

Cash *inflows* from investing activities are:

- collections of principal on debt instruments of other entities
- cash proceeds from the sale of equity investments
- cash received from the sale of productive assets

Cash *outflows* from investing activities are:

- cash paid to acquire debt instruments of other entities
- cash payments to buy equity interest in other entities
- disbursements made to purchase productive assets

In Chapter 17 we examine a cash flow statement for two competitors.

What Stories Does the Cash Flow Statement Tell You?

Although the format of the cash flow statement is nowhere near as straightforward as the formats of the balance sheet and the income statement, you can still glean some important information from it.

One key story you can derive from the cash flow statement is how the company is generating its cash. Is it from providing goods and services (our favorite method), from selling equity in the company or incurring debt, or from investment activities? We would love to see a company generating plenty of cash from day-to-day operations with minimal reliance on external financing.

The cash flow statement also gives us a sense of how the organization used its money. Where do the priorities of the company lie? Is it in growth mode, spending large sums on equipment, or is it selling off its equipment? Does it like to distribute the wealth to owners, or does it use it to spur further growth?

We can also see how liquid the organization is. How much cash does it have at the end of the year and how does this compare with previous years? Cash flow statements are usually presented for the current year and two previous years.

But the key question the cash flow statement answers for us is "Is the net income reported on the income statement ever realized in cash?" If the operating income figure on the income statement and the operating cash figure are

miles apart, you need to ask some tough questions. It may be that the entity is inflating income or deflating expenses—or both.

Quiz

1. The cash method of accounting is the most commonly used method among large corporations.
   T or F

2. The cash method of accounting recognizes accounts receivable and accounts payable.
   T or F

3. When you incur an expense but do not pay it in cash, it is recorded, under the accrual method of accounting, as
   (a) an accounts receivable
   (b) an accounts payable
   (c) a fixed asset
   (d) a long-term liability

4. A sale that has not yet been collected in cash is
   (a) an accounts receivable
   (b) an accounts payable
   (c) a fixed asset
   (d) a long-term liability

5. Profit and cash are different because of
   (a) timing
   (b) the double-entry system of accounting
   (c) banking regulations
   (d) IRS rules

6. The indirect method is the most user-friendly method for creating a cash flow statement.
   T or F

7. The indirect method has line items that disclose the increase or decrease in working capital items such as inventory, receivables, and payables. T or F

8. Cash outflows for financing activities include
    (a) cash disbursed to repay principle on long-term debt
    (b) cash disbursed to repay principle on short-term debt
    (c) dividends paid to common shareholders
    (d) purchase of fixed assets
    (e) purchase of common stock of another entity
    (f) all of the above
    (g) a, b, and c
    (h) a, b, c, and d

9. Cash inflows from investing activities include
    (a) cash proceeds from the sale of equity investments in other entities
    (b) cash paid to acquire the debt instruments of other entities
    (c) cash proceeds from the sale of stock

10. The cash flow statement can tell you
    (a) how a company is generating its cash
    (b) how the organization used its cash resources
    (c) how liquid the organization is
    (d) whether the income reported on the income statement is realized as cash
    (e) all of the above

CHAPTER 5

How the Financial Statements Are Related

How the Income Statement, Cash Flow Statement, and Balance Sheet Are Related

Remember that the balance sheet is the mother of all financial statements and that the income statement and cash flow statements are babies.

HOW THE INCOME STATEMENT LINKS TO THE BALANCE SHEET

The income statement is the detail on how earnings were generated. The basic formula of the income statement is:

$$\text{revenues} - \text{expenses} = \text{profit}$$

Please don't ever forget that formula. If I ever meet you on the street and you tell me that you've read this book, I'll be asking you for that formula!

So all that matters for the income statement are transactions that are considered revenue and expenses. It doesn't matter when cash was impacted. It doesn't matter when you buy a fixed asset or incur a long-term debt. Those belong on the cash flow statement and the balance sheet, respectively.

The final net income figure on the income statement (the proverbial "bottom line") is added to retained earnings on the balance sheet. Let me repeat that concept another way. The income statement (Figure 5.1) is linked to the balance sheet (Figure 5.2) through the retained earnings figure.

Income Statement	Balance Sheet	
Sales Less cost of goods sold	**Assets**	**Liabilities**
Gross margin Less operating costs	Cash Investments Accounts Receivable	Accounts Payable Long-Term Debt
Operating margin Less taxes, other	Inventory Fixed Assets Intangibles	**Equity** Stock
Net income or net profit margin		Retained Earnings

Figure 5.1 Income statement net income   **Figure 5.2 Balance sheet** retained earnings

HOW THE CASH FLOW STATEMENT LINKS TO THE BALANCE SHEET

For the cash flow statement (Figure 5.3), all that matters is what happened to cash. It is the detail of the item on the balance sheet called *cash*. It doesn't matter if you made a sale but haven't collected payment in cash yet. It doesn't matter if you incurred an expense but haven't paid it in cash yet. The income statement accrues for these things; the cash flow statement ignores transactions until they impact cash.

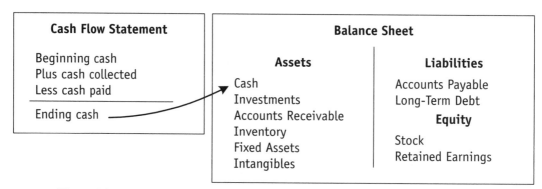

Figure 5.3 Cash flow statement

What Each Financial Statement Tracks

Remember: the balance sheet is the mother of all financial statements. It tracks all the big categories of items.

THE BALANCE SHEET

The balance sheet keeps track of all the assets the business holds:

- cash
- investments
- accounts receivable
- inventory
- fixed assets
- intellectual property

The balance sheet tracks the amounts the business owes other people:

- accounts payable
- long-term debt

The balance sheet tracks the equity the owners have in the business:

- stock
- retained earnings

THE INCOME STATEMENT

The income statement tracks only:

- revenues
- expenses

THE CASH FLOW STATEMENT

The cash flow statement tracks only:

- cash

Simple Transactions and How They Impact the Three Key Financial Statements

Before we get into discussing debits and credits, I want you to get a sense of how simple transactions impact the three key financial statements—a bird's-eye view, if you will.

Let's say that you make cement birdbaths and you have an inventory of 100 in stock. Each birdbath cost you $20 to make. So your total balance on the balance sheet in inventory is $2000.

Cash Sale

Today you were lucky enough to sell two birdbaths to a bird enthusiast for $60 cash. What happens to your financial statements?

First, go to the income statement (Figure 5.4), because you made some income. You record revenue of $60 and realize an expense of $40 ($20 per birdbath). This increases your net income by $20.

Income Statement

Sales	60
Cost of Goods	40
Gross Profit	20
Operating Expenses	0
Operating Profit	20
less Taxes/Other	0
Net Income	20

Figure 5.4 Income statement

Next go to the cash flow statement. Cash goes up by $60.

Cash Flow Statement

Beginning Cash	
+ Cash Collected	60
−Cash Paid	0
Ending Cash	+60

Figure 5.5 Cash flow statement

Now go fill out the balance sheet.

Balance Sheet

Assets ☺		Liabilities ☹	
Cash	+60	Accounts Payable	
Accounts Receivable		Long-Term Debt	
Inventory	−40		
Fixed Assets		**Equity ☺ or ☹**	
Intangibles			
		Stock	
		Retained Earnings	+20
	+20		+20

Figure 5.6 Balance sheet

Cash goes up by $60. Inventory goes down by $40. Retained earnings go up by $20.

Does your little balance sheet balance? Yes, miraculously! That crazy double-entry system works.

On the left side of the balance sheet, the asset side, you increased one asset—cash—by $60 and reduced another asset—inventory—by $40. That leaves you a total increase to the left side of the balance sheet of $20.

On the other side of the balance sheet, you increased retained earnings by your net income for $20.

Now each side of the balance sheet has gone up by $20. The transaction flowed through the financial statements and altered them appropriately.

Credit Sale: Part One

Now let's make this a bit more complicated. Let's instead say that you made a sale on credit. You don't get to collect cash right away.

I'm also going to change the numbers a little bit. Let's say that this time you sell 100 birdbaths to a local nursery on credit. The nursery takes the birdbaths and agrees to pay you for them in 30 days.

Now what happens to the financial statements?

First, go to the income statement, because you made a sale. Revenues increase by 100 times the $30 selling price or $3000. Then you realize an expense for the birdbath of $20 per birdbath or $2000. Revenues of $3000 less expenses of $2000 equal an increase in net income of $1000.

Income Statement	
Sales	3,000
Cost of Goods	2,000
Gross Profit	1,000
Operating Expenses	0
Operating Profit	1,000
less Taxes/Other	0
Net Income	1,000

Figure 5.7 Income statement

What happens on the cash flow statement? Nothing! The cost of manufacturing the birdbaths hit the cash flow statement months ago, so it has already been accounted for. No cash changed hands today, so the cash flow statement stays dormant.

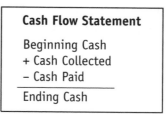

Figure 5.8 Cash flow statement

What happens on the balance sheet?

Balance Sheet		
Assets ☺		**Liabilities** ☹
Cash		Accounts Payable
Accounts Receivable	+3,000	Long-Term Debt
Inventory	– 2,000	
Fixed Assets		**Equity** ☺ or ☹
Intangibles		
		Stock
		Retained Earnings +1,000
	+1,000	+1,000

Figure 5.9 Balance sheet

You increase accounts receivable by $3000 for the amount the nursery owes you. You decrease inventory by $2000 for the birdbaths sold. You increase retained earnings by $1000.

Same scenario as last time. Assets on the left side of the balance sheet are increased by $1000 ($3000 less $2000) and equity on the right side of the balance sheet is increased by $1000. Whew! You balance again.

Credit Sale: Part Two

In a month's time, you collect payment from the nursery, a $3000 check. What happens to the financial statements now?

First, you ask if the income statement is impacted. No, it is not. You didn't make a new sale or incur a new expense. This is all old, already recorded revenues and expenses, so you skip the income statement.

Income Statement
Sales
Cost of Goods
Gross Profit
Operating Expenses
Operating Profit
less Taxes/Other
Net Income

Figure 5.10 Income statement

You go directly to the cash flow statement. Cash is increased by $3000.

Cash Flow Statement	
Beginning Cash	
+ Cash Collected	3,000
– Cash Paid	
Ending Cash	+3,000

Figure 5.11 Cash flow statement

On the balance sheet (Figure 5.12), you increase cash by $3000 and decrease accounts receivable by the amount you just collected, $3000. That gives you a net effect of zero on the left side. Nothing happened on the right side, so you're OK.

How are we holding up? If that is just enough detail for you, or maybe almost too much detail, I suggest you skip the next chapter because it goes into debits and credits—the super detail of accounting.

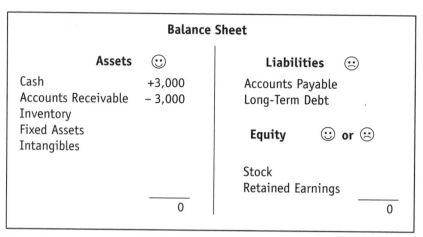

Figure 5.12 Balance sheet

Purchasing a Fixed Asset

Now let's say that you want to purchase a $5000 color copier to help you create ads and brochures to market your birdbaths. What happens to your financial statements now?

Well, it depends on whether you capitalize it or expense it.

EXPENSING

When you buy a fixed asset, such as a copier, you might have the option of expensing it rather than capitalizing it. Generally, if an asset is under $5000, many large organizations will forgo recording it as a fixed asset and instead just expense it entirely.

So if you decide to expense a $5000 copier, it would flow through the financial statements in this way.

Income statement (Figure 5.13): expenses are increased by $5000 and net income is reduced by $5000.

Income Statement

Sales	
Cost of Goods	_____
Gross Profit	
Operating Expenses	5,000
Operating Profit	
less Taxes/Other	_____
Net Income	– 5,000

Figure 5.13 Income statement—expense the copier

Cash flow statement: cash is reduced by $5000.

Cash Flow Statement

Beginning Cash	
+ Cash Collected	
– Cash Paid	–5,000
Ending Cash	–5,000

Figure 5.14 Cash flow statement—expense the copier

Balance sheet: cash is reduced by $5000 and retained earnings are reduced by $5000—you balance!

Balance Sheet

Assets ☺		Liabilities ☹	
Cash	–5,000	Accounts Payable	
Accounts Receivable		Long-Term Debt	
Inventory			
Fixed Assets		**Equity ☺ or ☹**	
Intangibles			
		Stock	
		Retained Earnings	–5.000
	–5,000		–5,000

Figure 5.15 Balance sheet—expense the copier

CAPITALIZING

If you decide instead to capitalize the copier—or, in simpler terms, record the copier as a fixed asset—here is what would happen to your financial statements on the day of purchase.

Income statement: no effect.

Income Statement
Sales
Cost of Goods
Gross Profit
Operating Expenses
Operating Profit
less Taxes/Other
Net Income

Figure 5.16 Income statement—capitalize the copier, day of purchase

Cash flow statement: cash is reduced by $5000.

Cash Flow Statement	
Beginning Cash	
+ Cash Collected	
– Cash Paid	–5,000
Ending Cash	–5,000

Figure 5.17 Cash flow statement—capitalize the copier, day of purchase

Balance sheet (Figure 5-18): cash is reduced by $5000 and fixed assets are increased by $5000.

Later in the year, the income statement is impacted because if we capitalize the copier, we necessarily have to depreciate it.

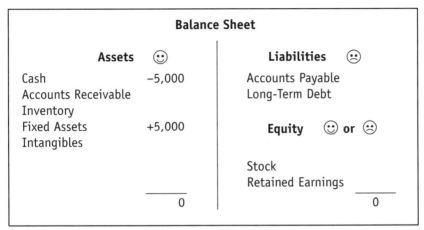

Figure 5.18 Balance sheet—capitalize the copier, day of purchase

---

What Is Depreciation?

It's a way of accounting for the loss in value of an asset. Depreciation allows businesses to acknowledge two truths about fixed assets.

First, fixed assets, as they age, are generally not worth as much as you paid for them; they lose value. Second, fixed assets are useful to the organization for more than one year. If you expense a fixed asset, you are in essence saying that you have used up its value in the year that you bought it. Most fixed assets are used for several years. A car, a computer, a piece of manufacturing equipment, and a copier all have value longer than a year.

So let's say that you've decided that the copier has a life of five years. If you used straight-line deprecation (the most simplified depreciation method possible: divide the cost of the asset by its useful life), you would recognize that you used up one-fifth or $1000 of its value every year.

So on our financial statements, at the beginning of the year, cash is down by $5000 and fixed assets are up by $5000. Now, at the end of the year, you recognize that the asset has been used up and the value of the copier is less. So you record depreciation expense. Key word—expense. Go to the income statement (Figure 5.19) and increase expenses by $1000, thereby reducing net income by $1000.

```
              Income Statement

     Sales
     Cost of Goods
                              _____
     Gross Profit
     Operating Expenses       –1,000
                              _____
     Operating Profit
     less Taxes/Other
                              _____
     Net Income               – 1,000
```

Figure 5.19 Income statement—capitalize, end of year

What happens on the cash flow statement? Nothing. Cash was impacted when you paid cash for the copier. Depreciation is what some fancy accountants call a *noncash expense*. It reduces net income without reducing cash in later years—years 2-5 in our example.

```
         Cash Flow Statement

     Beginning Cash
     + Cash Collected
     – Cash Paid
     _____
     Ending Cash
```

Figure 5.20 Cash flow statement—capitalize, end of year

On the balance sheet, you now need to decrease fixed assets by the $1000 in depreciation and decrease retained earnings by the $1000 decrease in net income flowing over from the income statement (Figure 5.21).

So at the end of year 1, your balance sheet reports:

- a decrease in cash of $5000
- an increase in fixed assets of $4000 ($5000 copier less $1000 depreciation)
- a decrease in retained earnings of $1000

So the balance sheet again balances. Assets are decreased by $1000 and retained earnings are decreased by $1000.

No matter what you do, you check to see that your balance sheet balances.

Balance Sheet

Assets ☺		Liabilities ☹	
Cash	−5,000	Accounts Payable	
Accounts Receivable		Long-Term Debt	
Inventory			
Copier	5,000	**Equity** ☺ or ☹	
Less accum. depr.	−1,000		
Fixed Assets	+4,000		
Intangibles		Stock	
		Retained Earnings	−1,000
	−1,000		−1,000

Figure 5.21 Balance sheet—capitalize, finalize end of year

At the end of year 2, your balance sheet (Figure 5.22) shows:

- a decrease in fixed assets of $1,000 for depreciation
- a decrease in retained earnings of $1,000 for depreciation expense

Balance Sheet

Assets ☺		Liabilities ☹	
Cash		Accounts Payable	
Accounts Receivable		Long-Term Debt	
Inventory			
Fixed Assets	−1,000	**Equity** ☺ or ☹	
Intangibles			
		Stock	
		Retained Earnings	−1,000
	0		−1,000

Figure 5.22 Balance sheet, end of second year

So depreciation, in effect, spreads the impact of your purchase on income and retained earnings over a longer time period. When you expense the purchase, it reduces retained earnings (a.k.a. net income) by $5000 in one pop. When you depreciate it, you reduce retained earnings and net income by just a little—$1000 in our scenario—each year (Figures 5.23 and 5.24).

Income Statement	
Sales	
Cost of Goods	_____
Gross Profit	
Operating Expenses	–1,000
Operating Profit	
less Taxes/Other	_____
Net Income	– 1,000

Figure 5.23 Income statement, capitalize copier

Income Statement	
Sales	
Cost of Goods	_____
Gross Profit	
Operating Expenses	5,000
Operating Profit	
less Taxes/Other	_____
Net Income	– 5,000

Figure 5.24 Income statement, expense copier

You really don't have a choice with most purchases.

In our example, we pretended that the organization had a choice between expensing and capitalizing a fixed asset. In most cases, this is not true. The IRS has a lot to say about whether an item should be depreciated and for how long.

Many organizations opt to expense small purchases, let's say under $5000 or $2500, but when you get up in the tens of thousands of dollars, the IRS frowns on expensing. You see, when you expense a fixed asset purchase, this reduces the taxable income you report to the IRS and the taxes you pay in the year of purchase.

So for tax reasons, expensing fixed asset purchases is often more attractive. But if you are trying to please the shareholders, capitalizing and then depreciating fixed assets is more attractive because you decrease your income only a little each year.

Now are you ready to talk about debits and credits? Hold onto your hats—Part Two is going to get very detailed!

Quiz

1. The mother of all financial statements is
   (a) the income statement
   (b) the cash flow statement
   (c) the statement of owners' equity
   (d) the statement of activities
   (e) the balance sheet

2. The formula of the income statement is (I can never ask this enough!)
   (a) revenues – less cash = profit
   (b) cash – profit = expenses
   (c) revenue – expenses = profit

3. The income statement is linked to the balance sheet, its mother, through
   (a) the fixed asset figure
   (b) the cash figure
   (c) the retained earnings figure
   (d) the accounts payable figure

4. The cash flow statement only cares about what happened to
   (a) revenues and expenses
   (b) fixed asset purchases
   (c) cash

5. The balance of intellectual property is included on which statement?
   (a) balance sheet
   (b) income statement
   (c) cash flow statement

6. The balance of accounts payable is reported on which statement?
   (a) balance sheet
   (b) income statement
   (c) cash flow statement

7. Retained earnings appear on which statement?
   (a) balance sheet
   (b) income statement
   (c) cash flow statement

8. Cash used to purchase a fixed asset appears on which statement?
   (a) balance sheet
   (b) income statement
   (c) cash flow statement

9. When we make a cash sale
    (a) the income statement records a sale
    (b) the cash flow statement records an increase in cash
    (c) the income statement is not affected
    (d) the cash flow statement is not affected
    (e) a and b
    (f) b and c

10. When we make a sale on credit
    (a) the income statement records a sale
    (b) the cash flow statement records an increase in cash
    (c) the income statement is not affected
    (d) the cash flow statement is not affected
    (e) a and b
    (f) b and c
    (g) a and d

11. When we collect on an account receivable,
    (a) the income statement records a sale
    (b) the cash flow statement records an increase in cash
    (c) the income statement is not affected
    (d) the cash flow statement is not affected
    (e) b and c
    (f) c and d

12. When we capitalize something, it means we
    (a) record it as an expense
    (b) record it as a liability
    (c) realize it in cash
    (d) record it as a fixed asset

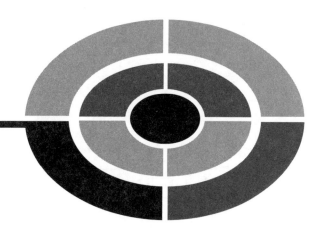

Test: Part One

1. Busting the covenants is when you
   (a) ignore the classic accounting equatio
   (b) run afoul of the agreement you made with the bank on a loan
   (c) stop tithing at church

2. A business can raise money by
   (a) selling stock
   (b) taking out a loan
   (c) selling goods and services
   (d) all of the above

3. What three things can happen to your profit?
   (a) pay dividends, pay taxes, and retain
   (b) pay dividends, pay taxes, and distribute
   (c) pay taxes, retain, and distribute to employees

4. The best source of resources to finance your company's operations is
   (a) issue stock
   (b) take out a loan
   (c) sell products and services
   (d) all of the above

5. Working capital
   (a) is current assets minus current liabilities
   (b) should be as small as possible
   (c) is the resources, or capital, you have working for you
   (d) all of the above

6. ABC stands for
   (a) activity burden calculation
   (b) activity-based calculation
   (c) activity-based costing
   (d) actual burden cost

7. The subtotal on the income statement that is the result of subtracting cost of goods sold from sales is
   (a) operating margin
   (b) gross margin
   (c) net margin

8. The subtotal on the income statement that is the results of subtracting cost of goods sold and operating expenses from sales is
   (a) operating margin
   (b) gross margin
   (c) net margin

9. The subtotal on the income statement that is the result of taking cost of goods sold, operating expenses, and other expenses such as taxes from sales is
   (a) operating margin
   (b) gross margin
   (c) net margin

10. In general, direct costs go into which category of expenses?
    (a) cost of goods sold
    (b) operating expenses
    (c) capital expenditures
    (d) unusual items

11. The indirect method
    (a) reconciles net income to cash
    (b) categorizes information into three general categories—operating, investing, and financing
    (c) is the most commonly used method
    d) all of the above

12. The three categories of cash flow disclosed on the financial statements are
    (a) operating, financing, and investing
    (b) operating, purchasing, and net income
    (c) financing, investing, and day-to-day operations

13. If operating cash from the cash flow statement and operating income on the income statement are vastly different, it may indicate that
    (a) the entity is not recognizing its sales in cash
    (b) the entity is using the cash method of accounting
    (c) the entity has a large balance of fixed assets
    (d) the entity is under investigation by the SEC

14. Interest paid to creditors is included in which category?
    (a) operating activities
    (b) financing activities
    (c) investing activities

15. Cash inflows for operating activities include
    (a) cash receipts for the sale of goods and services
    (b) cash receipts for the collection of operating receivables
    (c) cash interest received
    (d) cash dividends received
    (e) all of the above

16. Long-term debt appears on which statement?
    (a) balance sheet
    (b) income statement
    (c) cash flow statement

17. Cost of goods sold expense appears on which statement?
    (a) balance sheet
    (b) income statement
    (c) cash flow statement

18. Total sales revenue appears on which statement?
    (a) balance sheet
    (b) income statement
    (c) cash flow statement

19. Cash paid to acquire equity investments in another entity appears on which statement?
    (a) balance sheet
    (b) income statement
    (c) cash flow statement

20. Cash collected from customers appears on which statement?
    (a) balance sheet
    (b) income statement
    (c) cash flow statement

21. The income statement includes
    (a) cash transactions
    (b) fixed asset purchases and long-term investments
    (c) revenues and expenses

22. The proverbial "bottom line" is
    (a) total net assets
    (b) total cash
    (c) net income
    (d) retained earnings

23. We record depreciation because we want to acknowledge
    (a) that the value of most assets decreases over time
    (b) that assets are used by the organization beyond the year in which they were purchased
    (c) both a and b

24. The IRS lets you expense or capitalize assets at will.
    T or F

25. In the second year of depreciating an asset, cash is not affected.
    T or F

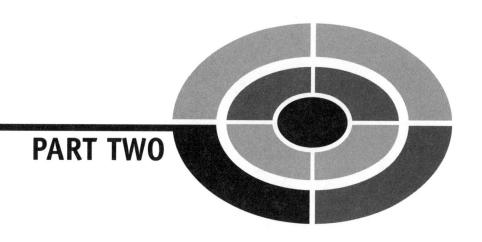

PART TWO

An Overview of Common Accounting Reports

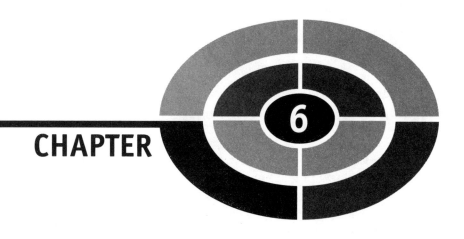

Different Systems, Different Reports

So far we have been talking about the general ledger and entries into the general ledger. The general ledger system is often called the *financial accounting system*. But the general ledger is not the only system that businesses use for counting. There are several other tools that businesses use to track financial results. These systems might or might not be linked to the general ledger. To get the systems to talk to each other, you have to invest in the technology that lets you do it.

Some organizations are reluctant to take advantage of technology—either because of the cost or because they don't like change. One of those "If it ain't broke, don't fix it" sort of attitudes. In 2004, a city manager of a small east Texas town told me that his bookkeeper is still keeping the city's records by hand! *Whoa!* There are all sorts of levels of financial record-keeping savvy.

Let me introduce you to a few other systems that track financial data that you might run into:

- cost accounting
- budgetary accounting
- tax accounting

Cost Accounting Systems

Cost accounting systems track how much it costs to create, market, sell, and distribute a product or service.

Imagine a cost accounting system for the manufacturing of a television set. The system would track how much each component of the TV cost as well as how many labor hours went into assembling the TV. The system would also track how many labor hours it took to quality-test the TV and how many TVs were rejected and reworked. It would track how much it cost to package the TV and how quickly it was shipped out to the customer. I could go on and on.

HOW IT DIFFERS FROM THE GENERAL LEDGER

This is much more detail than included in the general ledger. The general ledger is kept at a higher level. The general ledger or the financial accounting system will record how much the team made in salaries for the week, but it won't break down that Bob spent 15 hours assembling big-screen TVs and 23 hours on portable TVs or that eight of Bob's portables were rejected because of poor quality. The general ledger only knows that Bob was paid (for his shoddy work!).

Some accounting software has modules that allow a company to link the cost accounting data to the general ledger and some do not. Don't be surprised if you have an entirely different team at your company tracking cost accounting data than you have tracking your general ledger transactions.

One of the major criticisms aimed at financial accountants is that their information isn't timely. By the time the information is posted to the general ledger, compiled, reviewed, and reported, the team that needs to make decisions with it has moved on. A good cost accounting system will be in real time, giving the frontline team daily or sometimes even hourly information on its progress.

STANDARD COST AND OTHER COST TERMINOLOGY

You might hear the terms *standard cost*, *indirect cost*, *direct cost*, *variable cost*, or *fixed cost* used by a cost accountant. I described what indirect costs, direct costs, variable costs, and fixed costs are in Chapter 3 in our discussion of the income statement.

Standard cost is the cost to which accountants hold the manufacturing team. It's the standard against which actual costs are compared. For instance, they might determine that it takes 1.2 hours of manufacturing labor to create a television. This becomes the standard by which all manufacturing efforts are measured. The cost accountant will track deviations from standard cost and require the manufacturing team to explain the variations.

Cost accountants are the folks who allocate the indirect costs discussed in Chapter 3 to the products and services. They might also work with activity-based costing (ABC).

Smith Industries, Bill of Activities					
Part Number: XYZ-123 **Planned Volume:** 10,000					
			Driver Attributes		
Activities	**Drivers**	**Cost per Driver**	**Value Added**	**Non-value Added**	**Total Cost**
Unit Level Activities					
Cut to Length	Direct Labor Hours	$11.44	$11.44		$11.44
Rough Turn	Direct Labor Hours	$11.06	$11.06		$11.06
Centerless Grind	Machine Hours	$11.20	$11.20		$11.20
Batch Level Activities Set-Up					
Cut to Length	Set-up Hours	$9.75		$9.75	$9.75
Rough Turn	Set-up Hours	$9.76		$9.76	$9.76
Centerless Grind	Set-up Hours	$10.25		$10.25	$10.25
Inspection					
Cut to Length	No. of Inspections	$0.14		$0.14	$0.14
Rough Turn	No. of Inspections	$0.20		$0.20	$0.20
Centerless Grind	No. of Inspections	$0.25		$0.25	$0.25
Material Movement Receive Material					
Freight in	Pounds	$0.22		$0.22	$0.22
Direct Material	Pounds	$5.20	$5.20		$5.20
Product Level Activities Engineering					
Process Evalution	Engineering Hours	$1.25	$1.25		$1.25
Marketing Direct Product					
Quotation	Proposal Hours	$10.75	$10.75		$10.75
Totals			**$50.90**	**$30.57**	**$61.47**

Figure 6.1 Example of cost accounting report

It Costs Time and Money to Be Cool

One key rule to keep in mind in looking at your organization's accounting systems is this:

The frequency and accuracy of information cost time and money.

You have to decide what the information is worth to you.

For instance, I consult with a high-tech manufacturer. A few years ago they decided that cost, marketing, and sales information were key to their success and that they needed it every day, not once a month.

On their internal computer information system, their intranet, they have a multilayered Excel spreadsheet that contains up-to-the-hour information on hundreds of key metrics.

Any decision maker can access this spreadsheet to find out how many units of each product sold that day and how they were sold—by Internet, by phone, or by third parties. They can find out how much each unit cost and how much margin was generated on each product line. They can also determine whether they were on track with daily, weekly, and quarterly goals and diagnose what to do if they miss their targets.

Some of the data is fed into the Excel spreadsheet from the general ledger system, some from the cost accounting system, some from the phone system, and some from the Internet sales tracking system. Creating and updating the spreadsheet was and continues to be a huge investment of time and money on the part of the company. So why do they do it? Because the up-to-date information lets them change course and respond to market demands and competitors actions within a day—not within a month or a quarter. Information is power!

Budgets

A budget is the translation of the plans of the entity into financial terms.

WHY HAVE A BUDGET?

Budgets are simply a management tool that lends focus and accountability to an organization.

Focus

Creation of a budget can focus your organization on what is important. Periodic monitoring of the budget gives an organization feedback on whether it is operating according to plan and *staying* focused on what is important.

For instance, at the beginning of the year, a hospital might decide that, in order to improve its services, it needs to renovate the emergency room and buy several key pieces of medical equipment. If by midyear, the renovation has not been done and the purchases have not been made, a monthly budget report will highlight the fact and alert management that action needs to be taken.

Accountability

A budget is also useful if you want to hold managers and staff accountable for their decisions and actions. A budget is nothing if it is not monitored, used, and taken seriously.

I once worked for an organization that spent two months creating a budget on several multiple-page Excel spreadsheets that filled a large binder. At the beginning of the year, every manager was given a copy of the binder—and that was the last we ever looked at it!

We spent what we spent, we sold what we sold, and no one was held accountable to it. You can imagine the respect that the managers had for the budget! *None*! In that case, it wasn't even worth having one. If you are using a budget right, you report periodically about whether or not the team is spending or generating revenue according to plan.

YOU MIGHT NOT NEED A BUDGET

Some organizations don't have them and don't really need them.

After teaching a budgeting seminar to CPAs a few years ago, a participant approached me and asked for my help. She was the controller for a rapidly growing Las Vegas business. Her company made the Plexiglas screens that decorate slot machines. (You know how they change every few years—one year the slots are decorated like Monopoly games and the next year it's "Viva Elvis!")

The owner of the company had recently attended a seminar for entrepreneurs. At the seminar, the instructors told him that he needed a budget. He had no idea what he would do with a budget, but he instructed his comptroller to go figure out how to pull one together for his company.

I stayed overnight in Vegas and met with the controller and her boss the next day. After a long discussion, I recommended that the organization not develop a budget right away. This owner did not want to keep managers informed of what they were spending; in fact, he wanted to keep it secret. He didn't want to create a yearlong projection of revenues and expenditures because he was growing so fast his projections would have been way off.

What he needed and wanted was better cost data. He needed to know how much it cost him to make each screen so that he would be sure to sell it at a high enough price. So the budgeting tool wasn't for him at all. His controller was relieved and promised to compile the cost data he was looking for.

A VARIETY OF BUDGET TYPES

There are also a variety of budget formats and philosophies. Each organization keeps its budget in its own unique way. I teach budgeting to CPAs and have them draw the format of their budget on flip-chart paper and share it with the rest of the class. The variety of formats and content is striking. There is no right or wrong approach.

Here are three common ones: line-item budgets, performance-based budgets, and zero-based budgets.

Line-Item Budgets

Many businesses use a line-item budget. The line-item budget is simply a list of all the revenue and expenditure categories applicable to the entity. It is the simplest approach. Figure 6.2 shows an example.

Performance-Based Budgets

My favorite type of budgeting is performance-based budgeting. It takes a lot more investment of time to create, but actually links the strategic plan to the budget. The plan comes first, then the budget. Performance-based budgeting also links performance metrics to dollars. So instead of just asking a department whether it spent within limits, it also asks whether it performed its functions well. Figure 6.3 shows an example of a performance-based budget format.

Salaries	$300,000
Office Supplies	$5,000
Travel	$24,000
Equipment Maintenance	$2,000
New Equipment Purchases	$3,000
Utilties	$2,000
Phone	$6,000
Other	$1,000
Total	**$343,000**

Figure 6.2 Line-item budget

Goals/Strategies	1994	1995
A. Goal: INDEPENDENT LIVING: To assist Texans who are blind live as independently as possible consistent with their capabilities.		
A.1. Objective: Increase the number of consumers achieving their independent living goals. **Outcome:** Pct avoding a dependent living environment	93%	93%
A.1.1. Strategy: To provide a statewide program of development independent living skills. **Outputs:** Number of adults trained	$3,695,823 3,079	$3,439,224 3,184
A.2. Objective: Increase the number of children who achieve their habilitative goals.		
A.2.1. Strategy: To provide habilitative services to blind and visually imparied children. **Outputs:** Number of children receiving services	$2,761,465 8,988	$2,869,277 9,266
B. Goal: MAINTAIN EMPLOYMENT: To assist Texans who are blind or visually impaired to secure or maintain employment in careers consistent with their skills, abilities, and interests.		
B.1. Objective: Increase the number of successfully employed consumers. **Outcome:** Pct consumers successfully rehabilitated with improved economic self-sufficiency	86.5%	86.5%

Figure 6.3 Performance-based budget (continued on next page)

Goals/Strategies	1994	1995
B.1.1. Strategy: To provide vocational rehabilitation to services to persons who are blind or visually impaired.	$28,351,959	$28,259,959
Outputs: Number of consumers served	12,888	12,831
B.1.2. Strategy: To provide translation services leading to successful transition from school to work.	$1,311,082	$1,781,861
Outputs: Number of students successfully completing program	72	72
B.1.3. Strategy: To provide employment opportunities in the food service industry for persons who are blind or visually impaired. **Outputs:** Number of consumers employed	140	145
B. Goal: Continuation of 1993 salary increase	720,302	
Grand Total, Commission for the Blind	$39,060,851	$38,307,441

Figure 6.3 Performance-based budget (continued)

Zero-Based Budgets

Zero-based budgeting is also a popular budget philosophy. In zero-based budgeting, you assume that you don't exist anymore and must build the budget up from that "zero base."

For example, let's say you are a copy center inside a large corporation and the corporation has instituted zero-based budgeting this year. Currently, you have seven employees who process 3600 copying projects for the company during the year, you take up 800 square feet of space, and you maintain $230,000 worth of equipment.

To implement a zero-based budget, you assume that you don't exist any more. You don't automatically get to keep all those wonderful people and stuff. You must justify every employee you have, every project you take on, every square foot of space you consume, and every piece of equipment you maintain. You don't just get to have the same budget as you did last year and add a new person and 500 new projects.

You propose your output at three levels—maximum, moderate, and minimum. The proposals are documented and put in a stack with every other division's proposals. The leaders of the company rank the proposals in terms of importance. The proposals at the bottom of the stack might not receive funding because they are low priority and the organization might be out of resources to fund the proposals.

Jimmy Carter popularized this type of budget in his run for the presidency in the 1970s. It was designed to cut government waste—to make all government programs justify their existence and not assume that they would continue along the same path year after year after year. Personally, I think this kind of decomposing of a program or department might work once or twice, but you shouldn't make people go through this every year. It might cut the fat out of your organization once, but employees will not take it seriously if they are made to do it every single year. It can be very tedious.

BUDGETARY INFORMATION IS MAINTAINED APART FROM THE GENERAL LEDGER

Usually the budgetary information is tracked separately and reported separately from the general ledger. Many accountants create and maintain the budget on an Excel spreadsheet.

They often keep these systems separate because of the difference between the general ledger and the budget in recognizing a revenue or an expense. The budget might recognize a commitment to spend money even though the general ledger might not have recognized an expenditure yet.

For instance, you might contract with a management consultant in a $3600 contract. The budget will recognize that $3600 of the budget for consultants has been consumed, but the general ledger may not pick up the $3600 as an expense until the consultant bills you.

Some general ledger systems allow you to input the yearly budget figures into the general ledger and then, as transactions are posted to the system, the budget is updated and reports can be generated. The line items on the budget must match the line items in the general ledger for this to work.

Tax Accounting

How the IRS says transactions are to be treated and the way GAAP treats them are often different. In my simple little business, I have a woman who keeps my general ledger and creates my financial reports and another woman who does my taxes. The skills and knowledge to do each are quite different.

GAAP doesn't change that often. Tax code does. Tax accountants have to keep very fresh on the latest laws that impact their clients' tax returns.

Here is an example. When a company entertains its clients, the entire cost is posted to the general ledger. However, in many instances, the IRS will let the company write off, or recognize, only a percentage of the cost of entertainment. Employee benefits, depreciation, and travel expenses are just a few of the differences between taxes and GAAP accounting, and they are treated differently in the general ledger than they are in the tax records.

My taxable net income in my business never looks the same as the net income my bookkeeper reports on my income statement.

Another factor to add to this complicated situation is state taxes. Some states charge personal income tax; some don't. Almost all states have some sort of corporate income tax, although it might be named something less direct. For instance, in Texas, corporate income tax is called a *franchise tax*. Then there is the issue of sales tax, estate tax, and property tax. Tax, tax, tax.

This is why many major corporations have an entire team of tax specialists who concern themselves only with the tax implications of different decisions. For instance, when the company is looking at whether to lease or to buy an asset, the managers look at the effect on the financial statements, but they also look at the short-term and long-term effects on taxes. No one likes to pay more taxes than necessary. Because we are all familiar with the beautiful IRS forms, I won't include one here.

Quiz

1. Cost accounting systems track how much it costs to create, market, sell, and distribute a product or service.
   T or F

2. Indirect costs are the costs that can be directly linked to the product—such as component costs and manufacturing labor.
   T or F

3. Standard costs are used in tax accounting to determine amortization of equipment.
   T or F

4. One of the major criticisms aimed at financial accountants is that their information isn't
   (a) accurate
   (b) timely
   (c) proper
   (d) added correctly

5. The frequency and accuracy of information cost time and money.
   T or F

6. The two main benefits of a budget are that budgets enhance
   (a) timeliness and responsiveness
   (b) planning and accuracy
   (c) control and accountability
   (d) focus and accountability

7. Every organization should use a budget as a tool for managing.
   T or F

8. Which type of budget links the strategic plan to the budget?
   (a) the line-item budget
   (b) the zero-based budget
   (c) the performance-based budget

9. A zero-based budget asks that you
   (a) cut 10 percent out of every line item on the budget
   (b) propose output at three levels
   (c) assume that you and all your stuff don't exist anymore
   (d) link your requests to the goals of the organization
   (e) a and b
   (f) a, b, and c
   (g) b and c
   (h) all of the above

10. Tax considerations include
    (a) federal tax
    (b) state tax
    (c) local taxes
    (d) sales tax
    (e) property tax
    (f) estate tax
    (g) personal income tax
    (h) corporate income tax
    (i) all of the above

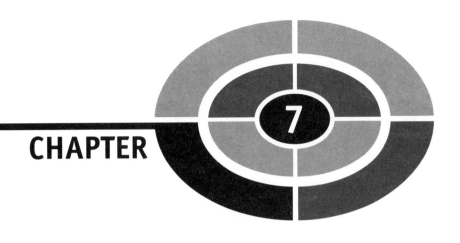

CHAPTER

Quarterly and Annual Financial Reports—A Tour

Every publicly traded company in the United States must publish several financial reports each year and submit them to the Securities and Exchange Commission (SEC). Only public companies are required to create financial statements and submit them to the SEC. A privately or closely held corporation doesn't have to create financial statements for anyone! Its financials are no one else's business.

Four of the most commonly used reports are the three 10-Qs—quarterly reports—and the single 10-K—an annual report summarizing the entire fiscal year.

The SEC dictates the disclosures that each section could contain and the title of each section. The SEC even tells corporations what size and type of font to use in the reports. The emphasis is on standardization and comparability of data. The SEC doesn't want any corporation looking any fancier than any other. Creativity is not valued here; all that matters is information.

The 10-K

The SEC documents are about as detailed as many corporations get—especially in their disclosures to outsiders. As we have discussed in Chapter 6 on cost accounting, budgeting, and taxation, there is a wealth of information that companies can generate and use internally to make financial decisions. If we are on the outside of the organization, we can't get our hands on any of this data.

So for this chapter, we are going to explore what we can get our hands on, the SEC document—the 10-K. (You can also get your hands on the 10-Q, but it covers only a quarter, not a year.) I suggest that you get one of these now so you have it next to you as we work through this chapter. I will include a few sample pages here and there, but it really would be best if you would get one yourself.

How Do You Get a 10-K?

How do you get a 10-K? Pick one of your favorite publicly traded companies and go on to its Web site and look for a menu option called "investor relations." Usually under this tab, you will find a PDF (Adobe) file of the latest 10-K. You can view, download, or print this document and have it handy as you read this chapter.

If you want someone else to print it, you can call or e-mail the investor relations department and ask them for a copy. They will be happy to mail you one—although this might take a little while. You can also log on to the Securities and Exchange Commission homepage (www.sec.gov) and find the filings for every company that is publicly traded.

Annual Reports Are Not 10-Ks

I need to point out here that an annual report and a 10-K are not the same thing. You might have encountered an annual report as an investor. An annual report is a magazine-style document. It is attractive, colored, and printed on slick paper. A good 70 percent of the document can be dedicated to marketing and giving the reader a warm fuzzy feeling about the company. The real financial data is usually included near the back of the report and doesn't last for more than 20 pages. ("No need to bore the investor with financial data" is the philosophy here, I guess.)

I definitely prefer the 10-K to the annual report as a document to analyze the financial results of a company. First of all, it is often 40 or more pages of good financial data and information on the company. It doesn't include any marketing hooey (not that I don't like marketing, mind you! I almost majored in it) or pictures of sweet puppies, gorgeous women, or small children to distract you. It is just information, information, information.

So go ahead and enjoy an annual report, but for real decisions, consult the 10-K or the latest 10-Q ,

---

Subscriptions Will Deliver Financial Info to You

If you have the money to pay for financial data, you can subscribe to any variety of financial services that will take the financial data published by a company and compile it, analyze it, and sometimes even make conclusions for you. These companies will save you on a lot of the grunt work. One such company, which is based here in Austin, is Hoover's (www.hoovers.com). For a monthly subscription fee, Hoover's will provide you with a wealth of financial information on a variety of companies.

The Cover of the 10-K

On this page, make sure to notice the date of the fiscal year-end. I have the Dell 10-K in my hands. I read about a quarter of the way down the page that Dell's fiscal year-end is January 30 (Figure 7.1).

This is important for me to know for several reasons.

One, I can use this date to gauge how old this information is. As I write, it is June, and so this information is already five months old. Dell has published several 10-Qs since then and, if I were doing a serious analysis, I would look at them to modify and update my understanding of what is going on in the business.

Second, I need to be aware that Dell's competitors do not necessarily have the same fiscal year-end. While Dell's 10-K is called the 2004 10-K because it is published for the fiscal year ending January 2004, the bulk of the report pertains to calendar year 2003. One of Dell's competitors, Gateway, has a fiscal year-end that corresponds with the calendar year-end—December 31, 2003. They call

UNITED STATES
SECURITIES AND EXCHANGE COMMISSION
Washington, D.C. 20549

Form 10-K

(Mark One)

☒ **ANNUAL REPORT PURSUANT TO SECTION 13 OR 15(d)
OF THE SECURITIES EXCHANGE ACT OF 1934**

For the Fiscal Year Ended January 28, 2005

or

☐ **TRANSITION REPORT PURSUANT TO SECTION 13 OR 15(d)
OF THE SECURITIES EXCHANGE ACT OF 1934**

For the transition period from   to

Commission File Number: 0-17017

Dell Inc.

(Exact name of registrant as specified in its charter)

Delaware	**74-2487834**
(State or other jurisdiction of incorporation or organization)	(I.R.S. Employer Identification No.)

One Dell Way, Round Rock, Texas 78682
(Address of principal executive offices) (Zip Code)

(512) 338-4400
(Registrant's telephone number, including area code)

Securities registered pursuant to Section 12(b) of the Act:

None

Securities Registered Pursuant to Section 12(g) of the Act:

Common Stock, par value $.01 per share
Preferred Stock Purchase Rights

Indicate by check mark whether the registrant (1) has filed all reports required to be filed by Section 13 or 15(d) of the Securities Exchange Act of 1934 during the preceding 12 months (or for such shorter period that the registrant was required to file such reports), and (2) has been subject to such filing requirements for the past 90 days. Yes ☒ No ☐

Indicate by check mark if disclosure of delinquent filers pursuant to Item 405 of Regulation S-K is not contained herein, and will not be contained, to the best of registrant's knowledge, in definitive proxy or information statements incorporated by reference in Part III of this Form 10-K or any amendment to this Form 10-K. ☐

Indicate by check mark whether the registrant is an accelerated filer (as defined in Rule 12b-2 of the Act). Yes ☒ No ☐

Approximate aggregate market value of the registrant's common stock held by non-
ffi a **liates as of July 30, 2004, based upon the closing price reported for such date on
The Nasdaq National Market** . . . . **$79.9 billion**
Number of shares of common stock outstanding as of February 25, 2005 . . . . **2,459,003,783**

DOCUMENTS INCORPORATED BY REFERENCE

The information required by Part III of this report, to the extent not set forth herein, is incorporated by reference from the registrant's definitive proxy statement relating to the annual meeting of stockholders to be held in July 2005, which definitive proxy statement will be filed with the Securities and Exchange Commission within 120 days after the end of the fiscal year to which this report relates.

Figure 7.1 Dell 10-K, page 1, 2005

their 10-K the 2003 10-K, but essentially, the Dell 2004 10-K and the Gateway 2003 10-K cover the same period.

Also notice on the bottom of this page that the aggregate market value of common stock held by the public is listed. This information allows you to get at the market value of the stock at a particular date—information you can't get anywhere else in the report. (This is the one of the few times that historical value is not used in a disclosure.) If you divide this number by the number of shares outstanding directly below it, you will be able to determine the market price per share as of the last day of the fiscal year. This number is used frequently by shareholders performing an analysis of the financial statements. Dell's aggregate market value is $75.6 billion and the number of shares is 2,530,660,582. This tells us that the market value of each share on January 30, 2004 is roughly $29.87.

Part I of the 10-K

The SEC dictates what will be included where in the financial statements. Part I of Dell's 10-K will contain similar information to Part I of Johnson & Johnson's 10-K, for example.

Part I is an overview of the business. It tells what the company is about, what sort of product it sells, and how it goes about doing business. The subtitles in Dell's Part I are:

- General
- Business Strategy
- Products
- Services
- Financial Services
- Sales and Marketing
- Manufacturing
- Product Development
- Patents, Trademarks, and Licenses
- Employees
- Government Regulation
- Backlog
- Geographical Areas of Operation
- Factors Affecting Dell's Business and Prospects

- Trademarks and Service Marks
- Website Access to Dell's SEC Reports
- Executive Officers of Dell

Why all this background information? Because it is important to educate the investor. Let's pretend you are a retired schoolteacher and you got a tip from your son-in-law that you should invest in a computer company. You know nothing about computer companies, but you know to read the 10-K! This section of the 10-K is very valuable to you: it allows you to compare the operating philosophy of Dell with the operating philosophies of its competitors. You can then decide which computer company you feel more affinity with or have more faith in.

Let's backtrack a bit and talk about a few of these subtitles and sections in Part I.

BUSINESS STRATEGY

Here is an excerpt from Dell's 10-K:

> The key tenets of Dell's business strategy are:
> *A direct relationship is the most efficient path to the customer.* Direct customer relationships provide a constant flow of information about customers' plans and requirements ....

This is a great section that allows you to set the company apart from its competitors and is a must-read. It will shape your expectations of financial results. For instance, Dell is unique in the computer business in that it sells products directly to customers. It does not sell its computers to stores that then sell the computers to customers.

This will cause the financial statements to look quite different from the 10-Ks of competitors that might incur commissions for sales intermediaries or suffer high return rates from stores. The makeup of inventory balances and the amount of inventory balances might also be affected.

The financial statements are there to tell a story: this is our "Once upon a time" section of the financials. Don't skip it.

FACTORS AFFECTING BUSINESS AND PROSPECTS

This is another must-read section of the financial statements. This section should sound tame or normal and not go on for tens of pages.

Once, I succumbed to greed. (OK, I have succumbed more than once, but I'm only going to tell you about a single instance in this book!) Remember the late 1990s when stock prices were flying high? I have a friend who is an attorney in Dallas and he and his wife were trading stocks on a daily basis. They'd buy something in the morning and sell it by the afternoon. They had $50K or more to play with in the market and several times I talked with him right after he had doubled their money.

I was thrilled for them and envious. I wasn't getting those fabulous returns on my investments and I didn't feel like I had the luxury of "playing" with the money I had invested for my retirement.

One day, near the end of the stock market party, I received a gift of $10,000 from a relative. I decided to invest about half of it in the stock market. I called my lawyer friend and asked him where I should put it. "Who is hot and how can I make a quick buck?" was my approach.

He said that if he advised me that I could never complain to him if I lost money. I agreed and he advised me to invest in a high-tech Internet-related software company. Do you know where this is going? I plunked my money down and watched over the next few weeks as my stock became virtually worthless. The next time that I receive any gift of money, I'm buying a couch!

After I had lost it all, I received the company's 10-K in the mail. As I thumbed through and started to laugh and cry, I read this section. The "Factors Affecting Business and Prospects" for my high-tech company was laughably awful. It said things like "We only have one customer and if this customer does not buy our product, we are toast." "We only have one product. We do not have a patent for this product. If a competitor steals our idea, we are toast." "We have not finished developing our product and are not sure that it will meet the customers' needs. If it doesn't work, we are toast." I am paraphrasing, of course, but you get the idea: my investment was toast.

Always read this section of the financial statements. The company is obligated and required to disclose anything it knows that could negatively affect its financial results. You, the investor, have to decide whether the risks that the company discloses in this section are palatable to you. For instance, Dell's 10-K says, "General economic, business, or industry conditions may result in a decrease in net revenue." This is the "A rising tide lifts all boats" sort of statement and in my mind is no cause for alarm.

What is the moral of this story? Read the 10-K before you invest in a company. If it is a good company, it won't matter that much that you waited a few hours, days, or weeks to invest.

EXECUTIVE OFFICERS

This is another good section to peruse. If you are a serious Wall Street investor, reading this list of the folks on the management team is like reading a basketball team's roster. You know who these men and women are, their past track records, and you have opinions as to whether they can win the game and make a profit.

You might read that the leaders of the company are recent graduates of a prestigious business school with no hands-on experience with business. Nothing against Harvard, but real business experience counts for something. If you had faith in these young leaders and knew them personally, then you could comfortably make the choice to invest. If you did not have this personal faith, a disclosure of their professional experience and credentials, as is detailed in this section, might cause concern.

ITEM 2—PROPERTIES

This tells about the real estate holdings of the company. This will disclose the physical location of their operations. Their headquarters might be in the United States, but they have manufacturing operations in South America. A shifting or unstable political environment in any country could have serious implications for the company.

ITEM 3—LEGAL PROCEEDINGS

Here the company is required to disclose any significant lawsuits in which it is involved. Dell's section is short and sweet. In other words, benign.

"Dell is subject to various legal proceedings and claims arising in the ordinary course of business. Dell's management does not expect that the results in any of these legal proceedings will have a material adverse effect on Dell's financial condition, results of operations, or cash flows."

Notice the "material adverse effect" phrasing. This means that the lawsuits are not significant financially and will not cause huge fluctuations in the financial results disclosed in the financial statements. There might be several smallish lawsuits in progress, but nothing major.

Now, Microsoft, during its battles with the federal government, would have had significantly more to say in this section. Gateway, the subject of our financial analysis in later chapters, discloses in this section several significant lawsuits and a conflict with the SEC.

This section is also a must-read.

ITEM 4—SUBMISSION OF MATTERS TO A VOTE OF SECURITY HOLDERS

If a corporation wants to change any of the documents that were created to form the corporation, such as the bylaws or the articles of incorporation, the shareholders must agree to the change. Think of the articles of incorporation and the bylaws as being akin to the U.S. Constitution. Whenever the Constitution is changed, our elected representatives must agree to the change. For instance, if the company wanted to issue more stock than was initially allowed in the articles of incorporation, the shareholders would need to say whether they agree. Issuance of additional shares of stock could affect the value of their holdings.

Part II of the 10-K

Part II is all about money and is the core of the 10-K. Some of the information disclosed in this section is a bit technical—but after reading this book, you should be able to understand a good 80 percent of it with a simple read-through.

ITEM 5—MARKET FOR REGISTRANT'S COMMON EQUITY, RELATED STOCKHOLDERS MATTERS AND ISSUER PURCHASES OF EQUITY SECURITIES

This section discusses who owns the company, how the equity is structured, and whether the company pays dividends.

ITEM 6—SELECTED FINANCIAL DATA

I love this table. This table gives us five years' worth of financial information for such key items as net revenue, gross margin, operating margin, net income, cash

provided by operations, and total assets. This table makes it easy for a person running financial analysis to trend key information. Just by looking at it, you can get a sense of the growth or decline of the business (Figure 7.2).

ITEM 7—MANAGEMENT'S DISCUSSION AND ANALYSIS OF FINANCIAL CONDITION AND RESULTS OF OPERATIONS

This is hands-down my favorite part of the 10-K—even above the financial statements themselves (which, please notice, we still haven't gotten to!). This section, also called the MD&A, is a narrative version of the financial information. It tells the story of the financial statements.

It's not numbers just sitting there on the balance sheet, incomes statement, and cash flow statement; this section tells you how they got there. The MD&A goes on for several pages: it starts with a summary of results of operations and then dissects and examines each component of the income statement (Figure 7.3).

First it describes why net revenue—or total sales—has increased or decreased over previous years. Here is an excerpt from Dell's section on net revenue:

> Dell's fiscal 2004 growth continued to exceed market growth as consolidated net unit shipments increased 26% year-over-year while industry growth for the calendar year was only 9% (excluding Dell).

A section on gross margin highlights that gross margin improved in each of the last three years and attributes this improvement to "four primary cost reduction initiatives: manufacturing costs, warranty costs, structural or design costs, and overhead or operating expenses."

A section on operating expenses breaks out the components of operating expense into three subcategories—1) selling, general and administrative, 2) research, development and engineering, and 3) special charges—and explains the behavior of each.

The MD&A goes on to discuss the following:

- Liquidity, Capital Commitments, and Contractual Cash Obligations
- Market Risk
- Factors Affecting Dell's Business and Prospects
- Critical Accounting Policies
- Recently Issued Accounting Pronouncements

ITEM 6 — SELECTED FINANCIAL DATA

The following selected financial data should be read in conjunction "Item 7 — Management's Discussion and Analysis of Financial Condition and Results of Operations" and "Item 8 — Financial Statements and Supplementary Data."

	Fiscal Year Ended				
	January 28, 2005(a)	January 30, 2004	January 31, 2003	February 1, 2002(b)	February 2, 2001(c)
	(in millions, except per share data)				
Results of Operations:					
Net revenue....................	$49,205	$41,444	$35,404	$31,168	$31,888
Gross margin	9,015	7,552	6,349	5,507	6,443
Operating income..............	4,254	3,544	2,844	1,789	2,663
Income before cumulative effect of change in accounting principle(d)	3,043	2,645	2,122	1,246	2,236
Net income	$ 3,043	$ 2,645	$ 2,122	$ 1,246	$ 2,177
Earnings per common share:					
Before cumulative effect of change in accounting principle:					
Basic......................	$ 1.21	$ 1.03	$ 0.82	$ 0.48	$ 0.87
Diluted....................	$ 1.18	$ 1.01	$ 0.80	$ 0.46	$ 0.81
After cumulative effect of change in accounting principle:					
Basic......................	$ 1.21	$ 1.03	$ 0.82	$ 0.48	$ 0.84
Diluted....................	$ 1.18	$ 1.01	$ 0.80	$ 0.46	$ 0.79
Number of weighted average shares outstanding:					
Basic......................	2,509	2,565	2,584	2,602	2,582
Diluted....................	2,568	2,619	2,644	2,726	2,746
Cash Flow and Balance Sheet Data:					
Net cash provided by operating activities	$ 5,310	$ 3,670	$ 3,538	$ 3,797	$ 4,195
Cash, cash equivalents and investments	14,126	11,922	9,905	8,287	7,853
Total assets...................	23,215	19,311	15,470	13,535	13,670
Long-term debt...............	505	505	506	520	509
Total stockholders' equity	$ 6,485	$ 6,280	$ 4,873	$ 4,694	$ 5,622

(a) During the fourth quarter of fiscal 2005, Dell recorded a tax repatriation charge of $280 million pursuant to a favorable tax incentive provided by the American Jobs Creation Act of 2004. This tax charge is related to Dell's decision to repatriate $4.1 billion in foreign earnings.

(b) Includes a pre-tax charge of $742 million. Approximately $482 million relates to employee termination benefits, facilities closure costs, and other asset impairments and exit costs, while the balance of $260 million relates to other-than-temporary declines in the fair value of equity securities.

(c) Includes a pre-tax charge of $105 million related to employee termination benefits and facilities closure costs.

(d) Effective January 29, 2000, Dell changed its accounting for revenue recognition in accordance with the SEC's Staff Accounting Bulletin ("SAB") No. 101, *Revenue Recognition in Financial Statements*. The cumulative effect of the change on retained earnings as of the beginning of fiscal 2001 resulted in a charge to fiscal 2001 income of $59 million (net of income taxes of $25 million). With the exception of the cumulative effect adjustment, the effect of the change on net income for the fiscal year ended February 2, 2001 was not material.

Figure 7.2 Dell 10-K, 2005, financial data table

ITEM 7 — MANAGEMENT'S DISCUSSION AND ANALYSIS OF FINANCIAL CONDITION AND RESULTS OF OPERATIONS

Overview

Dell — through its direct business model — designs, develops, manufactures, markets, sells, and supports a wide range of computer systems and services that are customized to customer requirements. These include enterprise systems (servers, storage, workstations, and networking products), client systems (notebook and desktop computer systems), printing and imaging systems, software and peripherals, and global services. Dell markets and sells its products and services directly to its customers, which include large corporate, government, healthcare, and education accounts, as well as small-to-medium businesses and individual customers. Dell conducts operations worldwide and is managed in three geographic segments: the Americas, Europe, and Asia Pacific-Japan regions. Within the Americas, Dell is further segmented into Business and U.S. Consumer.

The following table summarizes Dell's consolidated results of operations for each of the past three fiscal years:

	Fiscal Year Ended				
	January 28, 2005	Percentage Change	January 30, 2004	Percentage Change	January 31, 2003
	(dollars in millions)				
Net revenue	$49,205	19%	$41,444	17%	$35,404
Gross margin	$ 9,015	19%	$ 7,552	19%	$ 6,349
% of net revenue	18.3%		18.2%		17.9%
Operating expenses	$ 4,761	19%	$ 4,008	14%	$ 3,505
% of net revenue	9.7%		9.7%		9.9%
Operating income	$ 4,254	20%	$ 3,544	25%	$ 2,844
% of net revenue	8.6%		8.6%		8.0%
Tax provision before repatriation charge	$ 1,122		$ 1,079		$ 905
% of income before income taxes	25.2%		29.0%		29.9%
Tax repatriation charge	$ 280		$ —		$ —
% of income before income taxes	6.3%		—		—
Income tax provision	$ 1,402		$ 1,079		$ 905
% of income before income taxes	31.5%		29.0%		29.9%
Net income	$ 3,043	15%	$ 2,645	25%	$ 2,122
% of net revenue	6.2%		6.4%		6.0%

During fiscal 2005, Dell maintained its position as the world's number one supplier of personal computer systems with performance that continued to outpace the industry. Dell's consolidated net unit shipments increased 21% as the company increased its share of worldwide personal computer sales by 1.1 percentage points during the calendar year to 17.8%. Consolidated net revenue increased 19% to $49.2 billion during fiscal 2005, with Dell's strong international performance being a key driver of this growth even as the company expanded its number one position in the U.S. During fiscal 2005, component costs continued to decline at a moderate pace that was relatively comparable to fiscal 2004. Dell utilized these cost declines to pass on cost savings to its customers and improve gross profit margin to 18.3% for the year. Dell's focus on balancing growth and profitability resulted in record operating and net income of $4.3 billion and $3.0 billion, respectively. Net income for fiscal 2005 includes a tax repatriation charge of $280 million pursuant to a favorable tax incentive provided by the American Jobs Creation Act of 2004. This tax charge is related to Dell's decision to repatriate $4.1 billion in foreign earnings. Dell's efficient direct business model and cash conversion cycle have allowed the company to generate annual cash flows from operating activities that typically exceed net income. During fiscal 2005, Dell continued to deliver

Figure 7.3 10-K, Dell, 2005, first page of MD&A (continued on next page)

strong liquidity with record operating cash flow of $5.3 billion and ended the year with record cash and investments of $14.1 billion.

Dell's objective is to maximize stockholder value while maintaining a balance of three key financial metrics: liquidity, profitability, and growth. Dell's strategy combines its direct business model with a highly efficient manufacturing and supply chain management organization and an emphasis on standards-based technologies. Dell's business model provides the company with a constant flow of information about trends in customers' plans and requirements. These trends have shown an increased use of standards-based technologies as well as a push towards standardization of services. Unlike proprietary technologies promoted by some of Dell's top competitors, standards-based technologies provide customers with flexibility and choice while allowing their purchasing decisions to be based on performance, cost, and customer service. Dell's business strategy continues to focus on the company's enterprise business and expanding its capabilities in that product group. Dell is also expanding into consumer electronics products such as plasma televisions while maintaining its leadership position in desktops and notebooks. Dell's superior execution in all product and service offerings has been demonstrated by progress in customer satisfaction ratings during the year, which is a key performance metric for the company.

Management believes that growth opportunities exist for Dell as the use of standards-based technologies becomes more prevalent and the company increases its presence in existing geographical regions, expands into new regions, and pursues additional product and service opportunities. During the year, Dell opened new facilities in the U.S., Canada, India, and El Salvador and expects to continue its global expansion in years ahead. Dell's investment in international growth opportunities contributed to an increase in Dell's non-U.S. revenue, as a percentage of consolidated net revenue, from 36% in fiscal 2004 to 38% during fiscal 2005.

While the current competitive environment continues to be challenging, management believes that there has been a steady improvement in business technology spending since the end of fiscal 2004. Management expects that the competitive pricing environment will continue to be challenging, and expects to continue to reduce its pricing as necessary in response to future competitive and economic conditions. Management is also focused on attracting and retaining key personnel as well as further investing in the company's global information technology infrastructure in order to address challenges that may arise with Dell's rapid global growth and the increased complexity of the company's product and service offerings.

Figure 7.3 10-K, Dell, 2005, first page of MD&A (continued)

Some of the topics do get a little technical, but it is worth your effort to read it.

ITEM 8—FINANCIAL STATEMENTS AND SUPPLEMENTARY DATA

Here, at last, are the financial statements. This section contains the auditor's opinion, the financial statements, and the notes to the financial statements.

The Auditor's Opinion

The first item is the auditor's opinion. This is an independent third party's appraisal of the forthrightness of the financial statements. Without it, you would just have to take the word of the company.

Auditors might have gotten a bad rap in recent years—some of it deserved—but they are all we have to make sure that the financials follow the standards.

I taught a course at a large state agency a few years ago. The purpose of the course was to help the agency employees read the financial reports submitted by small businesses that received state grants. The small businesses had to prove that they were financially stable and meet other financial requirements before this state agency would grant them funds.

The state agency made a weak policy decision because it did not require these small businesses to have their financials audited. I couldn't believe the mess that these small businesses were sending in.

Things that never would happen in any world showed up on the financial statements. Things like negative cash of $400,000-plus. Some companies that we knew had to have inventory listed no inventory. Others added personal items like jewelry to the financials and turned in a balance sheet that didn't balance.

Obviously, the state agency could not rely on these financial statements. And, looking from a big-picture perspective, it was silly for the state to even to ask companies for the financials if this was what they submitted.

Types of Opinions

Auditors can express one of three opinions, and the opinion is obvious in the first line of the opinion letter.

An *unqualified* opinion is the best one. It says, in essence, that the financial statements followed GAAP. Here is what the Dell opinion letter dated February 12, 2004 by PricewaterhouseCoopers LLP says:

> *In our opinion, the consolidated financial statements listed in the accompanying index present fairly, in all material respects, the financial position of Dell Inc. and its subsidiaries at January 30, 2004 and January 31, 2003, and the results of their operations and their cash flows for each of the three fiscal years in the period ended January 30, 2004, in conformity with accounting principles generally accepted in the United States of America.*

That is the best opinion possible.

The second opinion is called a *qualified* opinion. It says something similar to the above language, except that it lists exceptions. It basically says, "The financial statements follow generally accepted accounting principles except in the following instances…" and then goes on to list the exceptions. With this sort of opinion, you, the user of the financial statements, will have to be the judge of whether these exceptions bother you or seem reasonable.

The last opinion type is the *adverse* opinion. An adverse opinion is bad. It says that the financial statements do not, in all material respects, follow GAAP. This means that the financial statements are not to be relied upon to make decisions. An adverse opinion is very serious and will have a negative impact on the reputation of a publicly traded company and, as a result, its stock price might plummet.

Because of the serious nature of this opinion, the auditor will usually tell the client what needs to be fixed in order for the auditor to issue an unqualified or qualified opinion and give the client a chance to change the financial statements to comply with GAAP. Most companies will choose to go with the auditor's recommendations rather than suffer an adverse opinion.

Not Everyone Is Audited

I do feel that I need to say here that not everyone is audited. For instance, my records are not audited. I can lie to myself all I like and no one other than my little family will be affected. Another point is that this has nothing whatsoever to do with an IRS audit. The IRS does not express an opinion on the accuracy of the financial statements; it just demands that you cough up what you owe if you have broken the rules.

The Financial Statements

Next comes the balance sheet, the mother of all financial statements. Now, accountants like to express themselves creatively, and we don't have much opportunity to do it, so many CFOs will alter the name of the three key financial statements to something they like better. So, for instance, Dell calls its balance sheet the "Consolidated Statements of Financial Position."

And even the innards of the statement can contain new and unique terminology. What one company will call "gross margin" on the income statement another will call "contribution margin." Now that you are familiar with the format of the three key financial statements, you will be able to tell which one you are looking at—the balance sheet, the income statement, or the cash flow statement—no matter what the title is or what the line-item titles are.

The balance sheet is followed by the Consolidated Statements of Income (the income statement) and the Consolidated Statements of Cash Flows (the cash flow statement).

The last statement, which we haven't talked about yet, is the Consolidated Statements of Stockholders' Equity. This statement gives us detail on the components of stockholders' equity on the balance sheet. It shows how retained earnings

has been built up by net income or torn down by net loss. It also shows transactions with treasury stock, stock outstanding, and employee benefit plans and trends it over a three-year period. When looking at your statement of stockholders' equity, pay close attention to the column headers and the row titles.

The Notes to the Financial Statements

Finally, the notes to the financial statements. This is the most exciting read in the whole document—*not!* If you ever have insomnia, pull this section of the financial statements out. What? You thought the rest of it was boring? You ain't seen nothing yet!

The notes to the financial statements started out as harmless little footnotes at the bottom of the balance sheet or the income statement. But over time users kept asking for more information. Can you tell me about that number? How about more detail on this number? Now they are so voluminous, they don't fit under the financial statements. Dell's notes go on for 20 pages—and that is not unusually long. And that's for only 15 notes, which tells us that many of the notes are several pages long.

So how do you wade through this stuff? Well, you hit the highlights. Some of it is so legalese and accountingese that even I have a hard time understanding what they are saying. You need a degree in accounting or finance to understand much of the detail that the notes provide. But here are some things you may want to spend time deciphering:

- Note: Financial instruments. This note discloses what sort of investments the company holds, if any. Are they in bonds, stocks, and foreign corporations? Why would you want to know this? Because you would want to know if the company is investing its excess cash wisely. What's wise? Whatever you think it is! That all depends on whether you are a risk taker or more conservative.
- Note: Capitalization. This note discloses information about the company's stock.
- Note: Benefit Plans. This is a good section to read if you are an employee of the company.
- Note: Commitments, Contingencies, and Certain Concentrations. This is a good note to read because it is all about risk. A *commitment* is an engagement to assume a financial obligation. For instance, a company might have committed a portion of its cash balance to repay debt. This would not necessarily

show up on the cash flow statement; you have to read about it in the notes. *Contingencies* are things that might happen that could have a material effect on the financial statements; the company is obligated to reveal these items in the notes. *Concentration* is, in essence, another term for risk, so read about any concentrations.

Some of the notes break down the items on the balance sheet and income statement into more detail. This can be interesting. For instance, the gross account "inventory" might be broken down into raw materials, work-in-progress, and finished goods. Another note breaks down financial information into quarterly results.

Signature Page

The final page is the signature page, showing the names of all who are responsible for the accuracy of the report, namely the members of the board of directors.

CONCLUSION: A USEFUL DOCUMENT

The 10-K is a pretty useful document, if not very pretty. After reading this book, you should be able to tackle most of it—excepting the most technical notes. The more you use it, the better you will be at it.

Quiz

1. SEC stands for
   (a) Securities Exposure Committee
   (b) Securities and Exchange Commission
   (c) Secret Exchange Commission

2. The SEC loves it when companies get creative in their annual financial filings.
   T or F

3. The SEC dictates the type of font to be used in financial filings.
   T or F

4. To get the 10-K, you can
   (a) print it off from the company's Web site
   (b) print it off from the SEC Web site
   (c) call investor relations at the company and request a copy
   (d) e-mail investor relations at the company to request a copy
   (e) all of the above

5. Fiscal year-ends are always December 31.
   T or F

6. To approximate the market price of shares of stock at the fiscal year-end
   (a) divide total market value of shares on the cover of the 10-K by total number of shares outstanding
   (b) divide total market value of shares on the third page of the 10-K by total number of shares outstanding as disclosed in the notes
   (c) call investor relations at the company
   (d) a and c
   (e) b and c

7. Part I of the 10-K is background information.
   T or F

8. Always invest based on a friend's advice without looking at the 10-K.
   T or F

9. Legal proceedings is one of many disclosures in Part I of the 10-K.
   T or F

10. Who has to approve any changes to the articles of incorporation of the company?
    (a) the IRS
    (b) the CPA
    (c) the shareholders

11. MD&A stands for
    (a) Minor Disclosures and Analysis
    (b) Management's Disclosures and Analysis
    (c) Management's Discussion and Analysis

12. The best opinion an auditor can issue on the financial statements is
    (a) an unqualified opinion
    (b) a qualified opinion
    (c) an adverse opinion

13. The auditor issues an adverse opinion when the entity does not follow GAAP and it results in a material misstatement in the financial statements.
    T or F

14. Companies use their own unique terminology for the titles and the line items on their financial statements.
    T or F

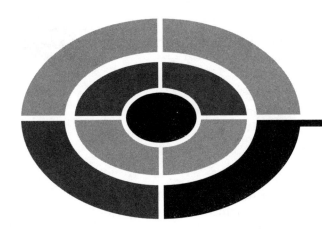

Test: Part Two

1. The general ledger tracks how many hours were spent manufacturing a product.
   T or F

2. Activity-based costing is a technique used by tax accountants.
   T or F

3. Which of the following are disclosed in Section I of the 10-K?
   (a) the balance sheet
   (b) the cash flow statement
   (c) the executive officers
   (d) the auditor's opinion on the financial statements

4. An annual report is the same thing as a 10-K.
   T or F

5. One of the major criticisms aimed at financial accountants is that their information isn't
    (a) accurate
    (b) timely
    (c) proper
    (d) added correctly

6. The notes to the financial statements contain information on the following:
    (a) employee benefit plans
    (b) investments
    (c) commitments
    (d) contingencies
    (e) all of the above

7. The 10-Q is the annual financial report that all publicly traded companies must submit to the SEC.
    T or F

8. MD&A stands for
    (a) Minor Disclosures and Analysis
    (b) Management's Disclosures and Analysis
    (c) Management's Discussion and Analysis

9. The frequency and accuracy of information costs time and money.
    T or F

10. Taxable income is often different than the income calculated in the general ledger because of differences between GAAP and the tax code.
    T or F

11. Which type of budgeting should be used only once in a while?
    (a) the line-item budget
    (b) the zero-based budget
    (c) the performance-based budget

PART THREE

Debits and Credits Detail—Rules, Rules, Rules

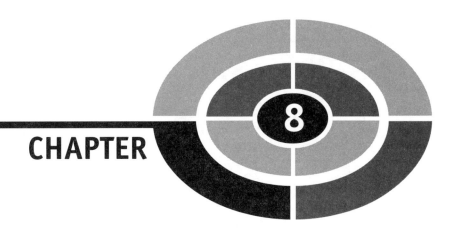

CHAPTER 8

How to Tell if Something Is a Debit or a Credit

When people study accounting, unfortunately they tend to get confused about debits and credits because of their experience with banks. When banks use the terms *debit* and *credit*, they have it all backwards, because they talk to you about your account from their perspective, not your perspective. So when they say they are crediting your account, the implication is that it's a good thing. Well, for you, it's good, but from their perspective, it's bad: it means they are losing money. If you were a bank and had to credit someone's account, you wouldn't be happy about it.

So before we can begin a serious discussion of debits and credits, please wipe from your mind the way that banks talk to you about debits and credits. They have it all backwards.

A Few Key Formulas

From Chapters 2 and 3 we learned a few key formulas that give us the basis of the balance sheet and the income statement. To understand debits and credits we have to look at those again.

The first formula is the basis of the balance sheet:

$$\text{assets} = \text{liabilities} + \text{equity}$$

The second formula is the basis of the income statement:

$$\text{revenues} - \text{expenses} = \text{net income}$$

As usual, the balance sheet is running the show. Remember: it is the mother of all financial statements. So the balance sheet formula is the root of our double-entry, debit/credit system.

An *increase* in *assets* is always a *debit*. A *decrease* is a *credit*.

An *increase* in *liabilities* is always a *credit*; a *decrease* is a *debit*. (See Figures 8.1 and 8.2.)

Now, how does the income statement formula fit in? The net income from the income statement increases our equity. An increase in our equity necessitates a credit. So when we increase net income, we record a credit.

Looking at the formula for net income, revenues increase net income so they must be a credit and expenses reduce net income and must be a debit.

To summarize:

$$\text{Increases in assets} = \text{debits}$$
$$\text{Increases in liabilities and equity} = \text{credits}$$
$$\text{Increases in revenues} = \text{credits}$$
$$\text{Increases in expenses} = \text{debits}$$

This is just something you need to memorize. It is not intuitive. It is just a rule. Write it on the back of your hand or in reverse on your forehead and look at it several times a day. Just commit it to memory and the rest will fall into place.

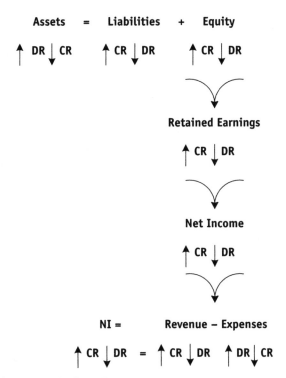

Figure 8.1 Debits and credits flow chart

	Increase	Decrease
Assets	Debit	Credit
Liabilities	Credit	Debit
Equity	Credit	Debit
Revenue	Credit	Debit
Expense	Debit	Credit

Figure 8.2 Table of debits and credits

A Special Way of Recording Transactions

Accountants even have a special way that they write down transactions. The debits are flush left and the credits are indented just a bit.

For example, let's say we bought a new car for $20,000 cash. The entry would be:

Fixed Asset	$20,000
Cash	$20,000

This tells us that the fixed asset was debited and the cash was credited. Just another funny thing to memorize. I'll add the notes DR for debit and CR for credit (these are standard abbreviations) to future entries, so they will look like this:

DR Fixed Asset	$20,000
CR Cash	$20,000

Chart of Accounts

Most companies have a chart of accounts—a listing of all the possible general ledger categories they could post transactions to. These accounts usually have simple numerical codes so that the accountant can refer to the account by just the code, or the code and the name, or just the name.

Figure 8.3 shows an example of a chart of accounts. In this organization, everything with a code starting with a 1 is an asset; everything whose code starts with a 2 is a liability; 3s are for equity, 4s are for revenues, and 5s and 6s are for expenses. We will use this chart of account for our examples for the remainder of the book.

Assets		
Cash (111000)		C
1111	General Checking Account	C
1112	Payroll Checking Account	C
1114	Money Market	C
1117	Cash in Registers	C

Figure 8.3 Chart of accounts, birdbath company (continued on pages 114 to 121)

Accounts Receivable (121000)			D
1219	Accounts Receivable -- Trade		D
1229	In Transit from Credit Card Processors		D
1240	Loans Receivable		D
1200	A/R Miscellaneous		D
Inventory (140000)			E
1400	Raw Materials		E
1420	Work in Process		E
1430	Finished Birdbaths		E
Prepaid Expenses, Deposits, and Other Current Assets (150000)			F
1510	Prepaid Expenses		F
	1511	Prepaid Insurance	F
	1512	Prepaid Rent	F
	1513	Prepaid Interest	F
	1519	Prepaid Other	F
1520	Deposits		F
	1521	Deposit -- UPS	F
	1522	Deposit -- Utilities	F
	1523	Deposit -- Rent	F
	1529	Deposit -- Other	F
1530	Other Current Assets		F
Total Current Assets (C + D + E + F)			**G**
Land and Buildings (160000)			H
1610	Land		H
1620	Buildings		H
1630	Land Improvements		H
1640	Building Improvements		H
1650	Leasehold Improvements		H

Furniture (170000)		H
1710	Furniture, Fixtures, & Equip	H
1720	Data Processing Equipment	H
1730	Data Processing Software	H
1740	Vehicles	H
Accumulated Depreciation (180000)		H
1810	Accumulated Depreciation – Building	H
1820	Accumulated Depreciation – Land Improvements	H
1830	Accumulated Depreciation – Building Improvements	H
1840	Accumulated Depreciation – Leasehold Improvements	H
1850	Accumulated Depreciation – Furniture, Fixtures, & Equip	H
1860	Accumulated Depreciation – Data Processing Equipment	H
1870	Accumulated Depreciation – Data Processing Software	H
1880	Accumulated Depreciation – Vehicles	H
Other Assets (190000)		H
1910	Intangible Assets	H
1911	Covenant Not-to-Compete – Previous Owner	H
1912	Goodwill	H
1913	Customer Lists	H
1918	Other Intangible Assets	H
1919	Accumulated Amortization	H
1920	Cash Surrender Value of Life Insurance	H
1930	Other Assets	H
Total Assets (G + H)		**H**
Liabilities		
Accounts Payable (211000)		K
2110	Accounts Payable – Merchandise	K
2120	Accounts Payable – Operating	K

2130	Customer Credits	K
Accrued Expenses (222000)		L
2210	Accrued Payroll	L
2220	Payroll Withholding	L
	2221 Federal Withholding	L
	2222 FICA Withholding	L
	2223 Medicare Withholding	L
	2224 State Withholding	L
	2225 Local Withholding	L
	2226 401(k)/Pension Withholding	L
	2227 Miscellaneous Withholding	L
2230	Accured Payroll Taxes	L
	2231 Accrued Payroll Taxes – FICA Employer's Share	L
	2232 Accrued Payroll Taxes – Medicare Employer's Share	L
	2233 Accrued Payroll Taxes – Federal Unemployment Tax	L
	2234 Accrued Payroll Taxes – State Unemployment Tax	L
2240	Sales Tax Collected	L
2250	Accrued Use Tax	L
2260	Accrued Retirement Plan Expense	L
2290	Other Accrued Expenses	L
Current Notes Payable (230000)		L
2310	Short-Term Obligation	L
2390	Current Portion of Long-Term Debt	L
Total Current Liabilities		
Long-Term Notes Payable (240000)		M
2410	Long-Term obligation	M
2420	Mortgage Note Payable	M
2430	Loan from Owner/Stockholder	M

2480	Other Long-Term Obligation		M
<2490>	Current Portion of Long-Term Debt		M
Total Liabilities (K + L + M)			
Owners' Equity/Net Worth			P
For a Sole Proprietor			P
3100	Capital		P
<3100>	Drawings (Close Out into Capital at End of Year)		P
3160	Retained Earnings		P
Total Liablities and Equity/Net Worth (N + P)			Q
Sales	(400000)		1
4010	Birdbath Sales		1
Total Net Sales			1
Cost of Goods Sold	(500000)		2
5010	Inventory Expense Birdbaths		2
Cost of Goods Sold			2
Gross Margin (Line 1 minus Line 2)			3
Operating Expenses	(600000)		
6010	Wages		4
6020	Vacation Pay		4
6030	Sick Pay		4
6040	FICA Tax		4
6045	Federal/State Unemployment Tax		4
6050	Group Health Insurance		4
6060	Workers' Compensation Insurance		4
6070	Disability Income Insurance		4
6075	Life Insurance		4
6080	Retirement (Pension/Profit Sharing/401(k))		4
6090	Other Benefit Expense		4

6710	Depreciation – Building	5
6720	Depreciation – Land Improvements	5
6730	Depreciation – Building Improvements	5
6740	Depreciation – Leasehold Improvements	11
6750	Depreciation – Furniture, Fixtures, & Equip	11
6751	Depreciation – Furniture, Fixtures, & Equip	11
6752	Depreciation – Data Processing Equipment	10
6753	Depreciation – Data Processing Software	10
6754	Depreciation – Vehicles	11
Travel and Entertainment	(680000)	12
6810	Business Travel	12
6820	Business Meals and Entertainment (50% Deductible)	12
6830	Food – Staff Meetings, etc. (100% Deduct., De Minimus)	12
Insurance	(690000)	
6910	Business Insurance	13
6920	Real Estate Insurance	5
6930	Vehicle Insurance	13
6940	Other Insurance	13
Credit Card and Other Service Charges	(700000)	
7010	Credit Card Service Charges	14
7011	Credit Card Service Charge Master Card/Visa	14
7012	Credit Card Service Charge Amex	14
7013	Credit Card Service Charge Discover	14
7014	Credit Card Service Charge Debit/ATM Card	14
7020	Bank Service Charges	16
7090	Other Service Charges	16
Dues and Subscriptions	(710000)	15
7110	Association Membership Fees	15

7120	Subscription Fees	15
7121	Subscription Fees – Professional Publications	15
Office Expense	(720000)	16
7210	Office Expense	16
Postage	(730000)	16
7310	Postage Expense	16
7311	Customer Package Charges	16
<7312>	Postage and Handling Fees Received	16
Taxes	(740000)	
7410	Inventory and Use Taxes	17
7420	Real Estate Taxes	5
7430	Business Licenses and Fees	17
7490	Other Business Taxes and Fees	17
Education	(750000)	18
7510	Education – Course Fees	18
7520	Education – Travel	18
7530	Education – Meals and Entertainment (50% Deductible)	18
7590	Education – Other	18
Equipment Rent	(760000)	
7610	Office Equipment Rent	16
7620	Store Equipment Rent	18
7690	Other Equipment Rent	18
Repairs and Maintenance	(770000)	
7710	Repairs and Maintenance – Building Equipment	5
7720	Repairs and Maintenance – Furniture, Fixtures, & Equip	18
7730	Repairs and Maintenance – Data Processing Equipment	10
7740	Repairs and Maintenance – Vehicle	18
7790	Repairs and Maintenance – Other	18

Other Operating Expense (780000)		18
7810	Bad Debts	18
7820	Collection Expense	18
7830	Cash Over/Short	18
7840	Classified Ads – Help Wanted	18
7850	Contributions	18
7860	Vehicle Expense	18
7870	Amortization Expense	18
7880	Penalties	18
7890	Franchise Fee/Royalty	18
7900	Miscellaneous Expense	18
Total Operating Expense (Sum of Lines 4 through 18)		**19**
Operating Income (Lines 3 minus Line 19)		**20**
Other Income (800000)		21
8100	Interest Income – Finance Charges Customers Accounts	21
8110	Interest Income	21
8120	Dividend Income	21
8130	Capital Gains Income	21
8140	Gain on Sale of Fixed Assets	21
8190	Other Income	21
Other Expense (820000)		
8210	Interest Expense	24
8220	Mortgage Interest Expense	5
8230	Loss on Sale of Fixed Assets	22
8240	Uninsured Casualty Loss	22
8290	Other Expenses	22
Net Income Before Taxes (Line 20 plus Line 21 minus Line 22)		**23**

Quiz

1. Banks talk about debits and credits from their perspective, not the customer's perspective.
   T or F

2. The formula of the balance sheet is
   (a) assets − equity = capital
   (b) capital + fixed assets = total assets
   (c) assets = liabilities + equity
   (d) assets = liabilities + retained earnings

3. The formula of the income statement is
   (a) sales − cost of goods = operating expense
   (b) sales − cost of goods = operating income
   (c) revenue − expenses = gross profit
   (d) gross profit − expenses = revenue
   (e) revenue − expenses = net income

4. An increase in assets is always a credit.
   T or F

5. An increase in liabilities is always a credit.
   T or F

6. An increase in equity is always a debit.
   T or F

7. An increase in revenues is a debit.
   T or F

8. An increase in expenses is a credit.
   T or F

9. When writing a transaction, debits are indented.
   T or F

10. Each organization's chart of accounts will be unique.
    T or F

A Few Simple Transactions

Let's run through a few simple transactions to get used to the double-entry system.

First, let's sell a birdbath. We have already gone through this example in Chapter 5, but we didn't consider how it affected the debits and credits.

You make cement birdbaths. You have an inventory of 100 in stock. Each birdbath cost you $20 to make. So your total balance on the balance sheet in inventory is $2000.

Cash Sale

Today you were lucky enough to sell two birdbaths to a bird enthusiast for $60 cash. What does the entry look like?

First, you get $60 cash. An increase in an asset is a debit. So you put:

    DR 1111   Cash $60

Then you get $60 in revenue. An increase in revenue is a credit. So you put:

    CR 4010   Sales revenue $60

Although we are all in balance, we are not finished yet. We have to recognize that we have reduced our inventory and incurred an expense in making the sale. A decrease in inventory is a decrease in an asset, which is a credit.

    CR 1430   Inventory $40

We have incurred an expense in order to make this sale of $40. An increase in an expense is a debit.

    DR 5010   Inventory Expense $40

When it all shakes out, the final, all-inclusive entry looks like this:

    DR 1111   Cash $60
    DR 5010   Inventory Expense $40
               CR 4010   Sales Revenue $60
               CR 1430   Inventory $40

Yeah! The entry balances: a total $100 debit and a total $100 credit.

From Chapter 5, let's look at what happens to your financial statements as a result of this entry. The income statement records a $60 increase in revenue, a $40 increase in expenses, and a $20 profit or net income (Figure 9.1).

Income Statement	
Sales	60
Cost of Goods	40
Gross Profit	20
Operating Expenses	0
Operating Profit	20
less Taxes/Other	0
Net Income	20

Figure 9.1 Income statement

On the cash flow statement, cash goes up by $60 (Figure 9.2).

On the balance sheet, cash goes up by $60, inventory goes down by $40, and retained earnings (your net income) go up by $20 (Figure 9.3).

```
          Cash Flow Statement

     Beginning Cash
     + Cash Collected          60
     –Cash Paid                 0
                               ____
     Ending Cash              +60
```

Figure 9.2 Cash flow statement

```
                    Balance Sheet

          Assets      ☺              Liabilities      ☹

  Cash                +60      Accounts Payable
  Accounts Receivable          Long-Term Debt
  Inventory           –40
  Fixed Assets                    Equity   ☺ or ☹
  Intangibles

                               Stock
                               Retained Earnings    +20
                     ____                          ____
                     +20                            +20
```

Figure 9.3 Balance sheet

Does your little balance sheet balance? Yep. Assets are up by $20 and so is equity.

Credit Sale: Part One

Now let's make this a bit more complicated. Let's instead say that you made a sale on credit. You don't get to collect cash right away.

I'm also going to change the numbers a little bit. Let's say that this time you sell 10 birdbaths to a local nursery on credit. The nursery takes the birdbaths and agrees to pay you for them in 30 days.

Now how do we record this? It is a very similar set of entries, except we don't collect from the customer right away in cash; we have to recognize an accounts receivable and collect in cash 30 days later. What does the entry look like?

First we recognize a $3000 receivable ($30 selling price times 100 birdbaths). An increase in an asset is a debit. So you put:

    DR 1210   Accounts Receivable $3,000

Then we get $3000 in revenue. So an increase in revenue is a credit. So you put:

    CR 4010   Sales Revenue $3,000

Although we are all in balance, we are not finished yet. We have to recognize that we have reduced our inventory by $2000 and incurred an expense of $2000 ($20 per birdbath) in making the sale.

A decrease in inventory is a decrease in an asset, which is a credit.

    CR 1430   Inventory $2,000

An increase in an expense is a debit.

    DR 5010   Inventory Expense $2,000

When it all shakes out, the final, all-inclusive entry looks like this:

    DR 1210   Accounts Receivable $3,000
    DR 5010   Inventory Expense $2,000
            CR 4010   Sales Revenue $3,000
            CR 1430   Inventory $2,000

Yeah! The entry balances: a total $5000 debit and a total $5000 credit.

Back from Chapter 5, let's look at what happens to your financial statements as a result of this entry. The income statement records a $3000 increase in revenue, a $2000 increase in expenses, and a $1000 profit or net income (Figure 9.4).

The cash flow statement (Figure 9.5) is not affected—yet!

On the balance sheet, accounts receivable go up by $3000, inventory goes down by $2000, and retained earnings (your net income) go up by $1000 (Figure 9.6).

Does your little balance sheet balance? Yep. Assets are up by $1000 and so is equity.

Income Statement

Sales	3,000
Cost of Goods	2,000
Gross Profit	1,000
Operating Expenses	0
Operating Profit	1,000
less Taxes/Other	0
Net Income	1,000

Figure 9.4 Income statement

Cash Flow Statement

Beginning Cash
+ Cash Collected
– Cash Paid

Ending Cash

Figure 9.5 Cash flow statement

Balance Sheet

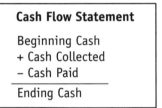

Assets ☺		Liabilities ☹	
Cash		Accounts Payable	
Accounts Receivable	+3,000	Long-Term Debt	
Inventory	– 2,000		
Fixed Assets		**Equity** ☺ or ☹	
Intangibles			
		Stock	
		Retained Earnings	+1,000
	+1,000		+1,000

Figure 9.6 Balance sheet

Credit Sale: Part Two

In a month's time, you collect payment from the nursery, a $3000 check. Now, what is your entry? You simply have to reverse out your accounts receivable and turn that asset into your favorite asset of all—cash.

DR 1111   Cash $3,000
          CR 1210   Accounts Receivable $3,000

What happens to the financial statements now?

First, you ask if the income statement is impacted. No, it is not. You didn't make a new sale or incur a new expense. This is all old, already recorded revenues and expenses, so you skip the income statement.

Income Statement

Sales
Cost of Goods

Gross Profit
Operating Expenses

Operating Profit
less Taxes/Other

Net Income

Figure 9.7 Income statement

You go directly to the cash flow statement. Cash is increased by $3000.

Cash Flow Statement	
Beginning Cash	
+ Cash Collected	3,000
– Cash Paid	
Ending Cash	+3,000

Figure 9.8 Cash flow statement

On the balance sheet, you increase cash by $3000 and decrease accounts receivable by the amount you just collected, $3000. That gives you a net effect of zero on the left side. Nothing happened on the right side, so you're OK (Figure 9.9).

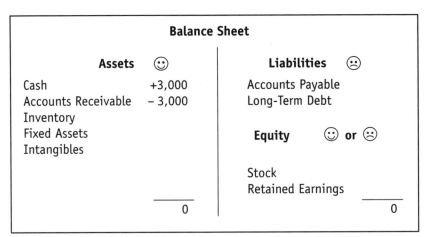

Figure 9.9 Balance sheet

Purchasing a Fixed Asset

Now let's say that you want to purchase a $5000 color copier to help you create ads and brochures to market your birdbaths. How do we record this?

Back from Chapter 5, you might remember that how we record it depends on whether we capitalize the asset or expense it. You are going to capitalize this copier, to record it as a fixed asset. And I am going to keep it simple and say that we paid cash for it.

So the entry must record an increase in fixed assets of $5000 and a decrease in cash of $5000.

DR 1710   Fixed Assets $5,000
          CR 1111   Cash $5,000

At the end of the period, we need to depreciate this copier. Using the simple straight-line method of depreciation and a life of five years, we can say we get $1000 of usage out of the copier every year. We will recognize this depreciation as an expense. An increase in expenses is a debit.

DR 6751   Depreciation Expense $1,000
          CR 1850   Accumulated
                     Depreciation $1,000

"Hey!" you might be saying. "What kind of curve ball is that, Accumulated Depreciation?"

Sorry, it is a bit strange. Accumulated Depreciation is what we fun, terminology-happy accountants call a *contra account*. It always is disclosed in the financial statements right underneath fixed assets, showing how much depreciation has been accumulated against (or contra) the fixed assets.

For example, you might have a balance sheet that looks like this:

Fixed Assets	$100,000
Less Accumulated Depreciation	$90,000
Net Fixed Assets	$10,000

This would tell us the fixed assets are old and used up, would it not? If the net fixed assets were $95,000, we would know this was some new stuff we were looking at here.

So, in a review of what we covered in Chapter 5, what is the effect on the financial statements?

On the day you purchase the copier, here is what happens to your financial statements:

Income statement: no effect.

Income Statement

Sales
Cost of Goods

Gross Profit
Operating Expenses

Operating Profit
less Taxes/Other

Net Income

Figure 9.10 Income statement

Cash flow statement: cash is reduced by $5000.

Cash Flow Statement

Beginning Cash	
+ Cash Collected	
– Cash Paid	–5,000
Ending Cash	–5,000

Figure 9.11 Cash flow statement

Balance sheet: cash is reduced by $5000 and fixed assets are increased by
$5000.

Balance Sheet

	Assets ☺		**Liabilities** ☹	
Cash	−5,000		Accounts Payable	
Accounts Receivable			Long-Term Debt	
Inventory				
Fixed Assets	+5,000		**Equity** ☺ or ☹	
Intangibles				
			Stock	
			Retained Earnings	
	0			0

Figure 9.12 Balance sheet

At the end of the year, when you depreciate the copier, the income statement
is impacted. So you record depreciation expense. Key word—expense. Go to the
income statement and increase expenses by $1000, thereby reducing net income
by $1000.

Income Statement

Sales	
Cost of Goods	
Gross Profit	_____
Operating Expenses	−1,000
Operating Profit	
less Taxes/Other	_____
Net Income	− 1,000

Figure 9.13 Income statement

What happens on the cash flow statement? Nothing. Cash was impacted when
you paid cash for the copier. Depreciation is what some fancy accountants call a
noncash expense. It reduces net income without reducing cash in later years—
years 2-5 in our example.

```
┌─────────────────────────────┐
│  Cash Flow Statement        │
│                             │
│  Beginning Cash             │
│  + Cash Collected           │
│  – Cash Paid                │
│  ─────────────              │
│  Ending Cash                │
└─────────────────────────────┘
```

Figure 9.14 Cash flow statement

On the balance sheet, you now need to decrease fixed assets by the $1000 in depreciation and decrease retained earnings by the $1000 decrease in net income flowing over from the income statement.

The final effect of all these transactions on the balance sheet at the end of the first year is:

- a decrease in cash of $5000
- an increase in fixed assets of $4000 ($5000 copier less $1000 depreciation)
- a decrease in retained earnings of $1000

```
┌────────────────────────────────────────────────────────────────────┐
│                          Balance Sheet                             │
│                                                                    │
│              Assets    ☺        │      Liabilities    ☹            │
│  Cash                 −5,000    │   Accounts Payable                │
│  Accounts Receivable            │   Long-Term Debt                  │
│  Inventory                      │                                   │
│    Copier              5,000    │      Equity    ☺ or ☹            │
│    Less accum. depr.  −1,000    │                                   │
│  Fixed Assets         +4,000    │   Stock                           │
│  Intangibles                    │   Retained Earnings   −1,000      │
│                       ──────    │                       ──────      │
│                       −1,000    │                       −1,000      │
└────────────────────────────────────────────────────────────────────┘
```

Figure 9.15 Balance sheet

So the balance sheet again balances. Assets are decreased by $1000 and retained earnings are decreased by $1000.

No matter what you do, you check to see that your balance sheet balances.

Depreciation and Amortization

Amortization is the same thing as depreciation, only for intangibles.

The reason we depreciate something is twofold: to recognize that the value of the fixed asset decreases over time and to recognize that we are getting the benefit of the fixed asset over a period of years, that the purchase doesn't benefit us just in the year in which we bought the fixed asset.

Amortization is the same concept as depreciation, except that depreciation is applied to fixed assets and amortization is applied to intangibles. Intangibles would include patents, brand names, and other intellectual property.

Another thing we amortize, or spread over time, is long-lived expenses, such as warranty expense. Instead of pretending that we are going to incur all the warranty expense for a product in the year in which we create and sell the product, we amortize that cost, spreading it out over the length of the warranty.

Lease versus Buy Decision

Should we lease that fixed asset or should we buy it? There are many factors to consider and there are whole books written on the subject and several software programs that can help you make the decision. Your lender and/or the company you are leasing equipment or fixed assets from should be able to help you in the analysis.

A lease is treated as an expense: it flows through the income statement and hence reduces retained earnings on the balance sheet. So you realize an expense each time you make a lease payment.

If you purchase an item, it is recorded as a fixed asset on the balance sheet and depreciated over the useful life of the asset. Depending on the useful life of the asset, you might be expensing the cost of the asset more slowly if you capitalize it than if you lease and expense it.

Here are some questions you need to ask before you can decide whether to lease or buy:

- What effect will a lease or a purchase have on cash flow?
  - Is a down payment required? Generally leases don't require a down payment; purchases do.
  - At the end of the lease, do you have the right to sell the asset and earn some cash? In general, at the end of a lease you don't own the fixed

asset; it reverts to the lessor. If you purchased the fixed asset, you might be able to realize a nice chunk of cash flow somewhere down the line when you sell it. Some leases allow the lessee to pay a chunk of cash at the end of the lease to own it outright. (Be careful with these arrangements, because accounting standards and IRS rules might consider such arrangements to be substantially a purchase and not a lease.)

  – Are you going to pay cash for the fixed asset now or finance it over time?
  – What is the effect on cash flow for each monthly payment, whether on the loan you used to purchase the fixed asset or on the lease?

- What effect will the lease or purchase have on income?
  – How fast will expenses be realized on each option? Under a lease, the entire payment is recorded on the income statement and reduces income. Under a purchase, the only expense realized is depreciation expense. How long is the useful life and how quickly will you realize the depreciation expense on the income statement?
  – What effect will each option have on taxes? That depends on your answer to the above question.

- What effect will the lease or purchase have on the balance sheet?
  – Will putting the asset on the balance sheet "bust the covenants" of a loan or skew key financial metrics? Do you have an outstanding loan that has restrictions on how much more debt you can incur or how much you can have recorded as fixed assets? Do your investors have expectations about your fixed asset balance and accumulated depreciation balance that would be negatively impacted by a purchase?
  – Will leasing the item be misleading to investors? Would disclosing it on the balance sheet as something the business needs to operate be a more realistic and reasonable representation of reality?

And don't forget the time value of money. This concept reminds us that $1 today is worth more than $1 in five years, because we could have invested the $1 and made some interest income from it. So the timing of cash inflows and outflows will have an impact on your decision. (For a metric that helps you examine cash flows, see internal rate of return in Chapter 15.)

Quiz

1. When you sell a birdbath for cash, you debit cash.
   T or F

2. When you sell a birdbath on credit, you credit accounts receivable.
   T or F

3. When you make a sale of a birdbath out of inventory for cash, you affect the income statement, the cash flow statement, and the balance sheet.
   T or F

4. When you make a sale of a birdbath out of inventory on credit, you immediately impact the income statement and the balance sheet. You do not immediately affect the cash flow statement.
   T or F

5. When you buy a copier, you debit fixed assets.
   T or F

6. As you depreciate the copier at the end of each year, you increase depreciation expense by recording a credit.
   T or F

7. Accumulated depreciation is a contra account to fixed assets.
   T or F

8. A lease is an expense and flows through the fixed asset account on the balance sheet.
   T or F

9. When you purchase an item, instead of leasing it, you record the purchase on the balance sheet under fixed assets.
   T or F

10. The time value of money concept says that a dollar today is worth more than a dollar tomorrow.
    T or F

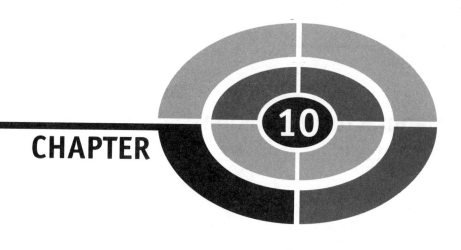

Inventory Valuation

Let's talk about another common transaction in business—the purchase, manufacture, and sale of inventory. But first, I want to distinguish between a service business and a manufacturing business in terms of inventory.

Service Business: Minimal or No Inventory

A service business has minimal or no inventory. Take my business, for example. I am an author, course developer, and speaker. All I have is intellectual property: the 20-plus courses I have developed plus a few books. When I make a sale, I am selling myself—I am selling myself going into an organization and teaching a class using the course material I have developed and to which I retain the rights. The only inventory I have is the books and manuals that I have written.

Manufacturing Business: Inventory, Inventory, Inventory

A manufacturing business, on the other hand, has several types of inventory. Let's go back to our birdbath business example.

You can imagine that the birdbath manufacturer will have a certain amount of stuff on hand for building the birdbaths—bags of cement, wire, and metal supports. Such stuff is commonly called *raw materials*.

You can also imagine that the manufacturer will have some birdbaths that are in the works, but are not finished. Maybe they are still drying or maybe on Tuesday we made 100 bowls and on Wednesday we started work on 100 bases and we haven't assembled them yet. This is called *work-in-process inventory* or *work-in-progress inventory*.

At some point, we have manufactured and assembled the birdbaths and they are ready for sale. This inventory is called *finished goods inventory*.

Some businesses spend a lot of effort and time tracking the balances in each of these categories. They might have a separate account for each of these categories on their books—one for raw materials, one for work in progress, and one for finished goods.

The way that inventory is valued is also of concern to manufacturing operations. Have you ever heard of LIFO and FIFO? They are not cute names for poodles; they are acronyms for methods of valuating inventory.

LIFO stands for "*last in, first out*." This method of valuing inventory assumes that any inventory you sell or use is from the last inventory purchased. So, looking at raw materials only for this example, we assume that the last bag of cement you bought is the first bag used to manufacture the birdbaths. This might not be true in reality, but it is the way the bag of cement is accounted for. This makes a difference in the cost incurred in making the birdbath. If the cost of cement is going up each time you buy a bag, then the LIFO method will cause the cement price to be at its highest and thus the cost of building the birdbath to be at its highest.

FIFO stands for "*first in, first out*." This method of valuing inventory assumes that any inventory you sell or use is from the first inventory purchased. In our example, accounting pretends that the oldest bag of cement is used in the manufacturing process. So if the price of cement is going up, the FIFO method would cause the cost of each birdbath to be the lowest cost possible.

There is a third method for computing the value of inventory. It is called the *weighted average method*. Here you take the total cost of all items in inventory and divide it by the total number of units in inventory:

$$\frac{\text{Total Cost of Goods for Sale at Cost}}{\text{Total Number of Units Available for Sale}} = \text{Weighted Average Cost per Widget}$$

This method tends to even out price fluctuations.

Here's an example. Suppose you purchase five bales of wire at $10 apiece and five bales of wire at $20 apiece. You sell five birdbaths.

Five bales at $10 each = $50

Five bales at $20 each = $100

Total number of bales = 10

Weighted average = $\dfrac{\$50 + \$100}{10}$ = $15

$15 is the average cost of the 10 bales.

So which method do you use? It is surprisingly a very complex decision. Several factors come into play. For one, if prices are going up and you use the FIFO method, your profit will be maximized on the sale of birdbaths (assuming low cost and stable pricing). This also means, because you are taxed on your profits, that your taxes are maximized.

Another factor that comes into play is your assumptions about the future. Do you believe that prices are going to continue to go up or go down? Predicting the future is impossible, but you might think you have a firm handle on it for the near term.

Unfortunately, you can't change between one method and the other as it suits your purposes. Once you pick a method, you are stuck with it. You can change it, but the accounting and paperwork nightmare the change causes is prohibitive.

So let's run through a simple example showing how inventory moves through a birdbath manufacturer and the effect on the financial statements.

Moving Inventory through Raw Materials, Work-in-Process, and Finished Goods

This is like one of those crazy word problems we had to do in eighth grade algebra, so if you didn't get into that, you won't get into this. I drew some pictures to help out.

On Monday, you have 10 bags of cement and 2 rolls of wire netting delivered by a local supplier. The supplier demands cash on delivery. A bag of cement costs $2.50 and a roll of wire costs $10.

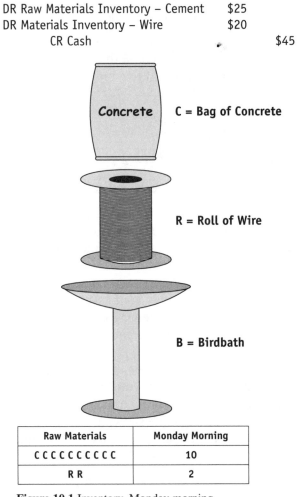

DR Raw Materials Inventory – Cement $25
DR Materials Inventory – Wire $20
        CR Cash $45

Concrete   C = Bag of Concrete

R = Roll of Wire

B = Birdbath

Raw Materials	Monday Morning
C C C C C C C C C C	10
R R	2

Figure 10.1 Inventory, Monday morning

Monday afternoon, the crew gets busy making birdbaths and goes through eight bags of cement—$20—and both rolls of wire—$20—to make four birdbaths. (As a rule, each birdbath takes a half roll of wire and two bags of cement to manufacture.) So each birdbath costs $10 ($5 for two bags plus $5 for a half roll).

DR Work in Process – Birdbaths $40
        CR Raw Materials Inventory – Cement $20
        CR Raw Materials Inventory – Wire $20

Raw Materials	Monday Afternoon
C C	2
Work in Process	
B B B B	4

Figure 10.2 Inventory, Monday afternoon

The birdbaths will be ready to sell by Tuesday afternoon at the earliest. Tuesday morning the supplier comes out to deliver more cement and wire. But the supplier would prefer that you buy more cement all at one time rather than have him deliver several times a week, so he cuts you a deal. If you buy 40 bags of cement, he'll sell it to you for $2.25 a bag. The cost of the wire stays the same. You think that sounds like a good deal, so you buy 40 bags of cement. You also buy 10 rolls of wire at $10 per roll (Figure 10.3).

```
DR Raw Materials Inventory– Cement      $90
DR Raw Materials Inventory – Wire       $100
        CR Cash                                $190
```

Tuesday afternoon, the crew makes six birdbaths. You decide to use the FIFO method of accounting for inventory, which means that the first inventory in is the first used. So you have two bags of cement that cost you $2.50 and 10 bags of cement that cost you $2.25. You also use up three rolls of wire. So one of your birdbaths cost $10 (using the original costing) and five of your birdbaths cost $9.50 ($2.25 x 2 = $4.50 plus $5) (Figure 10.3).

```
DR Work-in-Process Inventory   birdbaths        $10.00
DR Work-in-Process Inventory   birdbaths        $47.50
        CR Raw Materials Inventory   Cement                $5.00
        CR Raw Materials Inventory   Cement                $22.50
        CR Raw Materials Inventory   Wire                  $30.00
```

Tuesday afternoon, you acknowledge that the birdbaths you made on Monday afternoon are ready to sell and you put them out on the floor. In other words, you move the work-in-process inventory of birdbaths to finished goods inventory (Figure 10-4).

```
DR – Finished Goods Inventory – birdbaths        $40
        CR – Work-in-Process Inventory – birdbaths        $40
```

Raw Materials	Tuesday Morning
C C C C C C C C C C C C C C C C C C C C C C C C C C C C C C C C C C C C C C	42
R R R R R R R R R	10
Work in Process	
B B B B	4

Figure 10.3 Inventory, Tuesday morning

Raw Materials	Tuesday Afternoon
C C C C C C C C C C C C C C C C C C C C C C C C C C C	30
R R R R R R	7
Work in Process	
B B B B B B	6
Finished	
B B B B	4

Figure 10.4 Inventory, Tuesday afternoon

Wednesday morning, a customer comes in to buy two birdbaths for cash. You sell each birdbath for $20.

```
DR   Cash                                          $40
        CR – Sales Revenue                                  $40
DR – Inventory Expense                             $20
        CR – Finished Goods Inventory – birdbaths           $20
```

What is the profit, then, on each birdbath sold on Wednesday morning? $20 per bath less $10. Later in the week, when they sell the birdbaths that used the cheaper cement, the profit would be $10.50—$20 per bath less $9.50.

Raw Materials	Wednesday Morning
C C C C C C C C C C C C C C C C C C C C C C C C C C C	30
R R R R R R R	7
Work in Process	
B B B B B B	6
Finished Goods	
B B	2

Figure 10.5 Inventory, Wednesday morning

Wow! That is a lot of record keeping! You can imagine that most folks wouldn't bother keeping track of their inventory in such great detail, especially if the turnaround is just in a matter of days. But you can see how the cost of the materials and the assumptions you make about which raw materials are used first in the process can make a difference to the proverbial bottom line (profit).

Quiz

1. A service business generally has a lot of inventory.
   T or F

2. Work-in-process inventory is inventory that is finished waiting for customers to pick it up.
   T or F

3. The three phases of inventory are
   (a) raw, working progress, and finished
   (b) raw, work-in-process, and done
   (c) raw, work-in-process, and finished

4. LIFO stands for
   (a) last in freaks out
   (b) last in first out
   (c) last included finds others

5. FIFO pretends that the newest raw material item is used in manufacturing products.
   T or F

6. The weighted average method of inventory valuation tends to even out price fluctuations in the accounting records.
   T or F

7. If prices are going up, the LIFO method will maximize your profit on each sale.
   T or F

8. Once you pick an inventory valuation method, you have to stick with it.
   T or F

9. When you purchase raw materials for cash, you debit cash.
   T or F

10. Raw materials inventory is
    (a) inventory that has not been turned into a product
    (b) inventory that is perishable
    (c) inventory that is uncooked

CHAPTER 11

Guiding Principles of Accounting and Adjusting Entries

In accounting, we have experts who spend large amounts of time theorizing about why we do what we do. Many of them are professors, some are partners in accounting firms, and others work for a standards-setting board. And these reasons for doing what we do have become what we call "accounting principles." I like to think of them as guides that help us make good choices in creating financial information. When in doubt about how to treat a transaction, you can consult these principles and concepts. If it is a very technical issue, you might have to consult with one of those thoughtful "experts"—a CPA or the FASB and the GASB.

Guiding Principles of Accounting

These are the basic accounting principles, concepts, and assumptions that we will cover in this chapter:

- business entity
- continuing concern
- conservatism
- objectivity
- relevance
- reliability
- time period
- revenue recognition
- cost
- consistency
- materiality
- full disclosure
- money measurement
- matching

BUSINESS ENTITY

The business—whether it is a sole proprietorship, a partnership, or a corporation—is a separate and distinct entity. The records of the business are not to mingle with other entities, including the owner of the entity. For example, if the owner of a partnership buys a house for his family, it does not go on the books of the partnership.

CONTINUING CONCERN

The business is assumed to live on and on unless expressly stated otherwise. This is known as the *continuing- or going-concern concept*, that the financial records are maintained on the assumption that the business will continue forever. When an auditor has doubt that the business will live much longer, he or she will report in the auditor's opinion that the business is a "*going concern*" and detail why the business is likely to fail or cease business.

CONSERVATISM

Until the Enron fiasco, I mistakenly believed that all accountants were trained to be conservative. (I know we were definitely trained to dress conservatively. When I graduated from college, white shirts, blue suits, and those little red ties that looked like whipped cream flowers were all the rage for female accountants.)

I was trained to record transactions only if they definitely had happened or were going to happen. And I was trained to record, when in doubt, the most conservative number—the worst-case scenario, if you will. If there was a choice between a high revenue number and a low revenue number, you go with the low revenue number. That way, if things turn out for the better, you can adjust upwards and make everyone happy. If things go bad, you've already faced it.

Conservatism asks that you don't overstate revenues or understate expenses. It also asks that what you record be fair and reasonable. Or, another way to look at it is that it asks us not to anticipate any profit unless realized but to provide for all probable losses.

OBJECTIVITY

All transactions entered into the accounting records should be based on evidence—not opinion. Instead of guessing how much a vendor is going to request as payment, we wait until we get the invoice and enter the bill amount. We don't just pull numbers out of the sky. If we are forced to do this for some reason, we disclose our method for guessing in the notes to the financial statements.

This is one of the reasons that accountants don't bother putting a value on a brand name, such as the Coca-Cola brand. It is impossible to figure out with any great accuracy how much that would be worth. The brand is worth millions, maybe billions, but until someone pays actual cash for it, we would just be guessing at its worth. Guessing makes us accountants uncomfortable, so we just don't do it.

RELEVANCE

Relevance means that the data provided will actually make a difference to decision makers. Relevant financial statements are issued in time for decision makers to use them. Creating timely and meaningful data is the main goal of every financial accountant.

Who Comes up with All This Stuff Anyway?

Congress created the Securities and Exchange Commission in 1934 as a reaction to the financial mess of the Great Depression. Before 1934 corporations were unregulated and insider trading and other funny business practices were common and legal.

The Securities Exchange Act of 1934 both created the SEC and directed corporations to present registration statements for new issuances of stock and to make a "full and fair" disclosure of financial information. Congress gave the SEC the power to regulate the accounting profession. The SEC handed this job off to the profession, which promptly formed a self-regulating body. This body has had many names, but is now called the American Institute of Certified Public Accountants (AICPA).

The AICPA then turned around and created several rule-making boards. The first board is the Financial Accounting Standards Board (FASB). The FASB was formed in 1973, has seven full-time members, and has issued 140 pronouncements that make up the bulk of generally accepted accounting principles (GAAP). The FASB's mission is to "establish and improve standards of financial accounting and reporting for the guidance and education of the public." In 1984, the AICPA created the Governmental Accounting Standards Board, which is similar to the FASB except that it issues GAAP for governmental entities.

So if you are wondering whose rules to follow in case of an accounting question, here is the list of the rule makers, with the most influential being at the top:

- the Securities and Exchange Commission (SEC)
- the American Institute of Certified Public Accountants (AICPA)
- the Financial Accounting Standards Board (FASB)
- the Governmental Accounting Standards Board (GASB)

For Public Companies Only

In 2002, after the Enron debacle, Congress passed the Sarbanes-Oxley Act, also known as the Public Company Accounting Reform and Investor Protection Act. This act requires all public companies to document their internal controls over financial reporting. (A public company is a company that sells share of stock to the public.) It also asks that directors of a company verify in writing that the internal controls are in place and functioning. Sarbanes-Oxley—called

Sarbox for short—also requires that these internal controls undergo a very stringent audit each year.

This is a major change in the auditing profession, and many companies are going to fail the audit for the first few years as their internal controls are not well documented or are not functioning well.

The Public Company Accounting Oversight Board (PCAOB) was created with this act; it has final audit standard-setting authority over public accounting. The PCAOB standards supersede AICPA and FASB standards and are much more stringent. The AICPA and the FASB are considering following suit and making all their requirements match those of the PCAOB.

RELIABILITY

Reliable means that the information is free of errors and bias and that it is verifiable.

TIME PERIOD

Have you ever heard of a fiscal year? This accounting principle says that all accounting periods should be of similar length. Many fiscal years will begin on January 1 and end on December 31, but a business can choose any time period.

Many companies choose a fiscal year end that ends when sales are at their peak, so the cash balance and other balances will look as attractive as possible. For instance, a school textbook publisher I worked with made the majority of its sales in August, when the school districts purchased their books, so its year-end was in September.

Some companies choose a fiscal year to end during a time that is not so busy for the accountants, so that the accountants will have time to prepare the financial statements. Whatever you choose, you have to stick with it, because of the consistency concept (discussed later).

REVENUE RECOGNITION

Revenue should be recorded when the transaction actually occurs. Generally, revenue is recognized when the customer is billed or cash is received.

Sometimes deciding when to recognize revenue is more complicated, such as when a service firm, say a consultant, is working on a long-term project. Remember that conservatism asks that we not overstate revenues.

Since the character and behavior of the revenue in different industries vary so much, it might be difficult to follow generally accepted accounting principles (GAAP) in this area. In other words, if you have a question on this, it can get very technical. You might have to wade through the FASB's accounting pronouncements.

COST

We don't work with *market value* much in accounting. Whatever was paid to purchase an item is its value until it is sold or disposed of. That makes things easier for the accountant—but not necessarily more accurate. For example, if your business purchased a warehouse in 1982 for $180,000, then the book value would remain at $180,000 less depreciation until you sold it or it burned down. Even if the warehouse is worth $500,000 in 2004, its value remains at $180,000.

This is one of the biggest drawbacks of the accounting model. All assets are valued at historical value and this might understate or sometimes overstate the value of the assets. But given our principle of objectivity, you can see the theoretical and practical dilemma. What evidence would we have of the market value of the warehouse?

In order to get a true market value, we'd have to offer it for sale and then have someone offer to buy it. Then we'd have to tell the buyer, "Oh, no, we were only kidding. We really don't want to sell." Or we'd have to employ a team of appraisers. Pretty silly and tedious, so we just don't bother.

If you are selling a business, you'd better believe the purchaser will require that you come up with a market value for all your assets. However, on a day-to-day basis in a company that is going to be around a while, you don't bother with market value.

CONSISTENCY

Changing your mind about how a transaction is treated from period to period is frowned upon in accounting. Once you make up your mind about something, you should stick with it. Otherwise, the financial statements won't be comparable and users of the financial information won't know what's going on from year to year. If you do change your mind, you must disclose the change in the financial statements.

The principle of consistency also means that the same accounting treatment is applied to similar events from period to period. Once you choose a fiscal year and a method for valuing inventory, for instance, you are stuck with those choices.

Are you getting a sense of what sort of personalities would be attracted to the accounting profession? Folks who don't mind doing the same thing every time, who want to record things only once, and who take the most conservative or pessimistic view are well suited to financial accounting. (I am going to get a lot of letters on that one.)

Internal Controls Aren't Vitamins

Internal controls are policies and procedures that help you get things accomplished. Thinking of this from a personal perspective, consider this question: How do you make sure that you get to work on time every day?

I have controls in place to make sure I am not late to teach my classes. One of my recurring nightmares when I am stressed out is that I show up for class three or four hours late. I then have to face hostile participants who are ready to go to lunch. To make sure this nightmare does not become a reality, I pick out and press my clothes the night before. I write down an estimate of how long it will take me to get ready in the morning and travel to the site. I factor in how long it will take me to set up the room. (Some of my classes require more setup than others.) I also pack my supplies, such as my laptop, my pens, my toys, etc., and put them by the front door. I set two alarm clocks, one battery-operated and the other electric; that way, even if one doesn't work, I have another. If I am at home, I tell my husband what time I need to be up; if he wakes up and I'm not up yet, he can get me up. If I am on the road, I call for a wake-up call from the hotel. And I could keep going with this…. My controls reduce my anxiety.

Organizations also have anxieties. They worry about whether their products or services will be delivered to the customer in good condition and on time. They worry about whether their financial statements will be accurate. They worry about whether their employees will get sent a payroll check each week. In order to get where they want to go and do what they need to do, they have to put controls in place. Controls are little procedures that ensure goals are met.

Sarbox requires that the internal controls that ensure that the financial statements are accurate and comply with GAAP be documented and audited. The hope is that these controls will keep shyster accountants from lying about financial results in the financial statements.

MATERIALITY

Here we accountants cut ourselves a little slack; we get a little rebellious. (Get out the Harley!) If you hear an accountant say that something is "not material," that means that it has no significant impact on the financial statements. This allows us to sometimes bypass GAAP rules, especially when the cost of complying with GAAP is prohibitive.

Auditors love to use the phrase "not material" in conducting their audits. Auditors can't examine every single transaction, so a purchase of a stapler in a multibillion dollar corporation will not usually come under scrutiny. Even if the stapler were accounted for improperly, who would really care? It isn't "material." Next time your significant other gives you a hard time about buying an expensive pair of shoes, tell him or her that the purchase was not material and to focus on the big picture.

FULL DISCLOSURE

This reminds accountants that all disclosures in the financial statements are considered complete unless stated otherwise. Information that might affect a user's understanding of the financial statements must be disclosed. A knowledgeable user should be able to make an informed judgment about the financial condition of the business given the information provided.

MONEY MEASUREMENT

Only transactions or events that can be measured in terms of money appear in the financial statements. This necessarily means that many important things that go on in the business do not appear in the financials. For example, if the company loses its most loyal and favorite customer, this won't show up in the financial statements. Revenue might decrease, but the user of the financial report might not know the reason why. I discuss this more in the chapters on financial analysis.

MATCHING

This principle says that the expenses incurred in generating revenue should be matched with the revenues they generate. Here is an example. Let's say that you use a software program to design custom birdbaths for your customers. The software might have been purchased several years before, but you are using it now to generate income. In accounting, we like to match the software expense to the revenue it helped generate. It is only fair. Why should the first year be the only year burdened with the cost of the software?

The matching principle is one of the main reasons we bother with depreciating things. A depreciation expense is recorded every year that an asset is used. This way the cost of purchasing the software is not recorded in a way that artificially reduces profit in the year of purchase and then artificially inflates revenues in future years. Matching evens out the resulting profit (revenues less expenses).

The accrual method of accounting helps ensure matching. Using the cash method could cause a mismatch of revenues and expenditures between fiscal years. For example, you could pay cash for a bag of cement in December to construct a birdbath that is delivered for Christmas. The customer pays you in February. Given a December 31 fiscal year-end, this causes profit to be unreasonably reduced in the first fiscal year (because you recognized this expense without the corresponding revenue) and artificially inflated in the next fiscal year (because you recorded revenue without the corresponding expense).

Accrual accounting records revenue when revenue is realized, not when cash is received. Using accrual accounting, the expense is recorded when you purchase the cement and the revenue is recorded at Christmas when the birdbath is delivered. The revenue did not come in as cash but instead is recorded as an accounts receivable that will be reversed out when payment is received the next year.

The matching principle also causes us to make adjusting entries at the end of the year to make sure we are fairly stating all accounts.

Adjusting Entries

ADJUSTMENTS TO THE GENERAL LEDGER AT THE END OF THE PERIOD

Accountants make what are called *adjusting entries* for three reasons:

1. to bring balances up or down to where they should be
2. to match expenses to the revenues that generated them and visa versa
3. to give the accountants a chance to rest

Adjustments to Ensure Accuracy

At the end of a period, the accountant often has to make adjusting entries to several accounts to better represent what the balance in these accounts should really be.

Here's an example. Let's say it's December 31, the last day of your fiscal year. The electric company usually bills you on the 20th of every month for the previous month. So the last bill you got was for November electricity. You don't know how much they are going to charge you for December electricity, but you should record an expense for the electricity at the end of the year so that the expense isn't understated for the fiscal year.

Now you have to do some estimating and make an adjusting entry. If your bill from November was $2700, then you might assume that the bill for December would be similar.

At the end of the year, you would make an adjusting entry as follows:

DR Electricity Expense $2700
    CR Utilities Payable $2700

This way the revenues for the year are matched accurately to the expenses that helped create them. When the real bill arrives during the next fiscal year, the accounts can be adjusted to the proper amounts.

Think about the concepts of materiality and objectivity discussed earlier in this chapter. You do not have objective evidence at December 31 of exactly what the electric company is going to bill. But you can guesstimate it based on previous December bills or assume that it will be similar to November's bill. That is pretty objective. An estimate will be just fine and you arrived at it in a fair, objective manner. The amount that your estimate is off from the actual electricity expense for December is not material to the overall financial statements of the entity.

Adjustments to Match Expenses to Revenues

Accrual accounting minimizes profit distortions. The matching principle requires that expenses be recognized along with the revenue they help generate. You cannot falsely reduce profits by paying a bunch of expenses in advance or artificially inflate revenue by having clients prepay for services or products.

Using the same example as above, you made sales and created your product or service using the electricity in December and you must recognize that fact by estimating electricity expense.

Adjusting Entries—Let the Accountant Rest

Another reason that adjusting entries occur is that accountants don't want to have to keep track of every little detail on a monthly basis. It is just easier to make year-end entries for some items instead of doing it every day, every week, or every month.

For instance, let's say that you have 100 printers in your office and they all use toner. When you buy the toner, it goes into office supply inventory as an asset. At the end of the year, an inventory is taken to determine how many toner cartridges are left. What is used during the year is recorded as an expense. An adjusting entry is made to reduce the inventory balance.

The toner is no longer a happy asset that you own; it is gone. You used it up, so it needs to be recognized as a cost of doing business, an expense. We wait until the end of the year to do this inventory and to adjust the expense because it would be tedious and time-consuming for the accountant to make an entry recording toner expense every time a toner cartridge is retrieved from the office supply cabinet.

Usually, low-dollar—or immaterial—items are not tracked daily. If we were instead talking about an inventory of $300 printers, you would make entries to account for them every month or every time one is taken out of the supply room.

EACH ORGANIZATION'S SITUATION IS UNIQUE

The information below about adjusting entries is not exhaustive. There are items that will be unique to your situation that you need to take into account. Remember: the goal is to update the accounts for all items that have occurred within the fiscal year.

COMMON ADJUSTING ENTRIES

Here are some items that usually require an adjusting entry:

* wages earned by employees but not yet paid
* payroll taxes due but not yet paid
* property taxes
* interest expense and principal payments on a loan
* prepaid insurance
* inventory on hand at the end of a period
* interest income earned but not yet received
* depreciation expense
* bad debts
* dividends payable
* income taxes payable
* income receivable
* expenses payable

SOME SAMPLE ENTRIES

Supplies

Let's go back to the toner example. Assuming that earlier in the year you recorded the purchase of the toner as an asset. You now need to recognize an expense for the toner that was used. So you reverse out or reduce the asset and record an expense. Because happy assets are recorded as debits, you credit the asset account and debit expenses. That works out well, because increases to expenses are always debits.

> DR Office Supplies Expense – toner $700
>   CR Office Supplies – toner $700

See how close these accounts sound? Office supplies expense and office supplies. This can get a little confusing. One is an expense and one is an asset. If you think this similar naming will cause problems in the future, you might want to come up with a more unique name for one or both of them.

Prepaid Insurance

You might, like I do, pay insurance for months at a time, in advance so you don't have to keep writing a check every month. Let's say you pay six months in advance in October. Each month costs $200, for a total of $1200 in insurance expense.

When you initially purchase the insurance, you record it as an asset. It is a happy thing that you will have the benefit of in the future. Here is what you do when you first buy the insurance.

DR Prepaid Insurance $1200
    CR Cash $1200

At the end of the year, you recognize that half of the happy asset has been used up and recognize an insurance expense. You enter:

DR Insurance Expense $600
    CR Prepaid Insurance $600

Wages Expense

Rarely will the end of the year fall conveniently on the same day that you pay payroll. So it is likely that your employees have worked hours that they have not been paid for. Here is the entry:

DR Wages Expense $5,704
    CR Wages Payable $5,704

You might also want to recognize all applicable payroll taxes and payroll deductions.

Depreciation Expense

Depreciation is one of those weird entries that never affect cash. We in accounting call it a *noncash* transaction. Depreciation is realized as you use up an asset. As the asset ages, its value is diminished and an expense for it should be recognized. This is similar in concept to the previously discussed examples of supplies expense and prepaid insurance expense.

For example, when you buy a copier in January, you make the following entry:

DR Copier $10,000
    CR Cash $10,000

So it is now recorded as a happy asset. But by the end of the year, you have used up some of the copier's useful life. Copiers only last so long before they have to be replaced. So let's say that we think the copier will last five years. At the end of the first fiscal year, in December, you recognize that one-fifth of the life of the copier has been used. $2000 of value has been consumed (using the *straight-line depreciation* method). So you make this entry:

> DR Depreciation Expense $2,000
>   CR Accumulated Depreciation $2,000

Whoa! Were you expecting that I would credit "copier"? That makes perfect intuitive sense. However, that is not the way we do it. This is a strange rule—for which we have a good explanation.

Remember from Chapter 9 that the account "accumulated depreciation" is a *contra account*. A contra account is listed next to another account in the financial statements. In other words, it is mated to another account. For example, accumulated depreciation is mated with the equipment asset and would be disclosed on the balance sheet like this:

> Equipment $10,000
> Less Accumulated Depreciation $2,000
>   Net Equipment $8,000

Why do we bother with this contra account thing? Because we want to show the original value of the asset. The contra account helps indicate the age of our assets. If the contra account were $10,000, we would know that this copier was at the end of its useful life and would soon have to be replaced.

The net equipment number is also called the *book value* of the asset. This is not necessarily the asset's real market value; it is simply the historical cost of the asset less accumulated depreciation. We might be able to sell that copier for $9000 at the end of the first fiscal year, but on the books, we stick with $8000. Remember the principle of historical cost from earlier in this chapter? We accountants don't like to mess with market value: it fluctuates too wildly.

Unearned Revenue

In a lovely, perfect world, your clients pay you in advance for all the work you do for them. Many businesses actually do work this way; advertising firms, for example. Let's say that I take on a three-month project to develop a finance training curriculum for a client that is due at the end of February and I accept a payment in advance of $7000 in November. In November, I make this entry:

Depreciation Types

Accounting standards give you a choice of how to depreciate or amortize an item. Not many choices, but a choice, nonetheless.

These methods are your choices:

Straight line (SL): Here you take the total value of the asset and divide it by the number of years of useful life. This results in the same depreciation charge each year.

For example, we have a $10,000 van that has a five-year life. Each year, we realize $2000 ($10,000 / 5) in depreciation.

Sum of the years' digits (SYD): This one is a little more fun for those who like math. This method results in a higher amount of depreciation in higher years.

Take our van again, with its five-year life. If we sum all of the years' digits (1 + 2 + 3 + 4 + 5), you get 15, which becomes our denominator. Then, in the first year we say that the van has five years of life left. So our numerator that year is 5 and our depreciation rate is 5/15. $10,000 x 5/15 = $3333 in depreciation for year one. In year two, we have four years left, so 4 becomes our numerator and our rate of depreciation is 4/15. This is the way the whole thing shakes out:

Year	Depreciable Cost Rate	Depreciable Expense	Accumulated Depreciation	Book Value
1	10,000 x 5/15	$3,333	$3,333	$6,667
2	10,000 x 4/15	$2,667	$6,000	$4,000
3	10,000 x 3/15	$2,000	$8,000	$2,000
4	10,000 x 2/15	$1,333	$9,333	$667
5	10,000 x 1/15	$667	$10,000	$0

Figure 11.1 Sum of Digits balance method depreciation

Double-declining balance (DDB): Under this method, the remaining book value (not the total original book value) is multiplied by double the straight-line percentage rate. In our example, the straight-line rate was 20 percent each year (100% / 5); double that is 40 percent. It is a method that leaves a residual value on the asset: the entire amount is not depreciated over the life of the asset. It is not a very popular method.

In the first year, we multiply the value of $10,000 by 40 percent and get a $4000 depreciation and a remaining book value of $6000. In year two, we take the remaining $6000 book value and multiply it by 40 percent ; we get $2400 of depreciation and have a $3600 book value left. And we repeat it and repeat it through year 5.

Year	Depreciable Cost Rate	Depreciable Expense	Accumulated Depreciation	Book Value
1	10,000 (20% x 2)	$4,000	$4,000	$6,000
2	6,000 (20% x 2)	$2,400	$6,400	$3,600
3	3,600 (20% x 2)	$1,440	$7,840	$2,160
4	2,160 (20% x 2)	$864	$8,704	$1,296
5	1,296 (20% x 2)	$518	$9,444	$778

Figure 11.2 Double-declining balance method of depreciation

Units of production: Instead of using time to calculate depreciation, this method uses units. For example, we estimate that a manufacturing machine will produce 200,000 units over its life. In the first year, it produces 50,000 units, so we depreciate a quarter of its value in the first year (50,000 units / 200,000 units life = 25%).

Modified accelerated cost recovery system (MACRS): This is the IRS system for depreciating assets. It is a two-step process. First, figure out how long the IRS says your asset will live. Second, use a handy-dandy table to get your rate. For example, assets that can be depreciated over three years include tractors and race horses over two years old. No, really! Five-year property includes autos, trucks, computers, and dairy cattle. And the list goes on.

Once you decide what the useful life of your property is based on the IRS list, then you refer to a MACRS table that tells you what the depreciation rate is in each year.

MACRS is an accelerated depreciation method, which means that more depreciation is taken in the first years than in the later years. This differs from straight-line depreciation, in which the same amount is taken every year, regardless of the age of the asset.

> DR Cash $9,000
>   CR Unearned Consulting Revenue $9,000

Unearned consulting revenue is a liability account. Interesting, eh? It acknowledges that I owe the client services and I have not yet delivered.

At the end of the year, I should acknowledge that I have completed a third of the project. I do this so the revenues are matched to expenses. In December, I make this entry:

> DR Unearned Consulting Revenue $3,000
>   CR Consulting Engagement Payable $3,000

In February, when I finish the project, the entry is:

> DR Consulting Engagement Payable $6,000
>   CR Consulting Revenue $6,000

Revenue Earned but Not Received

The opposite of the above scenario could also happen. Let's say that the client has not paid me in advance, but instead will give me a check the day I finish the project in February. I am still making an effort to complete the project and incurring expenses related to the project in the current fiscal year. So in December, I need to recognize some consulting revenue receivable. Because receivables are assets, I debit the account to increase it:

> DR Consulting Revenue Receivable $3,000
>   CR Consulting Revenue $3,000

The next year, in February, I will make the following entry:

> DR Cash $9,000
>   CR Consulting Revenue $6,000
>   CR Consulting Revenue Receivable $3,000

That one was a little complex. It has three legs. I had to increase cash because the client paid me with a nice check for $9000. Then I had to reverse the receivable of $3,000 because the bill is all paid up—it is no longer receivable. Finally, I had to recognize the remaining revenue of $6,000. Whew!

Closing the Books

Each of the financial statements acts differently at the end of the year. The income statement is refreshed, the balance sheet is tweaked, and the cash flow statement is flipped. (That sounds like a good day at the spa to me!)

The income statement is refreshed every year. It is zeroed out. We start each year with zero revenue and zero expenses. Throughout the year, we build up the balances in the revenue and expense accounts and calculate the resulting profit (revenues less expense). The resulting profit is posted to the balance sheet in the retained earnings account. For this reason, revenues and expenses are sometimes called *temporary accounts*.

All of the balance sheet accounts, in contrast, are called *permanent accounts*. The balance sheet is not wiped clean every year; it is tweaked. The accounts on the balance sheet are just adjusted—either increased or decreased—throughout the year. The asset, liability, and equity accounts always have a balance.

The cash flow statement is, in effect, flipped every year: the ending balance of cash for this period is used as the beginning balance of cash for the next period.

Now why does all this matter? Because you should understand what the term *closing the books* means. It's the process of closing out the temporary accounts—revenues and expenses—and posting the results to the balance sheet.

Many software programs will automatically do this whole process for you. The program will automatically impact the retained earnings each time you make an entry for a revenue or an expense. This way the balance sheet is always up to date.

When, at the end of the year, you command the software to "close the books," it will wipe out the revenue and expense accounts and might make it impossible to enter any more revenue or expense transactions for the year you are working on. So be *very* careful to push this button only after you have recorded everything you want to for the period. Otherwise, you will have to make *adjusting journal entries*—not a huge deal, but not as easy as just entering expenses or revenues.

TRIAL BALANCE

A *trial balance* is a list of all the accounts in your chart of accounts with their respective balances listed in a debit or credit column. The debit column and the credit column are totaled at the bottom of the report.

The reason it is called a trial balance is because it is used to prove that your debits do indeed equal your credits. If they do not, your trial did not work and you have some investigating and adjusting of accounts to do.

You might have heard stories of accountants spending days trying to track down 84 cents that was throwing their books off balance. One cool thing about the latest accounting software is that it will not allow you to make any unbalanced entries. Your debits must equal your credits each time, so the ending balances are sure to work and your accountant doesn't have to waste his or her time tracking down trivial amounts.

Quiz

1. FASB stands for
   (a) Financial Accounting Settings Body
   (b) Financial Accounting Standards Board
   (c) Federal Accounting Standards Board

2. The guiding principle of continuing concern advises us that organizations are assumed to
   (a) operate as if they were concerned about continuing
   (b) continue to live on
   (c) concern only those who continue to invest

3. Conservatism asks that you
   (a) overstate revenues
   (b) understate expenses
   (c) neither of the above

4. The principle that prevents accountants from putting a value on brand names is
   (a) conservatism
   (b) business entity
   (c) objectivity
   (d) cost

5. Data is relevant when it
   (a) makes a difference to the decision maker
   (b) makes a difference during the fiscal year
   (c) is free of errors or bias

6. Fiscal years always end on December 31.
   T or F

7. Accountants are encouraged to disclose the market value of all assets.
   T or F

8. The financial statements record and track only transactions and events that can be measured using money.
   T or F

9. The matching principle asks that
   (a) revenues be matched to the depreciation expense from prior periods
   (b) expenses be matched to the revenue they generate
   (c) income from the income statement be matched to retained earnings on the balance sheet

10. Sarbox is the nickname that accountants and auditors have given to the new law that requires all public companies to document their internal controls over financial reporting and have them audited.
    T or F

11. An example of a contra account is
    (a) fixed assets
    (b) cash
    (c) accumulated depreciation
    (d) net income

12. Revenues and expenses maintain balances year after year.
    T or F

13. The ending balance of cash one year becomes the beginning balance of cash the next year.
    T or F

14. MACRS stands for
    (a) modified accelerated cost recovery system
    (b) modified accumulated cost recovery system
    (c) modified actual cost recovery system1

15. The double-declining balance method of depreciation is not a popular method.
    T or F

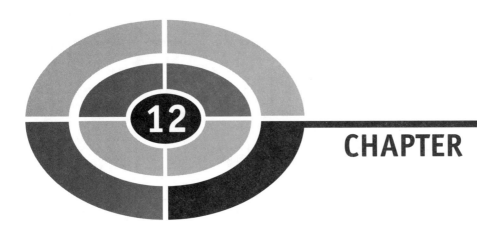

Governmental and Not-for-Profit Accounting

Now that you know the basics and before we get into applying them, I should say a few things about two aberrant types of accounting—government and not-for-profit.

Governments and not-for-profits have different operating objectives than for-profit entities.

For-profit—or proprietary—entities are in it for the money. They want to earn profit and cash so that they can distribute it to the owners so that the owners can live well.

Governments take money from their owners (the citizens) to provide services to their owners. Governments build and maintain roads, provide fire and police protection, educate our children, etc. To pay for all of this, governments collect taxes. They are not supposed to make a profit from their collections! Every dime collected is supposed to be used for the benefit of the citizens.

Not-for-profits are not governments: they do not collect taxes and they do not exist to benefit any owners. Not-for-profits are designed to use their resources to help specific people or groups. For instance, a not-for-profit might collect donations to run a home for troubled teenagers. All donations collected are to be used for the benefit of the troubled teenagers—not distributed to any owners or accumulated in a Swiss bank account.

In this chapter, I want to highlight some of the key differences between proprietary (or commercial) accounting and governmental and not-for-profit accounting. Because of their different operating objectives, they also have different financial reports and financial terminology. So far, we have been talking about proprietary or for-profit accounting. Again, I am not going to drill down to a lot of detail. I am going to give you a big-picture view.

Key Differences between Proprietary and Governmental and Not-for-Profit Accounting

Governmental and not-for-profit accounting is different from proprietary accounting in several key ways. Both:

- Both avoid the word "profit."
- Both pool resources into categories, programs, or funds.
- Both require retitled and reformatted financial statements.

GAAP for Government and Not-for-Profits

Governmental accounting and not-for-profit accounting also differ in who sets their standards. Governmental entities, such as municipalities, counties, and states, use generally accepted accounting principles (GAAP) promulgated by the Governmental Accounting Standards Board (GASB). Many not-for-profits follow GAAP promulgated by the Financial Accounting Standards Board (FASB). Some that operate like government entities might choose to use GASB standards.

With that said, let's start with an overview of governmental accounting.

Governmental Accounting

THE FUNDS

One of the unique features of governmental financial statements is that governments use pools or funds to track and report on their resources. When you look at a huge proprietary conglomerate, like IBM, you will see all the revenues and expenditures consolidated into one huge category. As far as the readers of the financial statements can tell, all the money is flowing in and out of one big purse.

Governments, on the other hand, keep track of their money in distinct pockets in the one big purse. (Think back to those huge, multipocket granny purses they used to sell on late-night TV in the 1970s.) They keep their funds separate so they can track the revenues and expenditures for different programs and functions.

They hate to commingle the resources of one fund with another fund. *Commingling* means that money out of one fund is being used to pay for another fund's program or project. For example, commingling occurs when you use money set aside to pay for school lunches to pay for the football team's new equipment. The federal government especially forbids commingling its funds with other funds because it wants federal grants to be used only for the purposes intended by Congress.

EXAMPLES OF FUNDS

For example, let's say that you run a county government and the new First Lady of the United States has a pet project that Congress is backing her on. She wants to build one new library per 200,000 children across the country. These funds will be funneled down to the local level through the counties. So you've received funding for three new libraries in your county from the feds.

The feds want to be sure that you don't use their money for any other purpose except to build libraries. If you do—if you use the library funds to fix a sewer line, for example—they will pull the plug on the program and take their money back plus a penalty.

So you create a separate fund to track this library grant until the libraries are finished. You do not commingle the fed's money with any other money. Each year that it takes you to build the library, you are able to report to the feds how much of their money was spent and on what items.

Here's another example: A highway near my house has taken literally 10 years to complete. This is because the city leaders did not specifically set aside money in their budgets or in a special fund to pay for the construction. Each year, they just use any surplus money out of sales tax revenues to work on the road. So, in essence, the road construction funds are commingled with other funds the city uses to operate. When an emergency comes up, as it always does, the city must use the money it planned to spend on the road to handle the emergency, such as to renovate a school or buy new vehicles for the police department.

If, instead, the city had issued bonds or debt to build the road and put the money aside in a special fund for the road, city leaders would less likely have been tempted to sacrifice the road construction for other immediately pressing needs. Currently, city leaders are telling citizens that all new road construction will be funded by tolls. In Texas, the land of cars and wide-open vistas, that is not going over well. Political heads are going to roll.

Types of Funds

So now that we understand the purpose of the government having funds, let's talk about the different types of funds. There are three supercategories of funds:

- fiduciary funds
- proprietary funds
- general funds

Each of these general categories has several fund types, and each fund type can have several fund titles. For example, the governmental fund supercategory contains several fund types—one being special revenue funds. A government may have as many special revenue funds as it likes, lumped under special revenue fund type. Here's an example:

- General Funds—super-category
  - Special Revenue Fund—fund type

- Federal Highway Construction Grant—fund title

Fiduciary Funds	Proprietary Funds	Governmental Funds
• agency funds • pension trust funds • investment trust funds • private purpose trust funds	• enterprise funds • internal service funds	• general funds • special revenue funds • capital projects funds debt service funds • permanent funds

Fiduciary Fund Supercategory

You have heard a bank referred to as a "fiduciary institution," right? This means the bank is entrusted with protecting your money. When you decide you want your money back, the bank has to give it to you.

This superfund category accounts for monies that the government is holding in trust on behalf of others. These monies are not to be spent by the government—ever.

Agency Funds

When you are an "agent" for someone else, you are acting on behalf of that person. A real estate agent acts on the seller's behalf. A sports agent acts on a baseball player's behalf.

Agency funds are simply monies held on someone else's behalf. The account will eventually be emptied out and distributed to the true owners.

For instance, when a county collects property taxes, not all of the taxes belong to the county. Some of the taxes are collected on behalf of the school district. When the county collects these funds on behalf of the school district, it deposits them in an agency fund and eventually gives the entire amount in the agency fund to the school district.

Pension Trust Funds

Pension trust funds are monies that employees set aside for their retirement. The monies are not to be spent by the government on roads, buildings, salaries, or anything else.

In Texas, we have two major retirement systems that are affiliated with the state: the Employees Retirement System and the Teacher Retirement System. Each has more than $20 billion in investments ready to fund its members' retirement. Every time we get a new legislative group in office, the question inevitably comes up as to whether state leaders can borrow from these pension trust funds just to get them through the latest budget crisis. Do you see any danger here?

Some poor accountant from the Comptrollers' Office has to go to the capitol every few years and meet with the new legislators and explain that the money is being held in a fiduciary capacity and cannot be spent.

Investment Trust Funds

Investment trust funds are created when one government makes investments on behalf of another government. Often governments will have excess cash for a few months of the year. As you can imagine, a county will be cash rich right after property taxes are assessed each year, but might be running low on cash several months later. Instead of letting that extra cash sit in the local bank making a puny return, the government might put it into higher-yield investments.

But wise investing is a skill that not all government managers have. So governments pool their investments and hand them over to one financially savvier government to choose the investments. This way they are getting a higher yield, but they don't have to worry about what to invest in.

The entity that is taking care of the pool cannot spend the pool. When the contributing government wants its money back, the investing entity must produce it immediately.

Private-Purpose Trust Funds

Private-purpose trust funds are funds that are set aside for specific uses for the benefit of specified individuals and organizations. For instance, let's say a rich widow dies and leaves her downtown Victorian mansion to the city. In her will she stipulates that the house must be used as a home for unwed mothers. Her house cannot be used for any other purpose but to house unwed mothers. The city cannot sell it and use the proceeds to renovate city hall or use it as offices for city employees.

Proprietary Funds

The proprietary funds supercategory accounts for activities that the government is involved in that mimic the commercial world. The term "proprietary" means owned.

Oddly enough, these funds are accounted for using commercial accounting standards and terminology rather than governmental accounting standards and terminology. This difference just makes governmental financial statements that much more fun to read!!!

Enterprise Funds

Enterprise funds account for activities that operate like business enterprises. These government-run businesses charge a fee for a service or product and can generate a profit. If they do generate a profit, their profits are often siphoned off to support other government activities. Examples of enterprise funds include public utilities and airports.

Be careful, however, not to assume that all enterprise funds generate a profit. Some show a loss every year and must be supported by appropriations from other governmental funds. An example of an enterprise fund that doesn't make money is a bus system. Very few bus systems in the United States actually turn a profit by charging rider fees. (The Citizens Area Transit in Las Vegas is one of them.) Tax revenues, federal grants, or private donations must supplement their operations.

Internal Service Funds

Internal service funds are businesses within the government. They do not transact with entities outside the government; instead, they support government operations. For example, the State of Texas has an agency whose function is to assist other state agencies in making purchases. It is called the Building and Procurement Commission. Instead of each state agency hiring staff to handle purchasing, the agencies can go to the Commission, pay a little fee, and have it all taken care of. Other examples include print shops and motor pools.

Governmental Funds Supercategory

The governmental funds supercategory is the catchall category for any fund that isn't fiduciary or proprietary. This supercategory accounts for a variety of governmental operations.

General Fund

The general fund accounts for all resources not accounted for in any other fund. Governments have only one of these and they usually account for a majority of the government's transactions. For most governments, this is the largest and most active fund.

Special Revenue Funds

Special revenue funds account for resources restricted for specific purposes. This restriction might be legal or administrative. For instance, a sin tax might be levied on cigarettes and the proceeds used to pay for ads to discourage teens from smoking. (Yes, that really is a true use of some of the cigarette tax in Texas.)

Or the federal government might grant funds to a state to be used for a special purpose, such as road construction. Many cities collect hotel and motel taxes and use the proceeds for economic development (a fancy way of saying that they use the money to bring more business into the area).

Capital Projects Funds

Capital projects funds account for resources being used to construct capital projects—one-time activities to acquire, constrvct, or improve (repair or renovate)

facilities. For instance, the funds a town sets aside to build a town hall or remodel the library would be accounted for in this fund. This way, the funds don't get lost or commingled in the general fund and possibly spent. This js where I wish my city had set aside funds to finish the road near my house.

Debt Service Funds

Debt service funds are like a savings account set aside to pay off bond debt. Instead of hoping that the general fund will have enough resources to cover the next bond payment, the government sets aside the money in a debt service fund.

Think of the potential problems here if this mooey is not separate from the other funds. It might be time to make the bond payment, but the city is out of money because it just spent it paying payroll and utilities. Many times, bond-holders require the government to create a debt service fund. If the government dpes not set the money aside, the bondholders have the right to call the entire debt immediately.

Permanent Funds

Here I think of the University of Texas, where I got my degree. A long, long time ago the University took the proceeds from the oil wells it owned and created per-manent funds. These permanent funds leave the principal always intact—hence the term "permanent."

The earnings are used to support the operations of the school. For many years, the tuition was very low because of these permanent funds. Now the cost of run-ning the school far exceeds the earnings of the permanent funds and tuition has gone up exponentially.

GOVERNMENT FINANCIAL STATEMENTS

All of these funds make government financial statements very, very thick.

In 2003 the State of Texas financial statements were 234 pages long—almost four times as long as Dell's 10-K. But why?

Well, it is the sheer number of financial statements. For one, each fund super-category gets its own set of financial statements. Add to that financial statements that combine various funds and financial statements that combine all funds. Before you know it, you have *X* financial statements instead of just three.

The GASB realized about a decade ago that these financial statements were getting out of hand: there were too many of them! So it set about looking for ways to make them more user-friendly.

As a result of study and intense debate (yes, this got governmental accountants up in arms!), another, more user-friendly layer was added on top of the fund financial statements. This layer rolls up the entire government into one summary set of statements, in essence treating the operations of the government—no matter what fund they are in—as one large fund. This additional layer looks much like a proprietary entity's financial statements. It is called the *entitywide perspective*. So instead of shortening the financial statements, governments actually added pages, thereby lengthening the documents. Hmmm. Compromise has its price.

WE MUST AVOID THE WORD "PROFIT"

Governments are very careful to avoid the word "profit" when referring to themselves. If the government earned a profit, it would indicate to citizens that it was collecting too much in taxes. Citizens prefer that governments run lean and mean and tax as little as possible.

And, because they also want to avoid the word "income," governments renamed the income statement as the "statement of revenues, expenditures, and changes in fund balances." And "net income" at the bottom of the statement was renamed as "excess (deficiency) of revenues over (under) expenditures." (See Figure 12.1.)

A NEW FINANCIAL STATEMENT

The GASB also added a new type of financial statement to the mix called the *statement of activities*. So, in addition to having a balance sheet, a statement of revenues and expenditures, and a cash flow statement for most funds, we add a fourth perspective. The statement of activities is, in essence, another slice at the statement of revenues and expenditures (see Figure 12.2).

A TURNED-AROUND BALANCE SHEET

Governments also often play around with the balance sheet and put it into another format. The components are the same; they just switch around the order.

The formula of the balance sheet is *assets = liabilities plus equity*. Governments prefer to express the ratio as *assets – liabilities = net assets*. And one version of the balance sheet is called the Statement of Net Assets. It is in essence a balance sheet with the elements flipped around (see Figure 12.3).

State of Texas
Statement of Revenues, Expenditures, and
Changes in Fund Balances- Governmental Funds
For the Fiscal Year Ended August 31, 2003 (Amounts in Thousands)

	General	State Highway Fund	Permanent School Fund	Nonmajor Funds	Totals
REVENUES					
Taxes	$25,906,873	$ 31,900	$	$	$25,938,773
Federal	20,311,966	2,659,108		46,371	23,017,445
Licenses, Fees, and Permits	1,983,152	828,484		109,253	2,920,889
Interest and Other Investment Income	96,776	22,599	1,023,803	974,770	2,117,948
Land Income	11,636	1,965	275,860	8,897	298,358
Settlement of Claims	554,023	8,949	7	25	563,004
Sales of Goods and Services	974,382	151,717		4,771	1,130,870
Other	1,451,149	6,084		6,403	1,463,636
Total Revenues	51,289,957	3,710,806	1,299,670	1,150,490	57,450,923
EXPENDITURES					
Current:					
General Government	1,827,031	10,649	597	122,335	1,960,612
Education	14,197,634			1,729,758	15,927,392
Employee Benefits	790			11,246	12,036
Health & Human Services	24,226,546			463,163	24,689,709
Public Safety & Corrections	3,602,176	347,464		116,928	4,066,568
Transportation	32,485	3,027,258		5,389	3,065,132
Natural Resources & Recreation	747,038			40,395	787,433
Regulation	260,148			50,886	311,034
Capital Outlay	128,021	2,415,145		111,093	2,654,259
Debt Service:					
Principal	3,937			362,951	366,888
Interest	163,975			196,124	360,099
Total Expenditures	45,189,781	5,800,516	597	3,210,268	54,201,162
Excess (Deficiency) of Revenues Over (Under) Expenditures	6,100,176	(2,089,710)	1,299,073	(2,059,778)	3,249,761
OTHER FINANCING SOURCES (USES)					
Transfer In (Note 12)	1,819,187	2,085,769		1,888,435	5,793,391
Transfer Out (Note 12)	(10,355,724)	(10,950)	(14,268)	(556,052)	(10,936,994)
Bonds and Notes Issued				383,418	383,418
Bond Proceeds for Advance Refunding				164,395	164,395
Payments to Escrow for Advance Refunding				(164,395)	(164,395)
Sale of Capital Assets	4,138	13,720		2,805	20,663
Increase in Obligations Under Capital Leases	4,079				4,079
Total Other Financing Sources (Uses)	(8,528,320)	2,088,539	(14,268)	1,718,606	(4,735,443)
Net Change in Fund Balances	(2,428,144)	(1,171)	1,284,805	(341,172)	(1,485,682)
Fund Balances, September 1, 2002	1,060,743	671,324	17,273,791	3,353,071	22,358,929
Restatements (Note 14)	83,613			(27,996)	55,617
Fund Balances, September 1, 2002, as Restated	1,144,356	671,324	17,273,791	3,325,075	22,414,546

Figure 12.1 Texas statement of revenues, expenditures, and changes in fund balance

WHAT IS "FUND BALANCE"?

Equity is not a meaningful concept in government, because nothing is owned. Governments prefer to use the term "fund balance." Fund balance is a concept similar to retained earnings. Fund balance is the amount left in revenues after all the expenses have been recorded plus the remaining excess of revenues over expenditures from previous years. This year's little excess fund balance is added to last year's little excess fund balance to come up with the total little excess fund balance. (Remember: retained earnings work the same way—current earnings are added to previous earnings to come up with total retained earnings.)

State of Texas
Statement of Activities
For the Fiscal Year Ended August 31, 2003 (Amounts in Thousands)

Functions/Programs	Expenses	Charges for Services	Operating Grants and Contributions	Capital Grants and Contributions
Primary Government				
Governmental Activities:				
General Government	$ 2,026,241	$ 1,378,735	$ 621,186	$ 49
Education	15,935,961	485,676	4,839,640	20
Employee Benefits	22,644	112		
Teacher Retirement Benefits	2,435,727			
Health and Human Services	24,742,714	821,773	16,792,451	
Public Safety and Corrections	4,207,856	148,420	315,520	
Transportation	3,562,159	974,627	80,025	2,570,556
Natural Resources and Recreation	835,139	437,834	148,780	9
Regulation	324,567	92,875	3,609	
Indirect Interest on Long Term Debt	366,847			
Total Governmental Activities	54,459,855	4,340,052	22,801,211	2,570,634
Business-Type Activities:				
Colleges and Universities	12,870,785	5,188,571	5,363,216	81,058
Texas Water Development Board Funds	158,881	3,002	265,588	
Veterans Land Board Loan Program Funds	94,941	25,699	100,148	
Texas Department of Transportation Turnpike Authority	57		14,129	81,933
Other Business-Type Activities	6,339,840	5,776,965	501,456	
Total Business-Type Activities	19,464,504	10,994,237	6,244,537	162,991
Total Primary Government	$ 73,924,359	$ 15,334,289	$ 29,045,748	$ 2,733,625
Component Units				
Component Units	$ 425,641	$ 265,724	$ 138,873	$ 1,160
Total Component Units	$ 425,641	$ 265,724	$ 138,873	$ 1,160

General Revenues
  Taxes:
    Sales and Use
    Motor Vehicle and Manufactured Housing
    Motor Fuels
    Franchise
    Oil and Natural Gas Production
    Insurance Occupation
    Cigarette and Tobacco
    Other
  Unrestricted Investment Earnings
  Federal Jobs and Growth Tax Relief Funds
  Settlement of Claims
  Gain on Sale of Capital Assets
  Capital Contributions
  Other General Revenues
Contributions to Permanent and Term Endowments
Extraordinary Items (Note 23)
Transfers--Internal Activities (Note 12)
  Total General Revenues, Contributions, Extraordinary Items,
  and Transfers

Change in Net Assets

Net Assets, September 1, 2002
Retatements (Note 14)
Net Assets, Setember 1, 2002, as Restated

Net Assets, August 31, 2003

Figure 12.2 Texas statement of activities (continued on next page)

| | Net (Expenses) Revenue and Changes in Net Assets | | | |
| | | Primary Government | | |
Governmental Activities	Business-Type Activities	Total		Component Units
$ (26,271)	$	$ (26,271)		$
(10,610,625)		(10,610,625)		
(22,532)		(22,532)		
(2,435,727)		(2,435,727)		
(7,128,490)		(7,128,490)		
(3,743,916)		(3,743,916)		
63,049		63,049		
(248,516)		(248,516)		
(228,083)		(228,083)		
(366,847)		(366,847)		
(24,747,958)	0	(24,747,958)		0
	(2,237,940)	(2,237,940)		
	109,709	109,709		
	30,906	30,906		
	96,005	96,005		
	(61,419)	(61,419)		
0	(2,062,739)	(2,062,739)		0
(24,747,958)	(2,062,739)	(26,810,697)		0
				(19,884)
0	0	0		(19,884)
14,349,758		14,349,758		
2,795,211		2,795,211		
2,790,936		2,790,936		
1,532,820		1,532,820		
1,531,275		1,531,275		
1,179,553		1,179,553		
583,159		583,159		
1,405,325		1,405,325		
239,198	28,020	267,218		4,578
354,535		354,535		
563,196	5	563,201		
6,359		6,359		228
600	1,318	1,918		
787,866	329,235	1,117,101		84,474
	235,997	235,997		
	36,532	36,532		
(3,069,447)	3,069,447			
25,050,344	3,700,554	28,750,898		89,280
302,386	1,637,815	1,940,201		69,396
69,476,046	25,396,411	94,872,457		118,300
293,502	37,554	331,056		27,390
69,769,548	25,433,965	95,203,513		145,690
$ 70,071,934	$ 27,071,780	$ 97,143,714		$ 215,086

Figure 12.2 Texas statement of activities (continued)

State of Texas
Statement of Net Assets
August 31, 2003 (Amounts in Thousands)

	Governmental Activities	Primary Government Business-Type Activities	Total	Component Units
ASSETS				
Current Assets:				
Cash and Cash Equivalents (Note 3)	$ 2,853,172	$ 3,491,719	$ 6,344,891	$ 228,733
Securities Lending Collateral (Note 3)	2,274,072	578,272	2,852,344	
Investments (Note 3)	379,912	1,051,461	1,431,373	76,573
Restricted:				
Cash and Cash Equivalents (Note 3)	3,169	1,012,463	1,015,632	29
Investments (Note 3)		733,790	733,790	
Loans and Contracts	260	53,782	54,042	48
Receivables:				
Taxes	1,565,535		1,565,535	
Federal	1,542,776	276,970	1,819,746	25,671
Other Intergovernmental	467,974	31,749	499,723	
Accounts	282,659	581,401	864,060	12,267
Interest and Dividends	164,672	204,366	369,038	3,859
Gifts		88,508	88,508	1,607
Investment Trades		182,380	182,380	
Other	47,751	630,184	677,935	19,443
From Fiduciary Funds	53,393		53,393	
Due From Primary Government (Note 12)				1,359
Due From Component Units (Note 12)	397	15	412	155
Inventories	224,687	100,662	325,349	1,087
Prepaid Items	2,221	79,976	82,197	3,734
Loans and Contracts	106,069	309,668	415,737	23,095
Other Current Assets	452	142,216	142,668	3,086
Total Current Assets	9,969,171	9,549,582	19,518,753	400,746
Non-Current Assets:				
Restricted:				
Cash and Cash Equivalents (Note 3)	1,014	303,425	304,439	623
Short Term Investments (Note 3)		894,058	894,058	
Investments (Note 3)		18,151,068	18,151,068	58,173
Receivables	126,222	490,045	616,267	
Loans and Contracts	569,591	2,448,582	3,018,173	1,835
Other	131	12,485	12,616	408
Internal Balances (Note 12)	7,366	(7,366)		
Loans and Contracts	441,217	2,841,961	3,283,178	55,164
Investments (Note 3)	19,030,954	4,117,544	23,148,498	343,046
Receivables:				
Taxes	464,003		464,003	
Other	121,315		121,315	
Gifts		159,516	159,516	
Capital Assets: (Note 2)				
Capital Assets - Non-Depreciable	42,089,185	4,296,256	46,385,441	6,832
Capital Assets - Depreciable	20,807,878	13,830,128	34,638,006	122,217
Accumulated Depreciation	(10,522,984)	(7,637,323)	(18,160,307)	(50,030)
Assets Held in Trust		55,223	55,223	
Net Pension Asset (Note 9)	155,580		155,580	
Other Non-Current Assets	21,253	94,662	115,915	3,945
Total Non-Current Assets	73,312,725	40,050,264	113,362,989	542,213
Total Assets	83,281,896	49,599,846	132,881,742	942,959

Concluded on the following page

Figure 12.3a Texas statement of net assets

State of Texas

August 31, 2003 (Amounts in Thousands)

	Primary Government			Component Units
	Governmental Activities	Business-Type Activities	Total	
LIABILITIES				
Current Liabilities:				
Payables:				
Accounts	$ 3,265,346	$ 1,232,242	$ 4,497,588	$ 16,113
Payroll	480,753	170,782	651,535	28
Other Intergovernmental	443,676	3,806	447,482	
Federal	3,560	62,340	65,900	19,305
Investment Trades		504,000	504,000	
Other	487,009		487,009	
To Fiduciary Funds	11,046		11,046	
Internal Balances (Note 12)	355,195	(355,195)		
Due To Primary Government (Note 12)				412
Due To Component Units (Note 12)	1,359		1,359	155
Deferred Revenue	606,223	1,468,208	2,074,431	28,401
Obligations/Reverse Repurchase Agreement	174,280		174,280	
Obligations/Securities Lending	2,274,073	578,272	2,852,345	
Claims and Judgments (Note 5)	96,148	16,408	112,556	
Capital Lease Obligations (Note 5, 7)	3,966	2,660	6,626	196
Employees' Compensable Leave (Note 5)	337,479	54,534	392,013	2,727
Notes and Loans Payable (Note 5)	15,906	767,364	783,270	59,326
General Obligation Bonds Payable (Note 5, 6)	128,626	103,775	232,401	
Revenue Bonds Payable (Note 5, 6)	67,936	429,014	496,950	11,369
Liabilities Payable From Restricted Assets (Note 5) *		393,197	393,197	2,781
Funds Held for Others		125,427	125,427	
Other Current Liabilities (Note 5) **		374,712	374,712	12,288
Total Current Liabilities	8,752,581	5,931,546	14,684,127	153,101
Non-Current Liabilities:				
Deferred Revenue		1,258	1,258	
Claims and Judgments (Note 5)	114,567	48,363	162,930	
Capital Lease Obligations (Note 5, 7)	47,738	20,702	68,440	152
Employees' Compensable Leave (Note 5)	155,344	341,459	496,803	1,327
Notes and Loans Payable (Note 5)	87,293	1,121,561	1,208,854	196,067
Liabilities Payable From Restricted Assets (Note 5)		3,201,321	3,201,321	151,390
General Obligation Bonds Payable (Note 5, 6)	3,055,957	2,495,422	5,551,379	
Revenue Bonds Payable (Note 5, 6)	670,981	8,847,899	9,518,880	161,649
Assets Held for Others (Note 5) ***		420,174	420,174	
Net Pension Obligation (Note 5, 9)	325,376		325,376	
Other Non-Current Liabilities (Note 5) ****	125	98,361	98,486	64,187
Total Non-Current Liabilities	4,457,381	16,596,520	21,053,901	574,772
Total Liabilities	13,209,962	22,528,066	35,738,028	727,873
NET ASSETS				
Invested in Capital Assets, Net of Related Debt	49,254,086	5,736,632	54,990,718	43,245
Restricted for:				
Education	458,788	1,611,811	2,070,599	13,492
Highway Construction	670,717		670,717	
Debt Service	252,369	123,167	375,536	
Capital Projects	148,557	214,431	362,988	220
Veterans Land Board Housing Programs		636,134	636,134	
Funds Held as Permanent Investments:				
Nonexpendable	18,558,596	12,205,937	30,764,533	
Expendable		304,598	304,598	
Other	756,692	71,509	828,201	35,223
Unrestricted	(27,871)	6,167,561	6,139,690	122,906
Total Net Assets	$ 70,071,934	$ 27,071,780	$ 97,143,714	$ 215,086

The accompanying notes to the financial statements are an integral part of this statement.

*   Of the $393,197, the current portion of Long-Term Liabilities is $328,209, and is reported in Note 5, whereas $64,988 is Current Liabilities.

**   Of the $374,712 reported by the primary government, $1,231 is the current portion of Long-Term Liabilities and is reported in Note 5, whereas $373,481 is Current Liabilities. Also, of the $12,288 reported by component units, $248 is the current portion of Long-Term Liabilities and is reported in Note 5, whereas $12,040 is Current Liabilities.

***   Of the $420,174, the non-current portion of Long-Term Liabilities is $107,290, and is reported in Note 5, whereas $312,884 is Non-Current Liabilities.

****   Of the $98,486, the non-current portion of Other Long-Term Liabilities is $95,206, and is reported in Note 5, whereas $3,280 is Non-Current Liabilities.

Figure 12.3b Texas statement of net assets

What Is a Deficit?

The term deficit means "deficiency in amount or quality; a falling short; lack; as, a deficit in taxes, revenue, etc." And it can be calculated in a variety of ways. That is why you will hear numbers for the federal deficit ranging from $7 trillion to $45 trillion. (That indeed is the range for 2003.)

Looking at just the year ended September 30, 2003, the federal government collected roughly $1.8 trillion in revenues, spent roughly $2.5 trillion, leaving it roughly $.7 trillion in the hole. Add this to the $6.8 trillion deficit accumulated in previous years and you have a $7.5 trillion deficit. (Please notice I am saying *trillion*, not billion and not million. One trillion dollars has 12 zeros— $1,000,000,000,000!)

Some of the difference might occur because of timing—commitments made to fund programs but not yet paid. But much of the difference must be made up with debt. The federal government still pays to run the $2.5 trillion in programs and must use debt to keep the funds flowing.

The high-end estimates of deficit are created when economists don't look at just one year of operations, but rather 5 or 10 years into the future. For example, *Atlantic Magazine*'s Nathan Littlefield projected the deficit at $45 trillion by looking out 10 years at the gap between the federal governments projected outlays (future spending plus current debt) and its projected revenues. Ouch!

What is incredible about the federal government is that their auditors—the Government Accountability Office (GAO, formerly the General Accounting Office, until July 7, 2004)—can't even express an opinion on the accuracy of the federal financial statements because financial systems and reports are so messy. So the $7.5 trillion deficit disclosed in the financial statements might not even be the right amount.

The way I look at deficit is as a negative fund balance. It cost more to run the government than the government brought in.

Not-for-Profit Accounting

Now, the not-for-profits did not fall into the fund trap, although they were using funds until relatively recently in their financial reports. Fortunately, the FASB put a stop to this. It said that not-for-profits can keep all of these funds separate

in their accounting system internally, but could not create monstrously long, fund-based financial statements to share with the public. Thank goodness!

In terms of financial statements, not-for-profits operate out of one pool of resources, and you will have only one set of financial statements. So not-for-profit financial statements are quite a bit thinner and simpler than the governmental financial statements.

Accounting standards say that a not-for-profit possesses the following characteristics:

- Resource contributors do not expect commensurate or proportionate pecuniary return.
- Operating purpose is other than to provide goods or services at a profit.
- Ownership interest is absent.

Organizations that clearly fall outside of these characteristics are businesses, governments, and investor-owned enterprises and entities that provide dividends, lower costs, or other economic benefit to their members, such as mutual insurance companies, credit unions, and employee benefit plans.

Here are some examples of not-for-profits:

- cemetery organizations
- civic organizations
- fraternal organization
- labor unions
- libraries
- museums
- other cultural institutions
- performing arts organizations
- political parties

NOT-FOR-PROFITS HAVE UNIQUE CONCERNS

Because not-for-profits have unique concerns, they also have their own Financial Accounting Standards Board (FASB) pronouncements. Their financial statements are uniquely titled and formatted, although they in essence contain the same sort of data as a proprietary business includes in its balance sheet, income statement, and cash flow statement.

Donations

Not-for-profits are unique in that they might operate from donations—and donations cause all sorts of accounting trouble.

Some donations are made with stipulations that the donation be spent in a specific way. Some pledges are made and never collected. (A CPA with a public television station once told me that one-third of the pledges they receive are never collected.) Some donations or pledges are not of cash but of time or other resources. These are just a few of the issues that cause revenue recognition to be a bit complicated.

You might hear terms thrown around such as "unrestricted funds," "temporarily restricted funds," and "permanently restricted funds." This relates to whether the funds are spendable now or sometime in the future. Usually, the terms of the donation will dictate whether they are restricted or not.

Sales of Goods and Services

Other not-for-profits actually sell a product or a service to generate revenues, but are not seeking earnings for an owner. All proceeds are to be used to further the mission of the not-for-profit. They run for the benefit of their clients.

Taxes

Not-for-profits are often exempt from many sorts of taxes. Revenues, payroll, and property may be tax-exempt. Often, not-for-profits don't have to pay sales tax.

FINANCIAL STATEMENTS

Not-for-profit financial statements need to demonstrate to their clients or beneficiaries that they are providing whatever services they can with the resources available—in other words, that beneficiaries are getting the most bang for the contributors' buck. However, this is often difficult to show with financial statements. It is possible, of course, to have accurate financial statements and spend all of the contributions, but still not be serving the clients in the most effective and efficient way.

This is why many not-for-profits include performance metrics in their annual reports. They might disclose how many clients were served and calculate a cost per client. They might also have metrics on how the quality of life of their clients has improved due to their assistance.

Again, not-for-profits have financial statements that are similar to the three key financial statements of a business enterprise, but with different names and in a slightly different format. Luckily for the reader, there are only three statements, not tens of statements as required for government:

- statement of financial position
- statement of activities
- statement of cash flows

The statement of financial position (Figure 12.4) is similar to a balance sheet. It must at least report the organization's total assets, liabilities, and net assets. Net assets are further broken out as to whether they are unrestricted, temporarily restricted, or permanently restricted.

The statement of activities (Figure 12.5) is a statement of revenues and expenses. It reports the change in the organization's net assets. The terms "fund balance" and "equity" are not used. The changes in net assets must be shown for each category: Change in Permanently Restricted Net Assets, Change in Temporarily Restricted Net Assets, and Change in Unrestricted Net Assets.

This statement most closely mimics the income statement we all know and love. Expenses are often grouped as management and general expenses, fundraising expenses, and membership development expenses.

Encumbrance

An encumbrance is an amount set aside for a commitment. For instance, a government might commit to hiring a trainer to come into the organization in four months to conduct a training session. The funds have not been paid to the trainer yet—and won't be until a month after delivery of the training session. So the cash won't actually go out for five months.

However, this is not money that the government can spend on anything else. So the estimated obligation is encumbered or—the way I think about it—burdened by this commitment. It is recorded in the general ledger as encumbered so that government leaders and managers won't mistake the funds for something they can use.

UNITED WAY OF MIAMI-DADE, INC.
STATEMENTS OF FINANCIAL POSITION
JUNE 30, 2004 AND 2003

ASSETS	2004	2003
Cash and cash equivalents, includes restricted cash of $0 in 2004 and $537,377 in 2003 (Note 8)	$ 10,806,905	$ 9,388,717
Investments (Note 2)	22,994,957	20,816,090
Pledges receivable, less allowance of $2,250,362 in 2004 and $2,137,500 in 2003	8,412,536	11,095,539
Donor-designated pledges receivables, less allowance of $1,623,076 in 2004 and $1,509,800 in 2003	4,917,511	4,837,434
Special contribution receivable (Note 12)	5,669,020	-
Other receivables (Note 3)	2,698,177	2,573,149
Prepaid expense and other assets	315,022	333,502
Prepaid pension costs (Note 6)	792,787	873,512
Property and equipment, net (Note 4)	7,964,902	7,378,183
	$ 64,571,817	$ 57,296,126

LIABILITIES AND NET ASSETS

LIABILITIES		
Accounts payable and accrued expenses (Note 7)	$ 2,264,681	$ 2,861,150
Approved allocations payable	15,405,206	16,387,313
Donor-designated allocations payable	9,683,078	11,262,410
Special contribution payable (Note 12)	5,669,020	-
Grants payable (Note 8)	197,336	418,947
Amounts held for others	488,115	481,732
Note payable (Note 7)	3,263,853	3,379,497
Total liabilities	36,971,289	34,791,049

COMMITMENTS (NOTE 9)

NET ASSETS (NOTE 10)		
Unrestricted	20,245,409	17,289,443
Temporarily restricted	7,099,888	5,054,863
Permanently restricted	255,231	160,771
Total net assets	27,600,528	22,505,077
	$ 64,571,817	$ 57,296,126

Figure 12.4 Miami-Dade United Way statements of financial position

A statement of cash flows (Figure 12.6) is no different from the statement used by proprietary entities.

All three of these statements must also disclose whether there are any donor restrictions on resources.

UNITED WAY OF MIAMI-DADE, INC.
STATEMENTS OF ACTIVITIES
YEARS ENDED JUNE 30, 2004 AND 2003

	2004				2003			
	Unrestricted	Temporarily Restricted	Permanently Restricted	Total	Unrestricted	Temporarily Restricted	Permanently Restricted	Total
Public support, revenue and other:								
Public support:								
Annual campaign, net of estimated uncollectible pledges of $4,212,391 in 2004 and $3,918,749 in 2003	$ 38,582,992	$ 4,355,560	$ -	$ 42,938,552	$ 37,331,550	$ 2,329,217	$ -	$ 39,660,767
Special contribution (Note 12)	-	5,669,020	-	5,669,020	-	-	-	-
Less: donor designations (Note 5)	(19,463,438)	6,914,135)	-	(26,377,573)	16,699,473)	1,088,072)	-	(17,787,545)
Annual campaign, net	19,119,554	3,110,445	-	22,229,999	20,632,077	1,241,145	-	21,873,222
Recovery of uncollectible pledges	1,430,247	16,000	-	1,446,247	1,146,595	-	-	1,146,595
Special events	1,232,663	-	94,460	1,327,123	1,521,287	188,226	60,771	1,770,284
Other contributions	590,238	-	-	590,238	342,879	-	-	342,879
Grants (Note 8)	362,733	34,747	-	397,480	420,553	-	-	420,553
Legacies and bequests	30,966	53,889	-	84,855	150,814	-	-	150,814
Total public support	22,766,401	3,215,081	94,460	26,075,942	24,214,205	1,429,371	60,771	25,704,347
Revenue:								
Investment income (losses):								
Interest income, net of investment fees of $85,575 in 2004 and $160,000 in 2003	531,673	-	-	531,673	569,993	-	-	569,993
Realized gains (losses) on sales of investment, net	483,448	-	-	483,448	(1,819,224)	-	-	(1,819,224)
Unrealized gains on investments, net	1,181,425	-	-	1,181,425	1,769,605	-	-	1,769,605
Other income, net	126,408	-	-	126,408	139,261	-	-	139,261
Total revenue	2,322,954	-	-	2,322,954	659,635	-	-	659,635
Other - net assets released from restrictions:								
Expiration of time restrictions	1,159,571	(1,159,571)	-	-	2,233,201	(2,233,201)	-	-
Total public support, revenue and other	26,248,926	2,055,510	94,460	28,398,896	27,107,041	803,830	60,771	26,363,982
Distributions and expenses:								
Distributions to agencies	14,953,922	-	-	14,953,922	15,458,308	-	-	15,458,308
Grant expenses	362,733	-	-	362,733	168,874	-	-	168,874
	15,316,655	-	-	15,316,655	15,627,182	-	-	15,627,182

Figure 12.5 Miami-Dade United Way statements of activities (continued on next page)

UNITED WAY OF MIAMI-DADE, INC.
STATEMENTS OF ACTIVITIES (Continued)
YEARS ENDED JUNE 30, 2004 AND 2003

	2004				2003			
	Unrestricted	Temporarily Restricted	Permanently Restricted	Total	Unrestricted	Temporarily Restricted	Permanently Restricted	Total
Payments to affiliated organizations:								
Payments to United Way of America	$ 345,480	$ -	$ -	$ 345,480	$ 346,500	$ -	$ -	$ 346,500
Payments to United Way of Florida	34,000	-	-	34,000	34,650	-	-	34,650
Total payments to affiliated organizations	379,480	-	-	379,480	381,150	-	-	381,150
Functional expenses:								
Program services	1,891,155	-	-	1,891,155	1,846,710	-	-	1,846,710
Supporting services	5,868,688	-	-	5,868,688	5,864,659	-	-	5,864,659
Total functional expenses	7,759,843	-	-	7,759,843	7,711,369	-	-	7,711,369
Other expenses	59,661	10,485	-	70,146	57,391	-	-	57,391
Pension plan (Note 6)	113,503	-	-	113,503	476,691	-	-	476,691
Fair market of derivative (gain) loss (Note 7)	(336,182)	-	-	(336,182)	389,617	-	-	389,617
Total distributions and expenses	23,292,960	10,485	-	23,303,445	24,643,400	-	-	24,643,400
Change in net assets	2,955,966	2,045,025	94,460	5,095,451	2,463,641 (	803,830)	60,771	1,720,582
Net assets, beginning of year	17,289,443	5,054,863	160,771	22,505,077	14,825,802	5,858,693	100,000	20,784,495
Net assets, end of year	$ 20,245,409	$ 7,099,888	$ 255,231	$ 27,600,528	$ 17,289,443	$ 5,054,863	$ 160,771	$ 22,505,077

Figure 12.5 Miami-Dade United Way statements of activities (continued)

UNITED WAY OF MIAMI-DADE, INC.
STATEMENTS OF CASH FLOWS
YEARS ENDED JUNE 30, 2004 AND 2003

		2004		2003
CASH FLOW FROM OPERATING ACTIVITIES:				
Increase in net assets	$	5,095,451	$	1,720,582
Adjustments to reconcile change in net assets to net cash provided				
by operating activities:				
Depreciation and amortization		243,755		251,165
Change in allowance for uncollectible pledges		226,138		127,800
Unrealized gains on investments, net	(	1,181,425)	(	1,769,605)
Realized (gains) losses on sale of investments, net	(	483,448)		1,819,224
Derivative fair value adjustment	(	336,182)		389,617
Change in operating assets and liabilities:				
Pledges receivables		2,570,141	(	1,613,887)
Donor designated pledges receivable	(	193,353)		3,514,250
Special contribution receivable	(	5,669,020)		-
Other receivables	(	125,029)		1,210,064
Prepaid expenses and other assets		18,480	(	96,289)
Prepaid pension costs		80,725		457,194
Accounts payable and accrued expenses	(	260,285)	(	331,519)
Approved allocations payable	(	982,108)	(	2,001,349)
Donor designated allocations payable	(	1,579,331)		17,935
Special contribution payable		5,669,020		-
Grants payable	(	221,611)	(	1,577,727)
Amounts held for others		6,383	(	8,559)
Total adjustments	(	2,217,150)		388,314
Net cash provided by operating activities		2,878,301		2,108,896
CASH FLOW FROM INVESTING ACTIVITIES:				
Proceeds from sale of investments		8,474,942		13,856,182
Purchase of investments	(	8,988,936)	(	14,811,002)
Purchase of property and equipment	(	830,474)	(	755,382)
Net cash used in investing activities	(	1,344,469)	(	1,710,202)
CASH FLOW FROM FINANCING ACTIVITIES:				
Repayment of note payable	(	115,644)	(	121,105)
NET INCREASE IN CASH AND CASH EQUIVALENTS		1,418,188		277,589
CASH AND CASH EQUIVALENTS - BEGINNING OF YEAR		9,388,717		9,111,128
CASH AND CASH EQUIVALENTS - END OF YEAR	$	10,806,905	$	9,388,717
Supplemental Disclosure:				
Cash paid during the year for interest	$	226,607	$	241,564

Figure 12.6 Miami-Dade United Way statements of cash flows

INTERNAL USE OF THE FUNDS

If you work for a not-for-profit, you might hear the accountant throwing around names of the funds. Until the 1990s, many not-for-profits were using fund accounting—a similar method to the governmental accounting discussed earlier in this chapter. Now, a not-for-profit may use fund accounting internally to keep different resources pooled in different pots, but for external reporting purposes all funds are combined into a single view of the entity. These funds are used for internal tracking and not reported in the financial statements given to stakeholders or external parties.

The funds that are generally needed by a not-for-profit include the following:

- unrestricted fund
- restricted funds
- endowment fund
- plant fund

The *unrestricted fund* is similar to the general fund in government. It is the money that the board of directors has to spend as they please.

Restricted funds are funds that must be used only for specific purposes.

An *endowment fund* is created when a donor gifts cash, investments, etc. to a not-for-profit organization for the purpose of providing income. Sometimes the principal of the endowment is permanent; sometimes it reverts to the donor.

The *plant fund* is where major capital assets and the debt incurred in obtaining them is reported.

Quiz

1. "Proprietary" means
   (a) owned
   (b) not-for-profit
   (c) governmental

2. Governments collect taxes in order to pay for
   (a) services for their citizens
   (b) trips to the Caribbean
   (c) raw materials in order to make products

3. Governments and not-for-profits avoid the word "profit."
   T or F

4. GASB stands for
   (a) Government Accounting Setting Board
   (b) Government Actuarial Standards Board
   (c) Government Accounting Standards Board

5. Not-for-profits always follow GASB standards.
   T or F

6. "Commingling" means that
   (a) the government is being friendly
   (b) the government has mixed up its objectives with the objectives of a proprietary entity
   (c) the government has used money out of one fund to pay for the program of another fund

7. Fiduciary funds can be spent by the government.
   T or F

8. Agency funds are monies held on someone else's behalf.
   T or F

9. Which of the following is not a fiduciary fund?
   (a) agency fund
   (b) pension trust fund
   (c) general fund
   (d) investment trust fund

10. Which of the following is not a proprietary fund?
    (a) pension trust fund
    (b) enterprise fund
    (c) internal service fund

11. An internal service fund runs programs that do business with entities outside the government to generate a profit.
    T or F

12. An enterprise fund may not generate a profit.
    T or F

13. The governmental fund supercategory is the catchall category for all funds that are not proprietary or fiduciary.
    T or F

14. A government should have several general funds.
    T or F

15. Which of the following is not a governmental fund?
    (a) capital projects fund
    (b) general fund
    (c) enterprise fund
    (d) permanent fund
    (e) pecial revenue fund

16. The GASB has recently lengthened the financial statements.
    T or F

17. Governmental financial statements have which two layers?
    (a) the entitywide layer and the fund layer
    (b) the user-friendly layer and the proprietary layer
    (c) the fund layer and the superfund layer
    (d) the superfund layer and the fund category layer

18. Fund balance is a concept similar to a proprietary entity's retained earnings.
    T or F

19. A deficit is created when the government spends more or plans on spending more than it collects or plans on collecting.
    T or F

20. The calculation of the federal deficit is questionable because the financial statements created by the federal government are questionable.
    T or F

21. Not-for-profits use funds in their financial statements.
    T or F

22. Not-for-profits can use funds for internal tracking purposes.
    T or F

23. IBM is a good example of a not-for-profit.
    T or F

24. An art museum is a good example of a not-for-profit.
    T or F

25. Permanently restricted funds are donations that you get to spend on whatever you want immediately.
    T or F

26. Which of the following is not a not-for-profit financial statement?
    (a) the statement of financial position
    (b) the income statement
    (c) the statement of activities
    (d the statement of cash flows

27. An encumbrance is funds set aside for a commitment.
    T or F

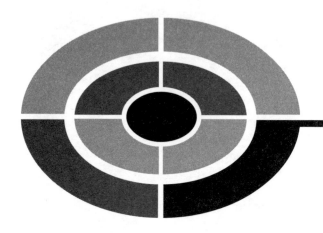

Test: Part Three

1. Which of the following are depreciation methods?
   (a) unit of production
   (b) MACRS
   (c) straight line
   (d) double-declining balance method
   (e) sum-of-the-years'-digits method
   (f) all of the above

2. Internal controls are a vitamin.
   T or F

3. Why are adjusting entries recorded?
   (a) to comply with the cost standard
   (b) to adjust balances to the proper amounts
   (c) to match revenues to expenses
   (d) to give the accountant a chance to rest
   (e) to reconcile net income to retained earnings
   (f) a, b, and c
   (g) b, c, and d
   (h) b, c, and e

4. The following are common items that require an adjusting entry:
   (a) bad debts
   (b) income receivable
   (c) inventory on hand at the end of the period
   (d) wages earned but not yet paid
   (e) depreciation expense
   (f) all of the above

5. The cash method of accounting can result in
   (a) a mismatch of revenues and expenditures
   (b) a miscalculation of true cost
   (c) a misstatement of investment market value

6. SEC stands for
   (a) Standards Efficiency Committee of the Treadway Commission
   (b) Securities Exchange Company
   (c) Securities and Exchange Commission

7. The PCAOB was created as a result of the financial and auditing scandals
   and failures of the late '90s and early '00s.
   T or F

8. Accounting principles and guidance encourage changing the way a transaction is treated from period to period.
   T or F

9. If an item is immaterial or not material, it means that
   (a) it doesn't weigh much
   (b) it does not have a significant impact on the financial statements
   (c) it' not made to last
   (d) it's inexpensive and cheap

10. When writing a transaction, credits are justified to the left.
    T or F

11. When you buy a new copier for cash, you would debit cash.
    T or F

12. When you buy a new copier for cash, you would debit fixed assets.
    T or F

13. Revenues and expenses affect net income and thus impact equity.
    T or F

14. A chart of accounts is a listing of the codes assigned to general ledger accounts.
    T or F

15. On the day you purchase a copier and recognize it as a fixed asset, you impact the income statement.
    T or F

16. Depreciation is a "non-cash" expense.
    T or F

17. Amortization is depreciation for intangibles.
    T or F

18. Intangibles include
    (a) goodwill
    (b) patents
    (c) trade names
    (d) all of the above

19. FIFO pretends that the newest raw material item is used in manufacturing products.
    T or F

20. The weighted average method of inventory valuation tends to even out price fluctuations in the accounting records.
    T or F

21. If prices are going up, the LIFO method will maximize your profit on each sale.
    T or F

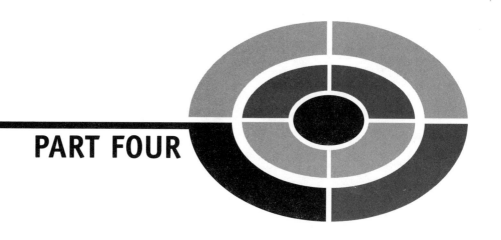

PART FOUR

Financial Indicators—Using Financial Information to Make Decisions

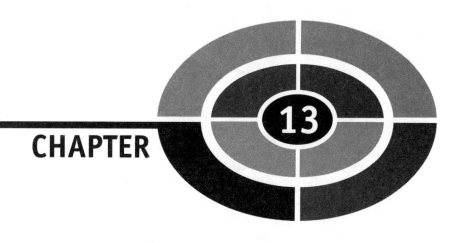

CHAPTER 13

Cautions about Financial Analysis

In the remaining chapters, we are going to look at how to conduct a financial analysis of an organization. After an introduction to the steps involved in an analysis, we are going to look at several tools for indicating the financial health of an entity. These tools include financial metrics. We will run financial metrics for two competing companies by using the financial data included in recent 10-Ks. But first, let me share some cautionary comments about financial analysis.

There Isn't One Number That Indicates Health

Over the years people have asked me, "What one number do I need to look at to determine whether my company is doing well or not?" Ah, if it were only that simple! There is not one magic number in the financial statements that will tell you how healthy an organization is.

You can be looking great on profit but have a weak cash flow. You might have a strong cash balance, but if it is all funded by debt, it will give you a weak balance sheet and impact your profitability because you have to pay interest.

All of the financial information works together, so you must look at the three key financial statements together. Each has a unique perspective that is important to understanding the entity. If you rely on only one financial statement for all your decisions, you are likely to make a mistake.

So in conducting a financial analysis, we are going to look at many metrics and many numbers, each derived from a different financial statement. After we have them all together, we can piece together a story and make some initial conclusions.

There Is No Such Thing as a Good or Bad Result

Anyone who tells you there is a perfect range for ratios is full of it. I once taught a course in finance for nonfinancial managers for a savings and loan. I was there to teach the loan officers how to read the financial statements submitted by their clients who were asking for loans. (No, they didn't already know how to read financial statements!)

The loan officers would always run a standard set of 10 metrics to see if a client's results would fall within a certain acceptable range. When the metrics did not fall within an acceptable range, the client's loan was rejected.

The loan officers had no idea what they were looking at or what the metrics meant. They only knew that if a metric fell outside of the range, it was bad.

This is a crazy way to do business. Obviously, they were not truly knowledgeable about how their clients' businesses worked. Each business has a unique business model and operating environment, and that must be taken into account when doing an analysis.

All the metrics do for you is paint you a picture of what is so. You cannot immediately judge a metric as good or bad based on some externally imposed scale. At the least, you must weigh it against other metrics, look at past results, and benchmark against competitors.

There Is No Standard That Dictates How Metrics Should Be Calculated

There is no GAAP for metrics, no principles that guide how they should be calculated. One text will tell you that you should use an average; another will tell you to use a year-end figure. One text will add depreciation back when working with net income; another won't. It all depends on what you read and who you listen to.

It also depends on what makes sense for the organization you are analyzing. For instance, the metric return on investment can be customized. The numerator of return on investment is income and the denominator is investment.

$$\frac{\text{income (return)}}{\text{investment}}$$

Which income figure are you going to use? Are you going to use net income after taxes or operating income? Or maybe EBIT—earnings before interest and taxes?

How about the bottom figure? What do you consider the investment? Is it working capital plus equity? What are you including in working capital? Does it include rainy-day cash? That can make a big difference to the result.

One company I analyzed in the late 1990s revealed in its annual financial report that return on investment was 316 percent. When I calculated it, using data from the annual report, I got 30 percent. I asked the accountants in the company to tell me why their number was so different, and they gave me a very detailed formula that had 20 components, not just the two I was working with. Is this kosher? Well, it is legal. Again, there is no standard against which to measure the measures.

This is why I recommend taking the metrics that companies disclose in their annual reports, on their Web sites, and in their investor relations marketing materials with a grain of salt. Recalculate them yourself.

Also, do not take the ratios we discuss in later chapters to be the gospel—the only way to approach the metric. Tweak them to your own needs, because there is no standard that dictates how you have to do them. I do, however, strongly suggest that you document how you calculated the ratio and do the same thing consistently over time so that the numbers are comparable.

There Is More to Business than Finance

Finance is just one piece of the story of an organization's success. If you really think about it, good financial standing is a result of doing many other things in the organization well. You can't generate a profit over the long haul if you don't have a good product or if you frustrate and drive off customers and employees. But because this is a book about accounting, we are going to look only at metrics that can be measured with dollars.

All that financial analysis can do for you is to give you clues of something else happening. It might indicate that customers are being driven away, but it won't tell you what is driving them away. The financial statements won't say customers are being driven away by a bad jingle for instance—all you will see is a decline in revenue over a period of years. When this happens, your next question is "Why did revenues decline?" The financial results were a clue and now you are going to have to do a little snooping around, asking tough questions of managers, customers, and possibly even suppliers.

THE BALANCED SCORECARD GIVES US A BROADER PERSPECTIVE

To get a broader sense of how successful and stable the company is, you might want to use the structure of the balanced scorecard model.

A professor at Harvard University, Robert Kaplan, invented the balanced scorecard model. He argues that businesses should create goals and metrics in four categories, not just one.

We are very good, after decades and decades of compiling financial information, at generating financial metrics. Most organizations have pretty good systems in place to gather, compile, and summarize financial information. And many times, unfortunately, it is the only set of metrics that organizations use to determine if they are successful.

In the balanced scorecard model, finance is just one of the four areas analyzed. Kaplan's balanced scorecard model includes four components:

- financial
- customer
- internal business processes
- learning and growth

The balanced scorecard encourages managers to take a more holistic view of the organization. Often, when companies are in a financial crunch, they put a stop to any training or travel for the employees. While this results in better short-term financial results, it might have a negative long-term impact on the learning and growth area. It might even hurt customer relationships or allow internal business processes to deteriorate.

The balanced scorecard is just that, a scorecard—a report card, if you will—that looks at a balance of areas and metrics. Ideally, systems would be in place to compile information and report on metrics in each of these four areas as often as possible. One organization I consult with calculates certain metrics daily. Others might report on the metrics monthly or quarterly.

Financial Component

In Kaplan's model, the financial component asks, "How do we look to our owners?" It asks, in essence, "Are the owners happy with the return they are getting on their investment in the organization?"

I teach a course on financial statement analysis to CPAs and in it we cover more than 70 metrics—a really long day, to say the least! We have been generating these types of metrics for centuries and are quite good at it now. It is the most fully developed area of the balanced scorecard. It includes the financial metrics we discuss in the remaining chapters.

Customer Component

The customer component asks, "How do customers see us?" Here we create goals and metrics to determine if we are going a good job pleasing our customers. We might ask, for instance, if our customers are loyal, repeat customers.

Many organizations already do a good job at collecting this sort of information. We have been concerned about customer satisfaction in this country for several decades now. Examples of metrics in this area include the following:

- market share
- customer acquisition
- customer satisfaction
- customer retention
- shares of the customer wallet
- response time
- convenient access
- brand recognition

The remaining two components are great to monitor but are sometimes hard to quantify. These are the least developed areas of the balanced scorecard. Many organizations ignore these aspects of a business's success entirely.

Internal Business Processes Component

Internal business processes asks, "What must we excel at?" In other words, how do our internal systems need to function in order to have happy customers and good financial results?

For instance, I was working for a high-tech company that had doubled in size each of the previous five years. At the quarterly meeting, the CFO congratulated everyone on the growth of the organization, but redirected everyone's attention to the problems that would keep them from succeeding in the future.

He likened the company to a sleek rocket ship racing to the moon. From the outside, everything looks perfect. However, when you open the cockpit door, you see a little fire in the nose of the ship and thin, haggard mice are running furiously trying to keep the rocket moving.

Yes, the company had grown, but the internal processes had broken down. The wrong products were being shipped to the customers, the quality of the products was slipping, and employees were not getting reimbursed for travel expenses for several months. He directed all managers to focus on cleaning up procedures and processes before chasing down additional market share and new products.

I once ordered all of my family's Christmas presents from one fabulous-looking catalog. It was full of all sorts of fun outdoor items that I hadn't seen anyplace else. The catalog company gladly took my money and promised delivery a week before Christmas. We waited...and waited. Finally, the gifts arrived—around Valentine's Day. Great products, great marketing, horrible execution. I will never order from that company again, no matter how tempting its products are.

Examples of metrics for this component include:

- amount of research done on emerging and future customer preferences
- percent of sales from new products
- new products introduced vs. planned
- percent of defects
- time customer must wait for delivery

Learning and Growth Component

This component of the balance scorecard asks, "Can we continue to improve and create value?" Here we ask if we have the infrastructure, the people skills, and the information systems to get us where we want to be in the future. This section asks whether you are set up for success. Are you investing in the skills of your people and in technology to get you where you want to be?

Under traditional, short-term financial measures, it is not in a manager's best interest to enhance the capabilities of subordinates, systems, or organizational processes. So sometimes this area is sacrificed in order to achieve short-term profit or cash flow.

For instance, a company might focus on profitability and cash flow to the detriment of long-term strategies. In one organization I worked with, the managers decided to stop offering employees training sessions because they were trying to cut expenses. In cutting expenses, they also were cutting customer service because the employees weren't being trained on how to handle customer complaints. Over time, the business lost several key customers, and hence their revenue went down even further. What was their solution to this problem? Cut training even more to reduce expenses and make up for lost revenues—a nasty downward spiral, wouldn't you say?

Possible metrics:

- employee retention
- competency upgrades of employees
- percent of employees who have access to customer information
- number of suggestions per employee
- percent of employees whose professional goals align with organizational goals
- percent of team-based relationships with other business units

To learn more about the balanced scorecard, I suggest you go to the Harvard Business School Press Web site (www.hbsp.harvard.edu) and purchase some of Kaplan's books or online courses.

There Is No Right or Wrong Way to Approach Business

Metrics will vary among competitors in the same industry for a variety of reasons.

Consider this simple analogy. You don't live the same way your siblings live, but who is to say who is living the better life? You are all functioning members of society, I hope, and your choices are just as good as their choices.

As an investor, owner, or employee of a business, you are looking for an affinity with a company. Does the company seem wise to you? What is wise to you might look scary to me. Financial analysis will reveal some of the values and choices that a company has made.

MATURITY OF THE COMPANY CREATES DIFFERENT RESULTS

The maturity of the organization makes a big difference in what you can expect financial ratios to look like and what the organization's goals are.

A Growing Firm

A growing firm will often consume more cash than it generates. It is like a baby needing to be fed all the time in hopes that one day it will become independent and be able to pay its own way. The company is fed by external investors, and all who are involved desire to grow the company's sales and market share. You will often see low profits, low cash, high debt, and high capital expenditures.

A Sustaining Firm

A sustaining firm has weathered childhood and is now just looking to clean up a few quirks here and there. You might liken this stage of maturity to a young adult who has a general sense of where he or she wants to go but hasn't learned some of the hard lessons of being a true adult. In these companies, the focus is on maintaining profitability and cash flow while cleaning up procedures, expanding capacity, and relieving bottlenecks. You will often see good profit, good cash flow, moderate debt, and high capital investments.

A Maturing Firm

A maturing firm is ready to reap the harvest, ready to take advantage of all the hard work of the earlier stages of its life and maximize cash flow and minimize investment. I liken a mature firm to a professional in her late 50s who is looking at retirement, is not looking for a career change, and is wanting to spend more time with the family and at her hobbies and not at the office. You will often see good profit, good cash flow, low debt, and low capital investments.

Quiz

1. Net income is the best indicator of the financial health of an entity.
   T or F

2. All metrics should fall within a predetermined, standard range.
   T or F

3. GAAP has rules regarding the calculation of metrics.
   T or F

4. Financial analysis can only give you clues about what is going on in an organization.
   T or F

5. The balanced scorecard has the following four components:
   (a) financial, compliance, operations, and internal control
   (b) financial, customer, internal business processes, and learning and growth
   (c) financial, customer, internal controls, and business metrics

6. An example of a customer satisfaction metric is
   (a) customer retention
   (b) customer acquisition
   (c) response time
   (d) convenient access
   (e) all of the above

7. The internal business processes component of the balanced scorecard looks at whether the organization's employees have the training and skills to help the company achieve its goals.
   T or F

8. An example of an internal business process metric is
   (a) new products introduced versus planned
   (b) time customer waits for delivery
   (c) employee retention
   (d) all of the above
   (e) a and b
   (f) b and c

9. The learning and growth component of the balanced scorecard asks if we have the infrastructure, the people skills, and the information systems to get us where we want to go in the future.
   T or F

10. Under traditional short-term measures of profitability, it is not in the managers' best interest to enhance the capabilities of employees or information systems.
    T or F

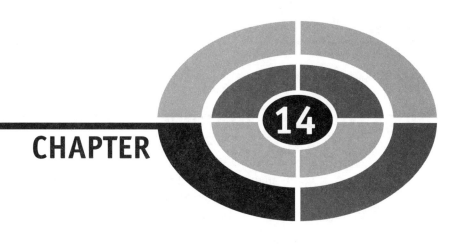

CHAPTER

14

Conducting a Financial Analysis— The Prep Work

In an ideal world, you have access to all sorts of wonderful information about the company before you start your financial analysis. In the real world, you might be lucky to get just a few things from the following list. Just because you can't get some of this information doesn't mean you should give up on running an analysis. Give it your best shot.

Also keep in mind the cost versus benefit of doing a superdetailed analysis of the organization. While it might be ideal to gather all the information I am recommending, it might be cost-prohibitive in terms of time—and time is money!

You can subscribe to services that will do some of the data gathering and analysis for you. If you are going to make a habit of doing financial analysis, paying for the help might be wise. A company that does good work on gathering and analyzing financial information is Hoover's (www.hoovers.com).

Things to Gather in Order to Do an Analysis

Here is a list of things it would be ideal to have when doing an analysis. If you are a company insider, you should be able to get all of this stuff. If you are doing an analysis from the outside, gathering this information will be a lot tougher and in some cases impossible. But give it your best shot; information is power.

Financing history. Find out how the organization has financed operations in the recent past, say the last five years. Has it relied heavily on debt to keep running, has it sold shares in its business to investors, or has it been able to generate money on its own? Also, are there any restrictive debt covenants or shareholder obligations that could impact the organization?

Terms of loans. If they have any outstanding debt, what are the terms of the debt? When is it payable? Is the interest rate favorable? When do they project they will retire the debt? Who is the debt payable to?

Distributions to owners. What is the organization's philosophy on sharing the wealth with owners? Many organizations like to plow their profits right back into the company in order to grow. Some prefer to give the owners the profits as they are made. Some are right in the middle: some percentage is invested back in the company and some is distributed. These decisions can make a huge difference in the organization's cash flow and equity position.

Age and types of payables. Who do they owe money to? Who are their key vendors and what are the terms with these vendors? Have they established credit with these vendors so they can hold onto their cash longer?

Age and types of receivables. Who owes the organization money? What is the mix of repeat vs. new customers? Who are its main customers and how creditworthy are they? How long do receivables remain outstanding?

Age and types of inventory. Does the organization hold a large amount of inventory? How old is this inventory? Do customers expect that products be available to them immediately upon demand? How does this impact inventory levels?

Details on cash—a cash flow statement. Get an audited cash flow statement. What do they do with their extra cash? Do they invest it or distribute it to owners? What do they invest in?

Audited versus Unaudited Financial Statements

I have a very serious warning about financial statements: if they have not been audited, you can't rely on them, period. Auditors confirm that the company is indeed following generally accepted accounting principles (GAAP). Without an auditor's blessing, there is no reason why the company would create accurate financial statements. Nothing prevents them from presenting information in its most flattering light. Heck, they might even make stuff up.

How Can Financial Statements Go Unaudited?

Some organizations are not required to publish financial statements. For instance, I have a small business and I am the sole owner. I do not share my financial results with anyone but my husband and my tax accountant. If you were a competitor of mine, you would have a hard time comparing what you do with what I do.

Some very large organizations are privately held. I once taught a seminar for a huge corporation in Tennessee that had been owned by a family for more than 80 years. They were involved in dozens of industries. One of their competitive advantages is that their competitors did not have access to their financial results and could not determine how—or if—they were making a profit.

Details on income—an income statement. Get an audited income statement. What was the gross sales figure? How much of gross sales did they get to keep in net income? What are the types of expenses involved in running the organization?

Competitor information. Find out who the organization thinks its main competitors are and get as much financial data on the competitors as possible. Gather all the items on this list for each competitor so you will have plenty of information to benchmark against.

Information on steady customers and steady vendors. Who are the significant vendors and customers for this organization? How is their industry faring? How are their companies faring? I know that if some of my steady customers go bust, I will also be in peril. Does the company rely heavily on just one customer or one vendor? If so, how solid is that relationship?

Factors that dictate the success of the entity. Each organization has its own definition of success and the route to it. For instance, the reason that Krispy Kreme Doughnuts is successful is different from the reason that Dunkin' Donuts is successful. Find out, through reading corporate promotional literature, media interviews, and Web sites and just plain talking to managers, why the organization is successful. Your next question is "How well is the organization doing at focusing on its success factors?"

Audited **financial statements.** I have to repeat it: audited financial statements are infinitely more reliable than unaudited financial statements. Yes, auditors have been shown up as fallible in the past decade, over and over and over, but a little assurance is better than no assurance.

Business plan or strategic plan. If you can get hold of the long-term strategies that drive the company and guide its leaders and employees, you will have a great deal of insight into why sacrifices are made and why the numbers might look like they do. However, many organizations operate without business plans or strategic plans. (This is not recommended, by the way.) Organizations that do operate using long-range planning of some sort will often sacrifice short-term returns for long-term goals. This will impact financial results.

Budget or standard to compare against. Budgets are simply the translation of the future plans of the organization into financial terms. You can tell a lot about the priorities of the organization by looking at its budget.

Things that interest you. Do you have specific concerns about the organization that I haven't covered? See what kind of data you can gather on these issues.

Financial Analysis, Step by Step

You can simply run a few metrics to start telling the story, but I want to teach you the "right" way to do it; the thorough way. This will harvest the maximum amount of interesting data.

So here are the steps to conducting a thorough financial analysis.

1. Consider the perspective of the users of your story. What questions would they like your story to answer? Are they an investor, manager, banker?

Your answer to this question will dictate what sort of metrics to run. For instance, investors are mostly concerned about profitability and return on their investment. Managers are usually concerned about things like inventory levels, production, and sales. They also worry about how well working capital is being managed. Bankers care about whether the organization has the ability to repay the loan. Banks often look at cash flow, other outstanding debt, and collateral.

2. Gain an understanding of environmental and market trends. Here you are going to have to do some research outside of the financial statements. The Management's Discussion and Analysis section of the 10-K and annual report might begin to give you clues about what is going on in the market, but you are going to have to do a little more work on finding out the answers to the following questions. This is not a complete list; use your noggin and get creative:

- Who are the competitors?
- What is this organization's standing against these competitors? How much market share does it have?
- What are customer perceptions of its product or service?
- Are the customers satisfied with the timeliness of service or product delivery?
- Is the demand for its product or service declining or increasing? Is the organization making divining rods out of sticks or global positioning systems?
- Who are the customers for the product? What kind of buying power do they have?
- What markets remain unexplored? Is there potential for growth?
- What is the organization's plan for the future?
- Is the company positioned for future success in its information systems and employee skills?
- What is the organization's reputation with suppliers?
- Have there been any major changes in management? Why?

3. Determine what you think the financials should look like. Here is where you apply all the knowledge you have learned so far in this book. You want to envision and physically sketch out what the balance sheet, income statement, and cash flow statement should look like for this entity. An airline's balance sheet will obviously look much different from an accounting firm's balance sheet. Here are some questions to answer to help guide your creation of scratch financial statements:

- How financially healthy is the entity?
- What would happen in case of liquidation?
- Where did the entity get its money and what did it do with it?
- Who owns the business?
- How profitable is the company?
- Where does the profit come from? Operations? Investing? Other?
- How much investment must the entity make in its product or service?
- How much does the entity spend in overhead?
- Is this profitability sustainable or a one-time fluke?
- Where did the cash come from? Operations? Investing? Financing?
- Is the entity realizing its profits in cash?
- Is the entity in a better or worse cash position than in prior years?
- How liquid are the entity's resources?
- Are working capital items increasing or decreasing? Inventory? Accounts receivable? Accounts payable?
- Are sales increasing or decreasing?
- Is the entity realizing cost efficiencies?
- What stage of the life cycle is the business in? Growth? Sustaining? Maturing? Declining?

Sketch out the balance sheet, income statement, and cash flow statement on paper. Use both dollar figures and percentages. (The percentages will be very telling in your later analysis.) For example, you might say that you think that on the asset side of the balance sheet cash should represent 10 percent of their assets, inventory 60 percent, and fixed assets 30 percent. You might predict that cost of goods sold is 70 percent of total sales. None of these documents have to be perfect; you are just doing an intuitive estimate.

Now, why are you doing this at all? Because you want to compare what you think the financials should look like with what they actually look like. If you are incredibly surprised, that tells you that either that you really don't know a whole lot about how the company runs, because you didn't do enough research, or that something funny is going on in the company.

Yes, it is a lot of work, but this is a high-yield activity!

4. Run a flux analysis on the financial statements—both horizontal and common size. *Fluctuation analysis*—or, in hip and cool accounting terms, *flux analysis*—is one of the best financial analysis tools around. In a fluctuation analysis, you stack up key numbers side by side and see how they have behaved over time.

Work with Both Dollars and Percentages

Relying on only dollars or only percentages can mislead you. For instance, you might see that sales have increased $1 million over the past year, but as a percentage, that is a minor 1 percent change because total sales are $100 million. Or the opposite might occur: you might see a huge percentage difference that is ultimately insignificant. For example, a 50 percent fluctuation in an account that has a very low dollar balance of $500 is only $250. So, if it goes up by $250, who cares?

There are two standard ways of doing a flux analysis—the common size approach and the horizontal approach. You should run both. If you plug the data from the financial statements into an Excel spreadsheet and then ask it to do the same calculations for each year, it won't be that much manual work.

How to Express a Metric

Metrics can be expressed in five main ways:

as a fraction	¼
as a percentage	25 percent
as a whole number	.25
as a ratio	1:4 (read as 'one to four')
as a multiplier	4 times per quarter

Each way of expressing the result is valid, but consider tradition and meaning when deciding on the method. For instance, return on investment is best expressed as a percentage. You might hear, "Return on investment for the project is 25 percent." It would not be as meaningful to say, "Return on investment is .25" or "Return on investment is one to four." You ultimately get to make the choice. Just try to be consistent in the way you express the metric so you don't confuse yourself or the users of your analysis.

COMMON SIZE ANALYSIS

In common size analysis, you turn everything into a percentage of a total. One item is 100 percent and the rest are a portion of this 100 percent. On the income statement, you turn sales into 100 percent and everything else becomes a percentage of total sales. Figure 14.1 shows an example:

Dell Income Statement, Fiscal Year
End January 2004, in billions

Sales	41,444	100%
Cost of goods sold	33,892	82%
Gross margin	7,552	18%
Operating expenses	4,008	10%
Operating margin	3,544	9%
Taxes and other	899	2%
Net income	2,645	6%

Figure 14.1 Common size analysis

I also think of this type of analysis as a pie chart analysis. You are asking, "How much of the total sales pie was consumed by cost of goods and how much by operating expenses?"

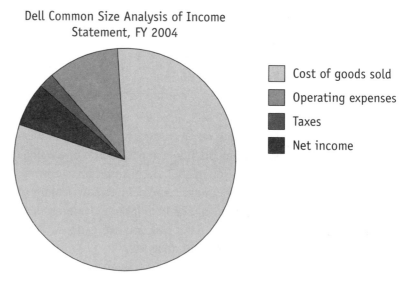

Dell Common Size Analysis of Income
Statement, FY 2004

- Cost of goods sold
- Operating expenses
- Taxes
- Net income

Figure 14.2 Common size analysis of the income statement

Now, what do you do with this information? Well, you want the pie to look better and better, not worse.

Going back to our income statement example, you see that in the first year the proportion of expenses and net income to total revenues is very similar.

Keeping all of the proportions stable while increasing sales is quite a feat and is a happy trend.

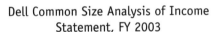

Dell Income Statement, Fiscal Year End January 2003, in billions		
Sales	35,404	100%
Cost of goods sold	29,055	82%
Gross margin	6,349	18%
Operating expenses	3,505	10%
Operating margin	2,844	9%
Taxes and other	722	2%
Net income	2,122	6%

Dell Common Size Analysis of Income
Statement, FY 2003

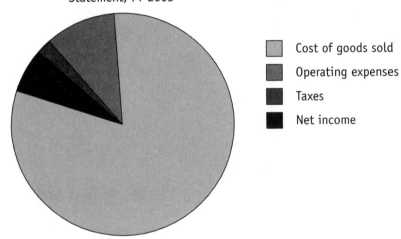

- Cost of goods sold
- Operating expenses
- Taxes
- Net income

Figure 14.3 Dell assets, common size analysis, 2003

When doing a common size analysis of the balance sheet, total assets are 100 percent on the left side of the balance sheet and total liabilities and equity are 100 percent on the right side of the balance sheet. You can also convert those to pies. For our example, I ran a common size analysis on just the asset side of the balance sheet (Figure 14.4).

Dell Assets from Balance Sheet, FY 2004 and 2003

	2004		2003	
Cash	4,317	22%	4,232	27%
Short-term investments	835	4%	406	3%
Accounts receivable	3,635	19%	2,586	17%
Inventories	327	2%	306	2%
Other current assets	1,519	8%	1,394	9%
Property, plant, and equipment	1,517	8%	913	6%
Investments	6,770	35%	5,267	34%
Other noncurrent assets	391	2%	366	2%
Total assets	19,311	100%	15,470	100%

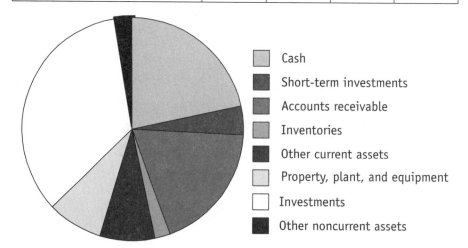

Figure 14.4 Dell's assets from the balance sheet, FY 2004

Here we see that cash has decreased between the years and appears to have been used on fixed assets and investments. Other proportions remain stable.

Running a common size analysis on a cash flow statement is difficult because some of the numbers are negative—or uses of cash—and some are positive receipts of cash. I don't recommend doing a common size analysis for the cash flow statement.

So some of the pieces of the puzzle are already coming together to form a picture of what is happening for Dell. We are piecing together a story.

HORIZONTAL ANALYSIS

With this second flux analysis technique, you choose one year as a base year and every other year is fluctuated off that year. In this case, a picture will substitute for a thousand words.

	2004		2003		Base Year: 2002	
Sales	41,444	133%	35,404	114%	**31,168**	**100%**
Cost of goods sold	33,892	132%	29,055	113%	**25,661**	**100%**
Gross margin	7,552	137%	6,349	115%	**5,507**	**100%**
Operating expenses	4,008	108%	3,505	94%	**3,718**	**100%**
Operating margin	3,544	198%	2,844	159%	**1,789**	**100%**
Taxes and other	899	166%	722	133%	**543**	**100%**
Net income	2,645	212%	2,122	170%	**1,246**	**100%**

Figure 14.5 Horizontal analysis, Dell income statement

Be careful which years you compare! Be careful that you compare valid numbers. Compare the fluctuating years only with the base year, not with each other.

So I chose 2002 as my base year. Every account in 2002 is 100 percent. 2003 and 2004 are fluctuated of this base year—not off each other.

Because of this, you cannot compare the 2003 numbers with the 2004 numbers. You can't say that sales in 2003 were 114 percent and sales in 2004 were 133 percent, so sales went up between 2003 and 2004 by 19 percent. That is not mathematically or logically valid, because sales between 2003 and 2004 actually increased by 17 percent ((41444 – 35404) / 41444). You can say that sales in 2003 were up 14 percent over 2002 and sales in 2004 were up 33 percent over 2002.

What I notice from the horizontal analysis is that Dell was able to increase sales by 33 percent between 2002 and 2004—a great thing in itself—and also increase net income by 112 percent. Yes, it doubled its net income. This is a concept called *scaling*. Scaling means that you were able to spend proportionally fewer dollars to make proportionally more income. Dell appears to be a scaling quite nicely!

After performing a common size analysis and a horizontal analysis, make notes about what you are seeing so far.

5. Decide which ratios are meaningful to the organization. Choose at least five ratios from each category—liquidity, profitability, and financing—and calculate them for the past three years

You can ratio any number against any other number in the financial statements. You can generate numbers and metrics until you are blue in the face. Some of the metrics will tell an interesting story and some will be entirely meaningless.

Be choosy about the metrics you run on your organization. Not all ratios will tell an interesting story about you. Some ratios might not even apply to you at all. So what you want to do is to look over the lists of ratios in Chapters 15, 16, 17, and 18 and decide which ones make sense for you. I suggest you choose to calculate at least five ratios in each category.

For our case study, I am going to run every metric listed in the chapter, whether or not it is a good, meaningful metric for our companies. I am doing this to drive home the point that not all metrics will work and not all metrics are worth worrying with.

The three categories of ratio are liquidity, profitability, and financing.

- *Liquidity* ratios tell us how flexible and powerful the organization is. Does the entity have enough liquid resources to cover its obligations?
- *Profitability* ratios tell us what kind of return the organization brings for its owners. Does the entity generate enough of its own funding to make it worth it for them to be in business?
- *Financing* ratios tell us how the organization is getting resources to operate. Is it generating its own resources, borrowing the resources, or selling equity to generate resources? Does the entity fund its growth and/or operations through profit *or* debt *or* contributions from owners?

6. Investigate. Now that you have raised so many questions with your flux analysis and ratio analysis, you need to start investigating why the numbers look as they do. If you are an outsider to the organization, you might not have anywhere else to go. You are then left to make educated guesses about what might have happened. You can also come up with a hypothesis and then watch to see if your hypothesis holds in future periods.

If you are on the inside, you should be able to ask the questions of the accountant and the managers to get an answer. But that is not always the case.

If it is a publicly traded company, read the Management's Discussion and Analysis section of the financial reports to see if the questions are answered. As we discussed in Chapter 7, the Management's Discussion and Analysis section of the financial statements is one of most important parts of the 10-K. It is the top managers' explanation of what happened over the past period and might even contain a little projection about where they think they are going in the near period.

Often, closely held organizations are also closed lipped. The owners are not accustomed to answer your questions, nor are they required to do so. For many managers, this is one of the biggest drawbacks of becoming a public company. When you go public, you have to answer the shareholders' questions. When you are private, you only have to answer to a few folks.

Even when you are analyzing a public company that issues 10-Ks and other annual reports, the numbers are so summarized or rolled up it is hard to get at the root cause of an issue.

Open Book Management

A company might benefit from sharing financial results with its employees. A philosophy called *open book management* recommends that managers educate employees about how the business makes money and the tools used to track a business's success. It also recommends that employees be told how the company is doing as often as possible and that employees share in the ownership of the company.

A man named Jack Stack popularized the philosophy. Stack was the manager of a division of a huge conglomerate. His division retooled engines. The huge conglomerate had decided that his division was not profitable and was planning to shut it down. It was the largest employer in a small town, and this would have had a disastrous impact on the whole community.

Stack was up nights worrying about what to do when he realized that he was doing everyone a disservice by keeping this problem to himself. He realized that only three other managers in the company understood what was going on and that the employees would be completely shocked when they lost their jobs.

The employees would blame Stack for all of their troubles because they were being kept in the dark. He decided to open up the books to the employees and train them on how to understand what was going on. He told them that to save their jobs they would have to become owners of the company and, as owners, they needed to concern themselves with the financial success of the company.

Jack came up with procedures, meetings, and even games that kept the employees involved. Once they understood the situation, the employees came up with a multitude of ideas to keep the business profitable. After two decades of open book management, the company is still going strong.

If you want to read more on this topic, pick up Stack's book, *The Great Game of Business*. It is fun to read—and educational to boot.

---

7. Make general conclusions about liquidity, profitability, and financing. Remember to highlight both the positive and negative trends. Run more ratios if necessary.

I recommend actually documenting your conclusions. Write down what you see in terms of liquidity, profitability, and financing. If you are anything like me, your memory is short. (I can't remember what I had for lunch last Wednesday.) And writing things down and stepping away for a little while will help you see themes or patterns in the data.

So, do yourself a favor in each of these steps: write your conclusions down so that you will have something to refer to.

8. Compare with benchmarks. The numbers, sitting alone, mean little. You must compare them against something—competitors, industry averages, or past history—in order to tell if the numbers are happy or sad.

My favorite comparison is against the company itself over time. As your mother always said, "Do your best!" Is the company doing its best? Are results improving over time?

No other company in the world operates exactly like the company you are examining, so comparisons with other companies are sometimes futile.

I was once tasked with summarizing the financial health of the State of Texas government in a magazine-style report, complete with graphics and color, for the legislature. My boss asked me to benchmark Texas against other states.

This turned out to be an impossible task. No other state runs like Texas. The other big states, like California, Florida, Pennsylvania, and New York, have completely different bureaucratic structures. The way they present their financial results was quite different. Some states allowed local government more of a hand in operations; some were highly centralized. I had to give up on comparisons.

It is like this in industry, also. In one of my classes on financial statement analysis, we compare Dell Computer with Gateway Computer and with Compaq (now HP). This comparison yields some interesting results, but it isn't completely meaningful because Dell and Gateway, while they might have similar business models, are different sizes. Dell has more market share. And Compaq doesn't even do business the way that Gateway and Dell do. To show you how challenging benchmarking is, I have done it with Dell and Gateway in the remaining chapters.

Other problems with benchmarking might arise when you are trying to benchmark in the following situations:

- **The company is part of a conglomerate** and its financial results are impossible to separate from the mother company
- **The company uses different accounting policies.** It might use LIFO instead of FIFO or recognize the cost of stock options while your company does not.
- **The company is a different size.** Sheer size of the organization might impact the way operating expenses, depreciation, and fixed assets look on the financial statements.
- **The company calculates its metrics differently.** There is no standard for calculating financial metrics. In other words, there is no GAAP for financial ratios. I recommend you calculate them for yourself rather than rely on the organization's disclosure. The metrics they calculate will always present the prettiest picture possible.
- **The company delays publication of results or does not publish at all.** You might desire to benchmark against your toughest competitor but cannot get any financial data on them because they do not share their results with the public.
- **The company likes to dress up its financial results.** Everyone likes to dress up! Many companies take action at the end of a quarter or a year to make their financial results as pretty as they can be. This might not hold in the middle of the period. So what anyone presents has to be taken with a grain of salt.

If you want to compare to industry averages, take a look at these resources:

- Dun and Bradstreet (www.dnb.com/us/)
- the Risk Management Association (www.rmahq.org)
- *Forbes* magazine (www.forbes.com)
- *Fortune* magazine (www.fortune.com)
- *CFO* magazine (www.cfo.com)
- PricewaterhouseCoopers industry reports (www.pwcglobal.com)
- *Almanac of Business and Industrial Financial Ratios* (annual, Prentice Hall)

9. Represent these conclusions graphically and narratively. Depending on who you are creating this analysis for, you might want to represent your conclusions graphically and narratively. You might want to create a user-friendly report summarizing your conclusions. The pictures, colors, and short stories I used in my magazine-style financial report went a long way to helping the legislature understand Texas finances.

Before embarking on this task, I recommend you do some reading about what makes reports and graphics user-friendly. If you present too much data, you can overwhelm and turn off your audience. One of my favorite books on the subject is *Say It with Charts: The Executive's Guide to Visual Communication* by Gene Zelazny (McGraw-Hill).

10. Consider making recommendations for improvements. Depending on your relationship to the organization, you might even go as far as to point out weaknesses and making recommendations for improvements.

Our Case Study—Dell and Gateway, 2004

WHY DID I CHOOSE DELL AND GATEWAY FOR OUR ANALYSIS?

I've been teaching financial analysis courses to CPAs for about eight years now. In 1998, I started using Dell, Gateway, and Compaq financial statements during my classes. I asked the CPAs to run some metrics and piece together a story about the companies.

For various reasons (one being the merger of Compaq and HP), I have been using the 1998 financial statements of Compaq, Dell, and Gateway during my classes up until now, 2004. Because HP is such a huge conglomerate, selling multiple products, I knew that after the merger I wouldn't be able to tell what in HP was the old Compaq and what was calculators or printers.

WHAT DID WE SEE?

What we always saw during our class exercise was that Compaq, because of the way it sold computers in stores and through intermediaries, was not able to manage its working capital and hence its cash flow very well.

Gateway had the same business model as Dell: it sold computers directly to the public without any stores or intermediaries. The big difference between Gateway and Dell was in the market share. Dell was a behemoth compared with Gateway, but Gateway was similarly profitable and a good manager of working capital and cash.

Dell came out looking the best of the three. Dell had good market share, although Compaq had more, and it managed working capital very well and had wonderful cash flow. Profits were stable even though the company was growing at a rapid rate.

A SHOCK IN 2004

What a surprise I encountered, then, in looking at Gateway's financial statements for fiscal year 2003. It turned out that Gateway has been experiencing significant losses for years. It has also decided to change its business model to start offering consumer electronics in addition to PCs. Its market share, as indicated by its net sales amount, has been falling off steadily year after year.

Gateway sold $3.4 billion in 2003, as compared with Dell's $41.4 billion. Quite a difference! Gateway sold $9.2 billion worth of product in 2000—the last year it was profitable. Because of Compaq's merger with HP and the variety of HP's offerings (calculators, printers, etc), I have left it out of the analysis.

Also, in the notes to the financial statements and the Management's Discussion and Analysis of Financial Position that precedes the financial statements in its 2003 10-K, Gateway discloses several legal proceedings and a conflict with the SEC. What a difference a few years makes to the financial story!

WE ARE GOING TO DO EVERY RATIO

I am going to run every ratio whether or not it makes sense. Why? So you can see why some metrics are not meaningful. I will take the more meaningful metrics and summarize them at the end of the chapter and make conclusions.

We are going to look at profitability metrics in Chapter 15, liquidity metrics and working capital in Chapter 16, liquidity metrics and cash in Chapter 17, and financing metrics in Chapter 18. We will conclude each chapter on one piece of the story for Dell and Gateway. At the end of the last chapter, we will conclude on the companies as a whole.

Quiz

1. Which of the following will you want to gather before you do a financial analysis?
   (a) terms of loans
   (b) age and types of receivables
   (c) information on competitors
   (d) strategic plan
   (e) all of the above

2. How the company decides to distribute its profits can have an impact on its cash flow and equity position.
   T or F

3. Organizations that operate using long-term plans will often sacrifice short-term returns for long-term goals.
   T or F

4. You can tell a lot about the priorities of an organization by looking at its budget.
   T or F

5. Investors are primarily concerned about what facet of financial health?
   (a) sales
   (b) profitability
   (c) debt
   (d) production

6. Banks want assurance that the organization
   (a) sells lots of product
   (b) has a cool product
   (c) can repay the loan

7. Internal managers are concerned with
   (a) working capital
   (b) profitability
   (c) sales

(d) production

(e) all of the above

8. Privately held organizations might not undergo an audit of their financial statements.
T or F

9. Metrics can be expressed as
   (a) fractions
   (b) percentages
   (c) whole numbers
   (d) colon fractions
   (e) multipliers
   (f) all of the above

10. Use dollars and percentages in your financial analysis because they lend perspective to each other.
T or F

11. In this sort of fluctuation analysis, you turn everything into a percentage of a total, such as total revenue or total assets:
    (a) horizontal fluctuation analysis
    (b) common size fluctuation analysis
    (c) vertical fluxional analysis

12. In using horizontal analysis, compare outlying years with the base year only.
T or F

13. The three categories of ratios are
    (a) profitability, liquidity, and financing
    (b) revenue, liquidity, and financing
    (c) liquidity, financing, and debt

14. The MD&A is a great place to start your investigation of why finances changed between years.
T or F

15. Open book management asks that employees be
    (a) educated about how the business makes money
    (b) informed of financial performance often
    (c) given ownership in the company
    (d) all of the above

16. Run a common size analysis and create a pie chart for the following data:

Sales	10,000
Cost of goods sold	8,000
Gross margin	2,000
Operating expenses	1,000
Operating margin	1,000
Taxes and other	400
Net income	600

17. You can benchmark financial results against
    (a) your own organization, over time
    (b) competitors
    (c) industry averages
    (d) all of the above

CHAPTER 15

Profit Ratios

Profit. Yeah! That's what capitalism is all about—taking something raw and/or unformed and turning it into something that others will pay a premium for. Profitable businesses put a little in and get a lot out; very profitable businesses put a dime in and get a dollar out.

The main financial statement that indicates profit is the income statement, sometimes called the *profit and loss statement* (P&L). So many of our ratios work from numbers derived from this statement.

The three categories of profit ratios are:

- margin ratios
- return ratios
- shareholder earnings ratios

Margin Ratios

Margins are subtotals. We already talked about gross profit and operating profit in Chapter 3 when we were discussing the income statement. The margins tell

us how much of our bar of soap (total sales revenue) we have left after taking out all expenses. Maybe you have a hotel-size bar of soap; maybe you have a sliver. These metrics turn the dollars into percentages.

NET PROFIT MARGIN PERCENTAGE

$$\frac{\text{net income}}{\text{net sales}}$$

The question this margin answers is "What percentage of sales was retained by the time we got to the bottom line of the income statement? How much profit did we walk away with at the end of the day?"

Margins vary widely by industry. Some organizations have a very high net profit percentage, such as custom home builders. They might generate 20 percent profits, *but* they might experience low dollar volume. So, although they retain a high percentage, they don't realize much in cold, hard cash. Some bigger operations, like Wal-Mart, do not have huge profit margin percentages. They might generate only a 3.5 percent profit, but 3.5 percent profit when you sell $256 billion is $9 billion. $9 billion is not easy to generate in any business.

Results for Dell

What is Dell's net profit margin percentage for some recent periods?

2004: net income of $2,645,000,000 / net sales of $41,444,000,000 = 6.38%
2003: net income of $2,122,000,000 / net sales of $35,404,000,000 = 5.99%

Results for Gateway

Net profit margin percentage is not calculable for Gateway, as it was not profitable in the past two years.

Conclusion

Dell is improving slightly year over year. When you are talking about gross sales of $41 billion, an increase of a tenth of a percent is a large chunk of change— $41 million ($41,444,000,000 x .001 = $41,444,000)—well worth the effort.

Dell's 6.38 percent of a bar of ivory soap is better than no soap at all—or negative soap, as with Gateway. Net profit margin percentage is such a summarized

figure. We need to break it down to diagnose whether it is component costs or operating expenses that are eating away at Gateway's profits. That is what gross profit margin and operating profit margin do for you.

GROSS PROFIT MARGIN

$$\frac{\text{gross profit}}{\text{net sales}}$$

Gross profit margin in dollars is one of the subtotals on the way to the bottom of the income statement. It is the result of taking total sales less cost of goods sold. Again, this metric indicates what percentage of sales has been retained to this point. It is a percentage, not a dollar figure. So to get it, we take the gross margin dollars and divide by total sales dollars.

Results for Dell

What is Dell's net profit margin percentage for some recent periods?

2004: gross profit of $7,552,000,000 / net sales of $41,444,000,000 = 18.2%

2003: gross profit of $6,329,000,000 / net sales of $35,404,000,000 = 17.9%

Results for Gateway

Here are Gateway's figures.

2003: gross profit of $463,564,000 / net sales of $3,402,364,000 = 13.62%

2002: gross profit of $566,205,000 / net sales of $4,171,325,000 = 13.57%

Conclusions

Here we see the beginnings of Gateway's overall net loss. Gross profit is the result of subtracting cost of goods sold from total sales; when Gateway does that, it is left with only a 14 percent profit margin percentage. Dell is doing better, retaining 18 percent of its total sales revenue by the time it gets to the gross margin. In other words, Dell has 18 percent left of its bar of soap and Gateway has only 14 percent. That's a 4 percent difference already—and with final, bottom-line profit margins at Dell only 6 percent and Gateway operating at a net loss, the 4 percent difference is significant. Why is Gateway's cost of goods proportionally higher than Dell's? I don't know and can't tell without further investigation.

OPERATING PROFIT MARGIN

$$\frac{operating\ profit}{net\ sales}$$

Operating profit margin percentage tells us what percentage of the bar of soap we have left after subtracting both cost of goods sold and operating expenses from total sales. In other words, the operating profit dollars are calculated by taking sales and subtracting cost of goods and operating expenses. You might want to refer back to the income statement in Chapter 3 for a breakout of these margin types. Again, what is good and bad is entirely dependent on the industry and the organization's historical results.

Results for Dell

2004: operating income of $3,544,000,000 / net sales of $41,444,000,000 = 8.55%

2003: operating income of $2,844,000,000 / net sales of $35,404,000,000 = 8.03%

Results for Gateway

Operating profit margin cannot be calculated because operating profit is negative.

Conclusion

Hmmm. Gateway's operating expenses ate up the rest of its profit. Dell is still left with 8 percent before unusual items. Only 10 percent of Dell's profit (18 percent – 8 percent = 10 percent) is eaten up by operations—and that's a very slim number for any business.

RELATIVE R&D (RESEARCH AND DEVELOPMENT)

$$\frac{\text{R\&D expense}}{\text{sales}}$$

This ratio asks, "How much is the organization investing in creating future products and services?" Again we will get a percentage here. If you see that the organization invests practically nothing in new product development, you might be concerned. This might mean trouble in the future. But then again, it might not mean anything. If the organization is a retailer, it might not spend any money in R&D because it does not develop products; it sells other people's products. Again, choose to run the ratio only if it makes sense to you.

Results for Dell

2004: research and development investment of $464,000,000 / sales of $41,444,000,000 = 1.11%

2003: research and development investment of $455,000,000 / sales of $35,404,000,000 = 1.28%

Results for Gateway

The 2003 research and development expense was not disclosed in the 10-K.

Conclusions

Wow, Dell spends very little on R&D—around 1 percent. We can assume that this figure is similarly small for Gateway because it doesn't even disclose it in the financial statements. It isn't material. This makes sense for both of these companies because they are not innovators; they are assemblers. They take whatever is selling on the market and package it and sell it. They don't invent anything.

Contrast that with Apple. Apple is an innovator. Its investment in R&D was $471 million, as compared with $6.207 billion in sales. So that is an investment of 7.6 percent—significantly higher.

Return Metrics

In these metrics we contrast profit with the investments that went into creating the profit. We want to invest as little as possible and generate the highest possible profit.

RETURN ON ASSETS

$$\frac{\text{net income}}{\text{total assets}}$$

Return on assets asks, "What sort of return did we generate for our investment in assets?" It is a very similar metric to return on investment (ROI). Some industries are very asset-heavy. For instance, the airline industry will have a huge investment in fixed assets in the form of jets and planes. This metric asks how much return or net income was generated as a result of putting those assets to work.

Results for Dell

2004: net income of $2,645,000,000 / total assets of $19,311,000,000 = 13.7%

2003: net income of $2,122,000,000 / total assets of $15,470,000,000 = 13.7%

Results for Gateway

Return on assets cannot be calculated, as net income is negative for Gateway.

Conclusions

Dell is holding steady on using assets to generate net income. This is a favorable result. Gateway's ratio is incalculable.

Be Wary of Aggregates

Here is another caveat about ratios: be wary of ratios that use elements that are aggregates of a bunch of numbers. For instance, notice how aggregated return on assets is. It takes into account *all* assets—cash, investments, inventory, accounts receivable, fixed assets, and intangibles. It might not make sense to look at all assets in relationship to return. Maybe just a few assets should be picked out and analyzed.

In our business, it might make sense to take rainy day cash out of the equation as we not plowing it back into the company to generate a return. Maybe for an airline, we should just look at net income compared with fixed assets, as we do in the following ratio, sales to fixed assets.

Try to refine any broad, aggregate numbers for your specific circumstances.

SALES TO FIXED ASSETS

$$\frac{\text{sales}}{\text{fixed assets}}$$

This might be a more meaningful ratio for an airline than return on total assets. Here we are asking about the relationship between fixed assets and sales. Hopefully, the top of this ratio is large in relationship to a lean fixed asset balance. This would tell us that the organization is efficiently using its resources to generate sales.

Results for Dell

2004: sales of $41,444,000,000 / fixed assets of $1,517,000,000 = 27.32

2003: sales of $35,404,000,000 / fixed assets of $913,000,000 = 38.78

Results for Gateway

2003: sales of $3,402,364,000 / fixed assets of $330,913,000 = 10.28

2004: sales of $4,171,325,000 / fixed assets of $481,011,000 = 8.67

Conclusions

This answer gets at a question similar to the one above: "How well were assets used to generate sales?" Gateway shows that it generated a return of less than 11 percent on its fixed assets in terms of sales for the past two years. Dell again is doing better, hovering around the 30 percent range. However, the percentage is declining—and the reason is the increase in fixed assets. Dell took some items that it was accounting for as leases and changed them to fixed assets. (I found this out by reading the notes to the financial statements.) I am not concerned about this number for Dell. I am concerned for Gateway. Their sales are slipping and they should have results similar to Dell, as they operate in a similar environment.

RETURN ON INVESTMENT

$$\frac{\text{net income}}{\text{long-term debt + equity}}$$

I have seen this ratio calculated in a variety of ways. In this particular example, we have net income (our return) on the top and our investment (long-term debt and equity) on the bottom.

The result will be a percentage that indicates how well the investment in the company is doing at generating a profit. Ideally, you would like to see the percentage return higher than the percentage return you would get if you put your money in the bank, say in a certificate of deposit (CD) or some other conservative instrument. If a CD rate is beating your company's return on investment, it might indicate that investors could do better investing their money elsewhere. Why should they risk giving you the resources when they can get as good a return on something much less risky and with a guaranteed payoff?

Why are long-term debt and equity considered our investment in the organization? Well, looking at the right hand side of the balance sheet, the only major thing we left out of the bottom of this equation is accounts payable. The argument might be that this should not be considered an investment because it has short turnaround: it will be paid off in the current quarter. I have also seen this ratio calculated with it included, so do whatever makes sense to you—but do it consistently!

Results for Dell

2004: net income of $2,645,000,000 / long-term debt of $505,000,000 + equity of $6,280,000,000 = 38.98

2003: net income of $2,122,000,000 / long-term debt of $506,000,000 + equity of $4,873,000,000 = 39.45

Results for Gateway

Return on investment cannot be calculated for Gateway.

Conclusions

Dell generates a healthy return on investment. Gateway does not generate a profit at all.

RETURN ON EQUITY

$$\frac{\text{net profit}}{\text{equity}}$$

This ratio asks, "Was the investment in the organization, in terms of equity, worth it?" Equity tells us how much of the company the owners own through stock and retained earnings. It contrasts return with total equity. Total equity will include stock and retained earnings.

Results for Dell

2004: net profit of $2,645,000,000 / equity of $6,280,000,000 = 42.12%

2003: net profit of $2,122,000,000 / equity of $4,873,000,000 = 43.55%

Results for Gateway

Return on equity cannot be calculated for Gateway.

Conclusion

Again, Dell is looking good and Gateway is not.

Shareholder Earnings Ratios

The following two ratios are very popular with shareholders. Undoubtedly, you've encountered both of these if you've read any books on investing.

EARNINGS PER SHARE

$$\frac{\text{earnings available to common stockholders}}{\text{average number of common shares outstanding}}$$

To calculate average number of common shares outstanding, take the beginning-of-the-year balance of shares and add the end-of-the-year balance of shares and divide by two.

This is a favorite metric of Wall Street. It simply expresses profitability in per-share terms. You might hear that earnings per share (EPS) were $.20 this past quarter. This metric simply takes the total dollar amount of profit and divides it by the number of shares outstanding during the period.

Companies love to project their earnings per share and announce their projections to the public and to Wall Street. If a company does not meet its projection, the selling price of its stock might suffer. This metric can be manipulated by changing the number of shares outstanding. The company can buy back and retire shares.

Results for Dell

2004: earnings available to common shareholders of $2,645,000,000 / average shares outstanding (2,721,000,000 shares [2004] + 2,681,000,000 shares [2003] / 2) = 98 cents

2003: earnings available to common shareholders of $2,645,000,000 / average shares outstanding (2,681,000,000 shares [2003] + 2,654,000,000 shares [2002] / 2) = 80 cents

Results for Gateway

Earnings per share cannot be calculated for Gateway.

Conclusions

The earnings per share for Dell went up over the years because the number of shares outstanding stayed the same while profit increased. This is a good thing. What can I say about Gateway that hasn't already been said?

What Is the Big Deal about EPS?

EPS is one of the key ratios for Wall Street analysts and investors and it is mostly about expectations.

Public companies project what their earnings will be for the upcoming four quarters. Those projections are communicated to the big investors—such as CalPERs (California Public Employees' Retirement System) and Fidelity Investments. These big investors can swing the price of the stock with one big purchase or sale.

If the company believes it might fall short of its earning projections, it starts communicating its shortfall to these institutional investors early. This way, the big investors are not surprised and make any fast moves in or out of the stock. If the justification for not meeting projections sounds reasonable to them, a shortfall might not affect stock price very much. That's what the company hopes, anyway. If earnings are way under projections and the large institutional investors do not appreciate the reasons, share price can drop precipitously.

Most public companies have a division called *investor relations*. Communicating with the large investors is one of the investor relations department's main jobs.

PRICE/EARNINGS RATIO

$$\frac{\text{market price per share of common stock}}{\text{earnings per share}}$$

This metric asks. "How much are the stockholders paying for the earnings?" Another way to look at this is "How expensive are the earnings? What multiple did the stockholders have to pay to own the shares?" It takes the market price of the share of stock and compares it with the earnings per share. You might get a result such as 35. This means that investors are willing to pay 35 times current earnings to purchase the stock. Is this good or bad? Again, it is subject to market conditions, the economy, and Wall Street's perceptions of the value of the stock.

Results for Dell

2004: market price per share of $29.87 per share (aggregate market value of $75.6 billion from the cover of the 10-K / number of shares of 2,530,660,582) / earnings per share of 98 cents = 30

2003: market price per share of $21.18 per share (aggregate market value of $54.4 billion from the cover of the 10-K / number of shares of 2,568,285,953) / earnings per share of 80 cents = 26

Results for Gateway

Price/earnings ratio cannot be calculated for Gateway.

Conclusion

Supposedly this number tells you that an investor in Dell is willing to pay 30 times earnings in 2004, as opposed to being willing to pay 26 times in 2003. But this number is affected by many factors.

Dell's earnings per share are up in 2004, but the number of shares outstanding is down by over 37 million. Market price is affected by many things other than the management of the company; it can be affected by politics, events, media exposure, etc. An increase in earnings per shareholder is something to be happy about—but as Dell increased its earnings it also decreased its outstanding shares. My conclusion: take this metric with a grain of salt. The elements of the equation are possibly more interesting and informative than the results of the equation.

Uncomfortable with Market Price per Share Information

We have all had a good dose of craziness in the 1990s. We saw how perceptions and hype can impact the price of stock. One good magazine article can send the price of the stock soaring. One small boo-boo can send stock prices down, down, down. We have seen companies sell their stock at exorbitant prices without any real profitability to back it up. We have seen liars and swindlers take their employees' benefit plans and cruelly zero them out.

After our stock market downturn in the early '00s, many companies that had gone public in the previous five years went private again so that they would not have to tolerate and bow to the expectations of uninformed investors and Wall Street. It is unrealistic to expect double-digit growth in sales and revenue every single quarter and every single year; however, this is what Wall Street often expects.

I am much more comfortable calculating metrics that have to do with an organization's internal operations and management's decisions than I am with data that is easily manipulated by the company and by investor expectations. For instance, I am wary of EPS and the price/earnings ratio because, in effect, they are out of the control of the organization's managers. These numbers can be manipulated by a stock split, in the case of earnings per share, or by a negative press release.

So What Can We Conclude about Profitability for These Two Companies?

Dell has maintained steady profitability while it has gained market share. Gateway is not profitable and is losing market share.

The margins in this business, even for a scrappy performer like Dell, are not crazy big—around 6 percent. What makes it in this business is volume. Dell has been increasing its sales volume year after year. Dell has maintained its profitability even as the selling price of its product has decreased. Gateway's volume is slipping—both in terms of dollars and in units.

Gateway has a proportionally higher cost of goods sold than Dell. Why is Gateway's cost of goods higher than Dell's? I don't know why. Sometimes sheer volume can mean savings on component costs: the more a company buys, the less each unit costs. So Gateway's slipping volume can affect its cost of goods sold. If I were internal to Gateway, I would investigate the cost of goods issue further.

Wal-Mart is another interesting company to look at in these terms. It sold $256 billion in product and generated $9 billion in bottom-line profit. That's a yield of only 3.5 percent profit. But it's still $9 billion. Volume is important.

Ratios for Projects

Internal rate of return (IRR), return on investment (ROI), and economic value added (EVA) are commonly used to evaluate the wisdom of projects. For instance, if you were going to purchase a new machine to increase production,

you would evaluate whether it was actually going to make a positive difference to your organization in terms of profit and cash flow.

One organization I work with uses all three metrics to evaluate projects. If the metrics do not meet certain minimum thresholds, the project is rejected.

INTERNAL RATE OF RETURN (IRR)

The formal definition of internal rate of return is "the rate of return that would cause the present value of all future cash flows to be $0." Ha, that's not very helpful!

The reason the definition sounds so bad is that internal rate of return takes into account the time value of money, which is one of those concepts that have caused many an accounting student to abandon the business school and go study English. The time value of money concept argues that a dollar today is worth more than a dollar five years down the line because you could have put that dollar to work and it would be worth more than $1.00 five years down the line.

IRR asks us, "What kind of return are we making on the project in the long run?" For our example, we have a software manufacturer that takes two years to create the software and then sells it for four years before it has to be revised or updated. So the life cycle of the software is six years. The first two years, the software developer experienced negative cash flow because it was paying to develop the software. Then the developer got a return on its investment in the product.

The result of calculating this metric is a percentage return. In our case, below, we end up with a 20 percent internal rate of return on a software project.

IRR is a very complex formula and not something you should try to calculate by hand. I suggest using an Excel spreadsheet command that will calculate the return for you given a series of future cash flows, because you get the number by taking each of the cash flows and discounting it back to the present. The interest rate that you have to assume to get all of those future cash flows to equal zero in the present is the internal rate of return. Was that Greek? You are not alone.

Here is what you really need to know about IRR:

- It gives us a sense of the return we will make on a project over a long period of time.
- It gets higher or better the faster the project recovers the cash. If the project recoups a huge amount of cash in the first few years of the project, IRR will be high. Conversely, if the project recoups a little cash in the first few years and the majority of cash in later years, IRR will be low.

- It gets higher or better the more cash the project earns. If the project recoups just a little cash throughout its life, IRR will be low.
- The less you invest in the project, the better IRR will be, because it is a rate of return. The less investment you have to cover with profits, the better.

RETURN ON INVESTMENT (ROI)

$$\frac{\text{net operating profit after tax}}{\text{invested capital}}$$

This is another way to look at return on a project, but it does not take into account the time value of money. It doesn't matter when the funds come in or in what amounts. All that matters is the final total return in dollars.

Hence, this metric is best used on short-term projects. If you are like our software developer and your projects have a long life cycle, ROI could possibly mislead you. If all of your cash flows come in year six and until then you are paying out cash, ROI will give you the same results as you would see if all your money came in year one and two and none came in year six. Obviously, you would rather have your money today than have to wait for six years.

In our first case study below, we have an IRR of 20 percent but a ROI of 40 percent. Quite a difference—and it is all due to the time value of money.

DOLLAR VALUE ADDED

net operating profit after tax – (cost of capital x capital employed)

Would you rather earn 12 percent or 55 percent? If you have your thinking cap on, the answer is "It depends!" It depends on the size of the project. I'd rather have a 12 percent return on a 10,000 project ($1200) than a 55 percent return on a $1000 project ($550).

Dollar value added is another way of looking at return. Instead of asking what percentage return is garnered on a project, dollar value added gives us a dollar figure. In its simplest terms, it is just the total dollars generated by a project. It does not take into account the time value of money either. It asks, "How much profit did you generate vs. how much the project cost you to implement?"

The tricky thing about dollar value added can be in the calculation of the cost of capital . But determining how much it actually costs a company to get more capital (i.e., the cost of capital) can be a complicated study.

If the company has limited resources, which we can assume is the case for almost all organizations, there is an opportunity cost involved in using resources on any particular project.

In other words, if the money is used for project A, then it can't be used for project B. The opportunity cost is the return that could have been generated on project B.

Along with opportunity cost, you have to factor in the cost of debt and equity. Making the calculations even more complicated.

Using the Three Metrics to Make a Decision

In our first case study below, EVA is $1,184, assuming a simple 12 percent cost of capital.

So these three metrics together give us a pretty good picture of the profitability of any project or undertaking. IRR is a great metric to use if you have a long life cycle. Because ROI does not take into account the time value of money, it is best used on short-term projects and decisions. And dollar value added gives you an actual dollar return.

Just like the fluctuation analysis we discussed earlier in this section, you want to run both dollars and percentages. For instance, a project might give you an IRR of 50 percent but a dollar value added of only $50. Probably not worth your time.

Here is some data from a mock company. Let's say that it creates software that takes two years to develop and then the software sells for four years after that. So the product's life cycle is six years. Figure 15.1 is a simple projection of their cash flows. What happens to IRR, ROI, and dollar value added in each of the following scenarios?

Base case study—6-year software project							
Cash Flows	**Year 1**	**Year 2**	**Year 3**	**Year 4**	**Year 5**	**Year 6**	**Totals**
Cash collected	—	—	$1,000	$2,000	$2,000	$1,000	$6,000
Cash paid out	$1,000	$1,500	$300	$600	$600	$300	$4,300
Net cash	($1,000)	($1,500)	$700	$1,400	$1,400	$700	$1,700
						IRR	**20%**
						ROI	**40%**
				dva = 6,000 – (4,300 x 1.12) =			**$1,184**

Figure 15.1 Case study: IRR, ROI, and dollar value added (continued on the next page)

Case study—6-year software project (continued)							
Cash Flows	Year 1	Year 2	Year 3	Year 4	Year 5	Year 6	Totals
Instead of $1,000 cash out in year 1—spend only $500							
Cash collected	—	—	$1,000	$2,000	$2,000	$1,000	$6,000
Cash paid out	$500	$1,500	$300	$600	$600	$300	$3,800
Net case	($500)	($1,500)	$700	$1,400	$1,400	$700	$2,200
						IRR	32%
						ROI	58%
				dva = 6,000 – (4,300 x 1.12) =			$1,744
Instead of 1,000 cash out in year 1—earn $2,000. In year 5, earn only $1,000 so that total cash flow reamins the same							
Cash collected	—	—	$2,000	$2,000	$1,000	$1,000	$6,000
Cash paid out	$1,000	$1,500	$300	$600	$600	$300	$4,300
Net cash	($1,000)	($1,500)	$1,700	$1,400	$400	$700	$1,700
						IRR	25%
						ROI	40%
				dva = 6,000 – (4,300 x 1.12) =			$1,184
Instead of only costing $1,000 in year 1, cash out is $1,500 in year 1							
Cash collected	—	—	$1,000	$2,000	$2,000	$1,000	$6,000
Cash paid out	$1,500	$1,500	$300	$600	$600	$300	$4,800
Net cash	($1,500)	($1,500)	$,700	$1,400	$1,400	$700	$1,200
						IRR	12%
						ROI	25%
				dva = 6,000 – (4,300 x 1.12) =			$624
Cost of goods sold—cash paid out in years 3-6 increases by 20% each year							
Cash collected	—	—	$1,000	$2,000	$2,000	$1,000	$6,000
Cash paid out	$1,000	$1,500	$360	$720	$720	$360	$4,660
Net cash	($1,000)	($1,500)	$,640	$1,280	$1,280	$640	$1,340
						IRR	15%
						ROI	29%
				dva = 6,000 – (4,300 x 1.12) =			$780.80

Figure 15.1 Case study: IRR, ROI, and dollar value added (continued)

Quiz

1. Margins are
   (a) subtotals
   (b) the result of taking revenues less expenses
   (c) what is left over after expenses are taken out
   (d) all of the above

2. Which of the following margins is also termed "the bottom line"?
   (a) gross margin
   (b) operating margin
   (c) net profit margin

3. Gross profit margin is the result of subtracting cost of good sold from
   (a) net profit
   (b) sales revenues
   (c) operating margin

4. Operating profit margin is the result of subtracting operating expenses from
   (a) net profit
   (b) sales revenues
   (c) gross profit

5. R&D stands for
   (a) research and discovery
   (b) research and development
   (c) ratios and denominators

6. Earnings per share is
   (a) profit divided by number of shares outstanding
   (b) gross margin divided by number of shares outstanding
   (c) gross margin divided by profit

7. The price/earnings ratio is best expressed as
   (a) a multiple
   (b) a percentage
   (c) a fraction

8. To increase IRR,
   (a) invest less on the front end
   (b) get cash out earlier
   (c) get more cash out in total
   (d) all of the above

9. ROI takes into account the time value of money.
   T or F

10. ROI is best expressed as
    (a) a whole dollar amount
    (b) a multiple
    (c) a percentage

CHAPTER

Liquidity and Financial Flexibility

There are three ways in which a company can use its money—spend it on fixed assets, spend it on working capital, or let it sit around as cash or investments.

In order to respond to unexpected opportunities or needs, the business needs to be as liquid as possible. Liquid means as flexible and as near cash as possible. This might be a good time for you to revisit the scale of liquidity discussed in detail in Chapter 2. Fixed assets are definitely not liquid. (See Figure 16.1.)

A building or vehicles will take a while to sell and you might not get your cash for days, maybe months. Working capital is the money you have tied up in things you hope to sell. It is more liquid than fixed assets, but still not as liquid as our favorite asset—cash.

In this chapter, we are going to look at ratios that have to do with working capital. In the following chapter, we will look at ratios have to do with cash balances.

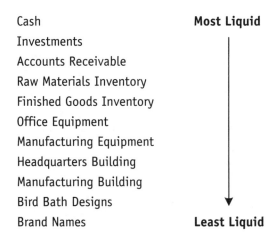

Figure 16.1 Scale of liquidity

Working Capital

current assets − current liabilities

Current assets are cash, accounts receivable, and inventory. Current liabilities are accounts payable. So another way to express the calculation is

cash + accounts receivable + inventory − accounts payable = working capital

Working capital is the money we have tied up in things we hope to sell. If we take out rainy-day cash from the equation, this number should be as small as possible because we want to minimize current assets (day-to-day cash needs, accounts receivable, and inventory) and maximize current liabilities (accounts payable).

If we have money tied up in working capital, we don't have that money tied up in cash—and when given the choice, we always prefer that money be in cash.

Now here is the dilemma if you are calculating this metric as an outsider to the organization. It will be virtually impossible for you to figure out how much of the cash is necessary for current needs and how much is rainy-day or reserve cash. So you are going to have to use the entire cash balance. If you are monitoring working capital from the inside, you should be able to get at the true daily cash needs.

Because we can't tell by looking from the outside what amount of cash the company actually needs to operate and how much is in savings, we just have to go with the lump sum. If we are on the inside, we should make every effort to

Rainy-Day Cash versus Daily-Needs Cash

There is a difference between the cash you need to have on hand to help you through a rainy day and the cash you need to operate on a day-to-day basis.

When we are looking at liquidity metrics, it would be great to know how much of a company's cash is in each category. This way we could get a better sense of how much it actually costs to run the entity and we could contrast that with its ability to generate cash or meet its debt obligations.

---

distinguish between rainy-day cash and daily-needs cash when calculating this our metric. We should run the majority of metrics in this chapter using daily-needs cash, not rainy-day cash. That makes the metrics much more meaningful.

Results for Dell

2004: current assets of $10,633,000,000 – current liabilities of $10,896,000,000 = –$263,000,000

2003: current assets of $8,924,000,000 – current liabilities of $8,933,000,000 = –$9,000,000

Results for Gateway

2003: current assets of $1,663,477,000 – current liabilities of $999,004,000 = –$664,473,000

2002: current assets of $1,955,372,000 – current liabilities of $940,349,000 = $1,015,023,000

Conclusions

Dell has a negative working capital figure while Gateway has a positive working capital figure. Because this working capital figure includes cash and we are unable to determine whether it includes rainy-day cash or not, I hesitate to judge either result too harshly.

The metric can easily be altered by either company's investment policy. If Dell chooses not to keep its excess cash in current assets, but instead invest it in long-term assets, working capital will be smaller. Maybe Gateway chooses to keep more of its cash in cash and short-term investments and less of it in long-term investments. The calculation of working capital affects several subsequent ratios.

How Hard Is Working Capital Working?

The next four ratios tell us how hard working capital is working at generating revenues. They indicate how lean and mean the organization is running.

WORKING CAPITAL TO SALES

$$\frac{\text{working capital}}{\text{total sales}}$$

This metric indicates how well working capital worked in generating sales. Ideally, you'd like to invest very little in working capital in order to make a load of sales.

Results for Dell

We cannot calculate a ratio for Dell because you can't have a negative number in either the numerator or the denominator. But Dell's negative working capital is good, so being able to generate sales with no investment in working capital is great. Dell is really able to have its suppliers and customers help finance its sales. This is not just good, but really good working capital management.

Results for Gateway

What is Gateway's ratio for the same period?

2003: working capital of $664,473,000 / total sales of $3,402,364,000 = 19.53 percent

2002: working capital of $1,015,023,000 / total sales of $4,171,325,000 = 24.33 percent

Conclusions

We cannot calculate Dell's working capital to sales ratio because the top of the ratio is negative. This indicates that Dell had to make a very small investment in working capital (even a negative investment in working capital) in order to generate sales. This is a happy result, although we cannot generate a ratio number.

Gateway's results are reasonable and improving. Again, working capital could be affected by its investment policy.

WORKING CAPITAL TURNOVER

$$\frac{\text{sales}}{\text{working capital}}$$

This is the same ratio as working capital to sales expressed in a different way. It is simply flipped. This tells you how efficiently working capital was used to generate sales. A lean, mean, fighting machine of a company would have a high turnover rate. This would mean that the organization put in a little in and got out a lot.

Results for Dell

We cannot calculate a ratio for Dell because Dell's working capital is negative.

Results for Gateway

2003: sales of $3,402,364,000 / working capital of $664,473,000 = 5.12 times

2002: sales of $4,171,325,000 / working capital of $1,015,023,000 = 4.11 times

Conclusions

Dell is a lean, mean, fighting machine because it generates sales with no investment in working capital. Gateway just doesn't end up looking as good, although its multiple has improved considerably.

Working Capital Contrast Ratios

CURRENT RATIO

$$\frac{\text{current assets}}{\text{current liabilities}}$$

If and only if you include rainy-day cash in this equation, do you want the top of this equation to be substantially larger than the bottom of the equation? In that case, you want current assets—cash, inventory, and accounts payable—to be larger than current liabilities. This would indicate that you have enough current resources to meet current obligations.

But if you take out rainy-day cash from the top, you want current assets to be small and you want current liabilities to be big, so the equation will not look as lopsided. Yes, the top might be slightly larger, but not terribly larger. To me, a very close ratio—say 1:1—would be positive.

Results for Dell

What is Dell's ratio for the last two years?

2004: current assets of $10,633,000,000 / current liabilities of $10,896,000,000 = .98 to 1

2003: current assets of $8,924,000,000 / current liabilities of $8,933,000,000 = .998 to 1

Results for Gateway

What is Gateway's ratio for the same period?

2003: current assets of $1,663,477,000 / liabilities of $999,004,000 = 1.67 to 1

2002: current assets of $1,955,372,000 / liabilities of $940,349,000 = 2.08 to 1

Conclusion

Dell is closer to the 1-to-1 ratio that I think is good to see. Gateway is improving its ratio over the years, but it is too soon to tell why this is happening.

QUICK RATIO

$$\frac{\text{current assets} - \text{inventory}}{\text{current liabilities}}$$

This ratio is also called the *acid test*. This is the same ratio as the current ratio, except that it takes inventory out of the top of the equation, leaving only accounts payable and cash. It is called *quick* because it takes the slow-moving asset—inventory—out of current assets. Inventory might or not be liquid. Some of the inventory might be obsolete or unsellable.

I like to run both the current ratio and the quick ratio together. If there is a vast difference between the two, say the current ratio is 2-to-1 and the quick ratio is .5-to-1, it would tell me that the organization has a large proportion of its resources tied up in inventory—maybe dangerously so.

Results for Dell

2004: current assets of $10,633,000,000 – inventory of $327,000,000 / current liabilities of $10,896,000,000 = .95 to 1

2003: current assets of $8,924,000,000 – inventory of $306,000,000 / current liabilities of $8,933,000,000 = .96 to 1

Results for Gateway

2003: current assets of $1,663,477,000 – inventory of $114,136,000 / current liabilities of $999,004,000 = 1.55 to 1

2002: current assets of $1,955,372,000 – inventory of $88,761,000 / current liabilities of $940,349,000 = 1.98 to 1

Conclusions

In 2004, Dell's current ratio was .98-to-1 and the quick ratio was .95-to-1. This shows that Dell has relatively little tied up in inventory—a first hint at very efficient working capital management. Gateway's 2003 current ratio was 1.67-to-1, contrasted with a quick ratio of 1.55-to-1. Again, a very close number, showing that Gateway also has very little inventory. So both companies are doing well in that regard.

The Inventory Component of Working Capital

INVENTORY TO WORKING CAPITAL

$$\frac{\text{inventory}}{\text{working capital}}$$

Because the denominator in the equation takes into account both positives and negatives, this metric does not provide a very valid comparison, although people do it all the time. This metric is intended to tell us what proportion of working capital is made up by inventory. I would prefer to use inventory to current assets.

Results for Dell

This calculation won't work for Dell because its working capital is negative.

Results for Gateway

2003: inventory of $114,136,000 / working capital of $664,473,000 = 17.18%

2002: inventory of $8,8761,000 / working capital of $1,015,023,000 = 8.74%

Conclusions

This might show that Gateway is building its inventory balance over time. From reading the Management's Discussion and Analysis section of the 10-K, I know that they are branching out to other products—to consumer electronics such as TVs. Maybe they have to keep a larger inventory of those items than they did for computers. We need more ratios on this issue.

DAYS' SUPPLY OF INVENTORY

$$\frac{\text{inventory}}{\text{cost of goods sold} / 365}$$

This is a very relevant metric for Dell and Gateway. It measures how many days' worth of inventory is sitting around. Obviously you want this number to be as small as possible. With my clients I have seen it as high as 400 and as low as two. When your money is in inventory, it isn't in cash—our favorite asset. The client with 400 days of inventory is constantly in a cash dilemma, while the client with two is a cash-generating machine.

Results for Dell

What is Dell's days' supply of inventory for some recent periods?

2004: inventory of $327,000,000 / cost of revenue of $33,892,000,000 / 365 days = 3.5 days

2003: inventory of $306,000,000 / cost of revenue of $29,055,000,000 / 365 days = 3.8 days

In the 2004 10-K Management's Discussion and Analysis of Financial Results section, Dell discloses that days' supply of inventory is three for both 2004 and 2003. This is very close to the number we got above, so maybe they are customizing the ratio a little bit, using averages on either the numerator or the denominator. Remember: there is no standard for how metrics are calculated, so there is nothing wrong with our numbers being different.

Results for Gateway

2003: inventory of $114,136,000 / cost of revenue of $2,938,800,000 / 365 = 14 days

2002: inventory of $88,761,000 / cost of revenue of $3,605,120,000 / 365 = 12 days

Gateway disclosed in the MD&A section of its 10-Ks that DSI was 14 in 2003 and 8 in 2002.

Conclusions

Aha! It's true—Gateway's inventory balance is slowly creeping up over time. Many moons ago, when I first started doing analysis of these two companies, Gateway's inventory balance rivaled that of Dell. This is not a happy development for Gateway.

Dell's result of having less than four days of inventory is very positive. In the computer industry, it is very important not to have a lot of inventory on hand because of obsolescence. Technology changes so rapidly that what sells today might not sell tomorrow and you end up stuck with a bunch of inventory you can't get rid of without discounting.

INVENTORY TURNOVER

$$\frac{\text{cost of goods sold}}{\text{inventory}}$$

This is another way to look at days' supply of inventory. Instead of saying days in inventory is 30 (a month's worth of inventory), you can say inventory turned 12 times, once each month.

Results for Dell

What is Dell's inventory turnover for some recent periods?

2004: cost of goods (cost of revenues) of $33,892,000,000 / inventory of $327,000,000 = 104 times

2003: cost of revenues of $29,055,000,000 / inventory of $306,000,000 = 95 times

Results for Gateway

2003: cost of goods (cost of revenue) of $2,938,800,000 / inventory of $114,136,000 = 26 times

2002: cost of revenue of $3,605,120,000 / inventory of $88,761,000 = 29 times

Conclusions

This is just another way of expressing days' supply of inventory, our previous ratio, so the same conclusions as for days' supply of inventory apply here.

The Accounts Receivable Component of Working Capital

ACCOUNTS RECEIVABLE TO WORKING CAPITAL

$$\frac{\text{accounts receivable}}{\text{working capital}}$$

Again, I have a problem with these types of metrics because the denominator contains both a positive and a negative. This ratio purports to tell us the proportion of working capital that is made up of accounts receivable. I have seen this one used more than a few times, so it is good to know about it.

Results for Dell

This calculation won't work for Dell because working capital is negative.

Results for Gateway

2003: accounts receivable of $210,151,000 / working capital of $664,473,000 = 31.63%

2002: accounts receivable of $197,817,000 / working capital of $1,015,023,000 = 19.49%

Conclusions

Accounts receivable for Gateway is proportionately larger than inventory and is creeping up as a percentage of working capital. We need to look at some absolute accounts receivable figures and metrics to further diagnose what is going on here.

DAYS' SALES OUTSTANDING (DAYS OF ACCOUNTS RECEIVABLE)

$$\frac{\text{accounts receivable}}{\text{net sales} \ / \ 365}$$

This is another of my favorite metrics. Here we are asking how long it takes us to collect from our customers. We definitely want this number to be as low as possible.

Results for Dell

What is Dell's days' sales outstanding for some recent periods?

2004: accounts receivable of \$3,635,000,000 / net sales of \$41,444,000,000 / 365 = 32

2003: accounts receivable of \$2,586,000,000 / net sales of \$35,404,000,000 / 365 = 26

Dell revealed in its Management's Discussion and Analysis section that DSO was 31 and 28 for the same periods. Again, our calculation is close.

Results for Gateway

2003: accounts receivable of \$210,151,000 / net sales of \$3,402,364,000 / 365 = 22 days

2002: accounts receivable of \$197,817,000 / net sales of \$4,171,325,000 / 365 = 17 days

Gateway disclosed the same numbers in its 10-K as I calculated.

Conclusions

Whoops! Just as was indicated in the previous metric, accounts receivable to working capital, Gateway's accounts receivable balance is creeping up or slowing. This is not a positive trend. It means that other people are using Gateway's resources.

Dell takes longer than Gateway in both years to collect on its receivables and its number is creeping up also. For both companies, I think this elicits further investigation. It might be that the customers that these companies are doing business with are making the metric worse. I know that if you sell products overseas,

the accounts payable cycle is abysmal. It is customary for Europeans to pay in 120 days and South Americans can be even worse. Possibly, as both companies expand into international markets, the average number of days it takes to collect worsens.

It might also be procedural. Maybe the companies aren't dedicating enough resources to collections. Sometimes you have to hire a team of irritating accounts receivable collection staff to follow up with slow-paying customers.

If I were internal to these companies, I would investigate and resolve the negative trend in this metric.

ACCOUNTS RECEIVABLE TURNOVER

$$\frac{\text{net credit sales}}{\text{accounts receivable}}$$

This metric is similar to days' sales outstanding, except that it is not expressed in days, but in turns. So, if it takes on average 60 days to collect from customers, accounts receivable turns is six, one turn every two months.

Results for Dell

For this metric to work for Dell, we had to assume that all sales were credit sales, that no one paid cash. We do not have access to the information on proportions of cash versus credit sales.

What is Dell's accounts receivable turnover for some recent periods?

2004: sales of $41,444,000,000 / accounts receivable of $3,635,000,000 = 11 times

2003: sales of $35,404,000,000 / accounts receivable of $2,586,000,000 = 14 times

Results for Gateway

2003: sales of $3,402,364,000 / accounts receivable of $210,151,000 = 16 times

2002: sales of $4,171,325,000 / accounts receivable of $197,817,000 = 21 times

Conclusions

This metric shows, using another expression of the same figures, that Gateway is better at collecting its receivables than Dell. However, its ability to collect is slowing from 21 to 16 times. I would watch this figure in future years. This difference between the two might be due to their customer base. Customers who pay with credit cards will pay within three days. Corporate clients pay in 30 or more days. If you do business in foreign countries, you can expect the collections to be much slower.

BAD DEBT PERCENTAGE

$$\frac{\text{allowance for doubtful accounts}}{\text{gross accounts receivable}}$$

This metric might give us an indication of how unreliable our customers are. Every time the financial statements are created, the company must estimate how much of its accounts receivable will go uncollected. I have—knock on wood—never experienced a bad debt; none of my customers have ever stiffed me. However, many organizations experience bad debt or sell to unqualified customers who didn't have the ability to pay in the first place. This metric tells us a little about the quality of the receivables.

You can imagine that a rent-to-own business that rents appliances might have plenty of customers who end up not paying. That is part of the reason it costs $300 a month to rent a couch!

Allowance for doubtful accounts has its own schedule at the end of the 10-K, Schedule II. It is also disclosed in a note to the financial statements—the note where balance sheet items are broken down in more detail.

Results for Dell

2004: allowance for doubtful accounts of $84,000,000 / accounts receivable of $3,635,000,000 = 2.3%

2003: allowance for doubtful accounts of $71,000,000 / accounts receivable of $2,586,000,000 = 2.7%

Results for Gateway

2003: allowance for doubtful accounts of $5,608,000 / accounts receivable of $210,151,000 = 2.67%

2002: allowance for doubtful accounts of $5,120,000 / accounts receivable of $197,817,000 = 2.59%

Conclusions

Both companies allow for less than 3 percent of their accounts receivable to go bad or be uncollectible. It makes sense that their numbers are similar, as they are both operating in a similar market with a similar business model. Hence, their customers are also similar—about 97 percent reliable.

The Accounts Payable Component of Working Capital

ACCOUNTS PAYABLE TO WORKING CAPITAL

$$\frac{\text{accounts payable}}{\text{working capital}}$$

This metric tells us the portion of working capital that is made up of accounts payable. As I explained for the ratios of accounts receivable to working capital and inventory to working capital, working capital is a mix of positive and negative numbers (rainy-day cash plus inventory plus accounts receivable less accounts payable). I think this makes this number squirrelly. But again, it is used quite a bit, so it is good to know of it.

Results for Dell

This metric won't work for Dell because of the negative working capital number.

Results for Gateway

2003: accounts payable of $415,971,000 / working capital of $664,473,000 = 62.60%

2002: accounts payable of $278,609,000 / working capital of $1,015,023,000 = 27.45%

Conclusions

For Gateway, while sales were decreasing between the years, accounts payable went up exponentially—$415,971,000 in 2003 versus $278,609,000 in 2002. This is another item that deserves investigation.

Is Gateway squeezing its vendors because it isn't doing so well? Does it mean that its new vendors of television components are used to operating on a stretched-out schedule? Or is Gateway simply slowing payments to its vendors because it is trying to hold onto as much cash as it can? This one needs further investigation, but it doesn't bode well.

DAYS' PAYABLES OUTSTANDING

$$\text{average purchases per day} = \frac{\text{Sales}}{365}$$

This measures the number of days that it takes you to pay your vendors. In general, you want to keep your own resources for as long as possible. So it is best to stretch accounts payable as far as you can without ruining your relationship with your vendors.

Results for Dell

What is Dell's days' payables outstanding for some recent periods?

2004: accounts payable of $7,316,000,000 / sales of $41,444,000,000 / 365 = 64 days

2003: accounts payable of $5,989,000,000 / sales of $35,404,000,000 / 365 = 62 days

Dell discloses its days' payables outstanding as 70 and 68 for these two years.

Results for Gateway

2003: accounts payable of $415,971,000 / sales of $3,204,364,000 / 365 = 45 days

2002: accounts payable of $278,609,000 / sales of $4,171,325,000 / 365 = 24 days

Gateway disclosed a DPO of 51 for 2003 and 27 for 2002 in the MD&A section of its 10-K.

Conclusions

Because Dell is a bigger animal, it can get away with stretching its payments out to vendors. Dell is the number-one PC maker in the world. If a vendor of LCD screens wants to sell a lot of screens, it will likely put up with Dell paying it later than the industry norm.

Gateway, because of its smaller market share, might not have that sort of leverage and might not be able to choose to stretch payments. Gateway is still a gentle company to do business with. It is not unusual for vendors to wait 45 days—but Gateway has almost doubled the time it took them to pay its vendors over last year. The vendors are going to feel this in their own checkbooks and might be none too happy about it. This metric deserves close scrutiny in the future.

ACCOUNTS RECEIVABLE TO ACCOUNTS PAYABLE

$$\frac{\text{accounts receivable}}{\text{accounts payable} + \text{accrued expenses}}$$

This is another way to look at liquidity or working capital items. In a traditional interpretation, you would want to see accounts receivable balanced by accounts payable. That way, accounts receivable could fund accounts payable. But if you are wisely managing your working capital items, you would have a stretched out or big accounts payable and a relatively small accounts receivable.

Results for Dell

2004: accounts receivable of $3,635,000,000 / accounts payable of $7,316,000,000 + accrued expenses of $3,580,000,000 = 33 to 1

2003: accounts receivable of $2,586,000,000 / accounts payable of $5,989,000,000 + accrued expenses of $2,944,000,000 = 29 to 1

Results for Gateway

2003: accounts receivable of $210,151,000 / accounts payable of $415,971,000 + accrued liabilities of $277,455,000 + accrued royalties of $48,488,000 + other current liabilities (in essence, all current liabilities) = 21 to 1

2002: accounts receivable of $197,817,000 / current liabilities of $940,349,000 = 21 to 1

It's interesting how stable this ratio is for Gateway.

Conclusions

I don't see either of these results as remarkable for these companies. I would not run this metric for these companies on a regular basis.

How All the Elements of Working Capital Add Up

CASH CONVERSION CYCLE

days' supply of inventory + days' sales outstanding – days' payables outstanding

This adds three key metrics for determining how well the organization is managing its working capital items—inventory, receivables, and payables. We want to minimize inventory balances, minimize receivables, and maximize payables.

When you add days' supply of inventory (DSI) and days' sales outstanding (DSO) and subtract days' payables outstanding (DPO), you end up with the number of days it takes the organization to turn an investment in its products and services into cash.

Results for Dell

2004: DSI of 3 + DSO of 32 – DPO of 64 = -29 days

2003: DSI of 4 + DSO of 27 – DPO of 62 = -31 days

Dell discloses -36 and -37 for the same period. All those little differences in my calculation of DSO, DSI, and DPO ended up making a big difference in this sum.

Results for Gateway

2003: DSI of 14 + DSO of 23 – DPO of 45 = -8

2002: DSI of 12 + DSO of 17 – DPO of 24 = 5

Gateway discloses –15 and –2.

Conclusion

What does Dell's -29 mean, anyway? It means that Dell has the use of other people's money for 29 days. In essence, Dell never has to reach into its own pockets to finance operations. It uses other people's money to finance operations and growth. Gateway is also efficiently managing working capital so that it has use of other people's money, but its number is not as deeply negative. It is now -8, an improvement over the previous year. Having a negative cash conversion cycle is ideal and both have it.

Back in 1996, Dell was a nearly $8 billion company. In 2004 it is a $41 billion company. A dollar's worth of other people's money when you are operating at a $41 billion sales volume is enormous. By both increasing sales volume and efficiently managing working capital, Dell has become a cash-generating machine. Gateway is also a cash-generating machine, but on a much smaller scale because its cash conversion cycle isn't as negative and it has a much smaller share of the market (i.e., total sales of $3.4 billion in 2003).

Overall Conclusions for Working Capital for Dell and Gateway

Dell has a cash conversion cycle of -29 and Gateway has a cash conversion cycle of -8. So Dell is using other people's money for a month and Gateway is using it for about a week. Both good results; Dell is better.

On inventory, Dell is holding pretty steady at a low number. Gateway's inventory is creeping up. This might be because it is selling TVs and not just computers. It might be because it is holding finished goods. It is hard to tell from the financials, but this is not a good trend for Gateway.

Both Dell and Gateway are collecting more slowly between the two periods. I would investigate why this is happening. Are they both doing more business with slower-paying clients? Are their collection procedures slipping?

Dell invests less overall in its working capital. All of Dell's metrics relating to inventory and accounts payable are improving. The only number that is improving for Gateway is accounts payable. And by "improving," I mean the company is stretching its accounts payables. This "improving" number might have a negative impact on its relationships with vendors.

Overall, again, Dell is doing better, although both are doing well and are good managers of working capital.

Quiz

1. Working capital is
   (a) current assets less current receivables
   (b) current assets less current liabilities
   (c) rainy-day cash plus daily-needs cash

2. Current assets include
   (a) cash
   (b) accounts receivable
   (c) inventory
   (d) accounts payable
   (e) all of the above
   (f) a, b, and c
   (g) b, c, and d

3. Working capital is monies you have tied up in things you hope to sell.
   T or F

4. You want working capital to be as big as possible if you include only day-to-day operating cash in your calculations and not include rainy-day cash.
   T or F

5. Working capital turnover measures
   (a) how many times working capital is used to generate accounts payable
   (b) how many times working capital is used to generate sales
   (c) how many times working capital is turned into inventory

6. Current liabilities include
   (a) accounts payable
   (b) inventory
   (c) accounts receivable

7. The quick ratio is also called
   (a) the acid test
   (b) the accounts payable turnover ratio
   (c) the inventory turnover ratio

8. Which of the two following metrics do you want to minimize in terms of days?
   (a) days' supply of inventory
   (b) days' sales outstanding
   (c) days' payables outstanding
   (d) all of the above
   (e) b and c
   (f) a and b

9. Which of the following is the correct equation for the cash conversion cycle?
   (a) DSO + DSI – DPO
   (b) DSO + DSI + DPO
   (c) DPO – DSO – DSI

10. A negative cash conversion cycle means that other people are using the organization's money.
    T or F

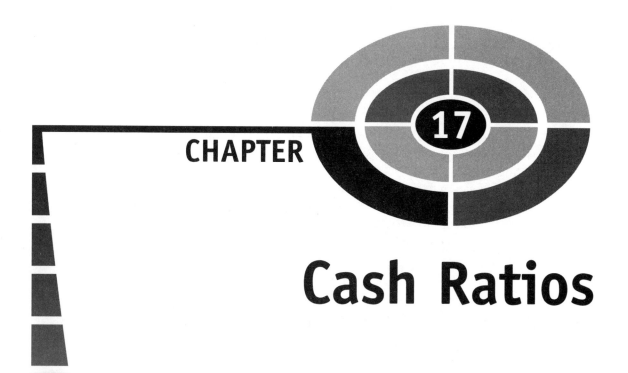

CHAPTER 17

Cash Ratios

Cash is our favorite asset because we can do so much with it. It is so flexible, so accommodating, so green. This chapter is all about examining our cash position. Many of the ratios use information from the cash flow statement.

But before we do the ratios, we should spend a little time "eyeballing" the cash flow statement. This will give us some insight into what Dell and Gateway are doing with the cash that they have.

Categories of the Cash Flow Statement

Every cash flow statement is divided into three categories of flows (both inflows and outflows): operating cash flows, investing cash flows, and financing cash flows.

Operating cash flows tell us how the company generated and used cash in creating products or providing services.

Investing cash flows tell how the company used its rainy-day cash to invest in other entities. This section also tells us whether the company has used its cash

to buy fixed assets or gained any cash from the sales of fixed assets. Fixed assets are considered a long-term investment. (I think this is a confusing and strange categorization of fixed asset purchases and sales, but I didn't write the accounting rules.)

Financing cash flows tell us how the company got financing to operate other than through operations. So this includes any debt or equity financing the company uses or pays back.

For more on this topic, you might want to revisit Chapter 4.

Eyeballing Dell's Cash Flow Statement

Let's first look at Dell's cash flow statement for FY 2004 (Figure 17.1).

FIRST CATEGORY—OPERATING CASH FLOWS

Dell generated $2.6 billion in net income in 2004 but had a positive effect on cash flows of $3.6 billion for the same period. Cool. Cash flows exceeded net income.

Remember that the accrual method of accounting will always cause a difference between net income and cash.

That is what all that detail is in between the top line of the cash flow statement and the net cash provided by operating activities line. It is a reconciliation of net income generated under the accrual method to true cash.

I don't want you to concentrate on the reconciling items. That can get pretty technical and it even confuses accountants! (I know this because I teach the statement of cash flows to CPAs.)

What we need to do is notice that cash from operations exceeds net income. This is a good trend and is due in large part to Dell's fabulous management of working capital, as described in Chapter 16.

DELL INC.
CONSOLIDATED STATEMENTS OF CASH FLOWS
(in millions)

	Fiscal Year Ended		
	January 30, 2004	January 31, 2003	February 1, 2002
Cash flows from operating activities:	2,645	2,122	1,246
Net income			
Adjustments to reconcile net income to net cash provided by operating activities:			
Depreciation and amortization	263	211	239
Tax benefits of employee stock plans	181	260	487
Special charges	—	—	742
(Gains)/losses on investments	(16)	6	17
Other, primarily effects of exchange rate changes on monetary assets and liabilities denominated in foreign currencies	(548)	(483)	178
Changes in:			
Operating working capital	872	1,210	826
Non-current assets and liabilities	273	212	62
Net cash provided by operating activities	3,670	3,538	3,797
Cash flows from investing activities:			
Investments:			
Purchases	(12,099)	(8,736)	(5,382)
Maturities and sales	10,078	7,660	3,425
Cash assumed in consolidation of Dell Financial Services L.P.	172	—	—
Capital expenditures	(329)	(305)	(303)
Purchase of assets held in master lease facilities	(636)	—	—
Net cash used in investing activities	(2,814)	(1,381)	(2,260)
Cash flows from financing activities:			
Purchase of common stock	(2,000)	(2,290)	(3,000)
Issuance of common stock under employee plans and other	617	265	298
Net cash used in financing activities	(1,383)	(2,025)	(2,702)
Effect of exchange rate changes on cash and cash equivalents	612	459	(104)
Net increase (decrease) in cash and cash equivalents	85	591	(1,269)
Cash and cash equivalents at beginning of period	4,232	3,641	4,910
Cash and cash equivalents at end of period	4,317	4,232	3,641

Figure 17.1 Dell's cash flow statement FY 2004

SECOND CATEGORY—INVESTING

Dell bought and sold investments in other organizations. Over the year, it bought $12 billion worth of investments and sold $10 billion worth. This gives it a net increase in investments of $2 billion. So we take last year's balance of short-term and long-term investments of $406 million and $5.267 billion ($5.673 billion) (from the balance sheet, the Consolidated Statements of Financial Position) and we add $2 billion to approximate current short-term and long-term investments of $835 million + $6.770 billion ($7.605 billion). That works!

So Dell took $2 billion out of operating cash and put $2 billion more into investments, giving it $7.6 billion in investments.

Dell also purchased $329 million in fixed assets and changed buildings accounted for as leases to buildings accounted for as fixed assets to the tune of $636 million.

All of these activities give us a net effect of using $2.8 billion of cash in investing activities.

THIRD CATEGORY—FINANCING

Here we see that Dell has used some of its cash—$2 billion—to buy back its own stock. Nice. As we said in earlier discussions, buying back your own stock has a wide range of positive benefits. All of the messages on Dell's cash flow statement are positive.

Eyeballing Gateway's Cash Flow Statement

Let's check out Gateway (Figure 17.2):

FIRST CATEGORY—OPERATING

Even though Gateway suffered a net loss of $514 million, it was still able to generate $72 million in cash from operations. This is due to its good management of working capital, as discussed in Chapter 16.

GATEWAY, INC.

CONSOLIDATED STATEMENTS OF CASH FLOWS
For the years ended December 31, 2003, 2002 and 2001
(in thousands)

	2003	2002	2001
Cash flows from operating activities:			
Net loss	$(514,812)	$(297,718)	$(1,031,062)
Adjustments to reconcile net loss to net cash provided by (used in) operating activities:			
Depreciation and amortization	163,973	159,458	199,976
Provision for uncollectible accounts receivable	11,297	11,139	23,151
Deferred income taxes	6,000	257,172	(27,282)
Loss on investments	808	30,272	186,745
Write-down of long-lived assets	66,397	52,975	418,304
Gain on settlement of acquisition liability	—	(13,782)	—
Loss on sale of property	6,052	—	—
Cumulative effect of change in accounting principle	—	—	23,851
Gain on extinguishment of debt	—	—	(6,890)
Other, net	1,941	(1,929)	(1,707)
Changes in operating assets and liabilities:			
Accounts receivable	(23,633)	11,020	301,630
Inventory	(25,375)	31,505	194,799
Other assets	306,258	(76,975)	21,729
Accounts payable	137,716	(59,856)	(442,312)
Accrued liabilities	(95,117)	(103,868)	(87,714)
Accrued royalties	(8,196)	(79,014)	(2,747)
Other liabilities	39,382	54,924	(40,810)
Net cash provided by (used in) operating activities	72,691	(24,677)	(270,339)
Cash flows from investing activities:			
Capital expenditures	(72,978)	(78,497)	(199,493)
Proceeds from sale of investment	—	11,100	—
Purchases of available-for-sale securities	(530,323)	(614,023)	(638,869)
Sales of available-for-sale securities	401,109	436,316	356,071
Proceeds from the sale of financing receivables	—	9,896	569,579
Purchase of financing receivables, net of repayments	—	—	(28,476)
Proceeds from notes receivable	20,045	—	50,000
Other, net	—	—	189
Net cash provided by (used in) investing activities	(182,147)	(235,208)	109,001
Cash flows from financing activities:			
Proceeds from issuance of notes payable	—	—	200,000
Principal payments on long-term obligations and notes payable	—	—	(3,984)
Proceeds from stock issuance	—	—	200,000
Payment of preferred dividends	(8,840)	(5,878)	—
Stock options exercised	1,794	367	9,431
Net cash provided by (used in) financing activities	(7,046)	(5,511)	405,447
Foreign exchange effect on cash and cash equivalents	—	—	2,893
Net increase (decrease) in cash and cash equivalents	(116,502)	(265,396)	247,002
Cash and cash equivalents, beginning of year	465,603	730,999	483,997
Cash and cash equivalents, end of year	$ 349,101	$ 465,603	$ 730,999

Figure 17.2 Gateway's cash flow statement FY 2003

SECOND CATEGORY—INVESTING

Gateway purchased $72 million in fixed assets and also bought and sold investments in other entities. Net effect was a use of operating cash of $182 million.

THIRD CATEGORY—FINANCING

Here we see that Gateway is obligated to pay $8.8 million in dividends to preferred shareholders. This, along with an exercise of stock options, gives Gateway a use of cash for financing activities of $7 million.

Bottom line: Gateway has $349 million in cash. If we add that to short-term and long-term investments from the balance sheet, we will get the total superliquid resources. Gateway has short-term investments (what it terms "marketable securities") of $739 million. It has no long-term investments. This gives the company $1.088 million in superliquid resources in FY 2003.

Contrast this with the figures in 2002: cash of $465 million plus marketable securities of $601 million for a total of $1.065 million. So Gateway is holding stable in its cash position. How Gateway did this is partially a matter of working capital management, discussed in Chapter 16, and partially due to the items we will look at in this chapter.

The Cash Ratios

OPERATING CASH INDEX

$$\frac{\text{cash from operations}}{\text{net income}}$$

Now this is a good metric. If the numerator is substantially different from the denominator, this might indicate that the organization has a hard time converting its profits into cash. Maybe it has stinky customers or it doesn't make much of an effort in collecting.

Results for Dell

What is Dell's operating cash index for some recent periods?

2004: cash from operations of $3,670,000,000 / net income of $2,645,000,000 = 1.39 to 1

2003: cash from operations of $3,538,000,000 / net income of $2,122,000,000 = 1.67 to 1

Results for Gateway

This ratio won't work for Gateway because of negative net income.

Conclusions

Dell's results are fabulous on this metric. Its ability to generate cash from operations, selling computers, exceeds its ability to generate net income. How can this happen? Through tight working capital management: through managing inventory, accounts receivable, and accounts payable. (See Chapter 16.)

CASH RATIO

$$\frac{\text{cash equivalents + marketable securities}}{\text{current liabilities}}$$

This ratio is the quick ratio less accounts receivable. It is truly just your current liquid resources contrasted against current liabilities. Again, the question this metric is supposed to answer is "Do we have enough liquid resources to cover our current obligations?"

Results for Dell

What is Dell's cash ratio for the last two years?

2004: cash of $4,317,000,000 + marketable securities of $835,000,000 + $6,770,000,000 / current liabilities of $10,896,000 = 1.09 to 1

2003: cash of $4,232,000,000 + marketable securities of $406,000,000 + $5,267,000,000 / current liabilities of $8,933,000,000 = 1.11 to 1

Results for Gateway

What is Gateway's ratio for the same period?

2003: cash of $349,101,000 + marketable securities of $739,936,000 / current liabilities of $999,004,000 = 1.09 to 1

2002: cash of $465,603,000 + marketable securities of $601,118,000 / current liabilities of $940,349,000 = 1.13 to 1

Conclusions

Dell's and Gateway's ratios stay close to 1 to 1, and both companies are similar in their results. Both companies have enough liquid resources to cover their current obligations. Both are good managers of working capital.

CASH TO WORKING CAPITAL

$$\frac{cash}{working\ capital}$$

This metric, the proportion of cash to total working capital, can be a little misleading because the denominator includes both positives (cash, accounts receivable, and inventory) and negatives (accounts payable). So I am not a huge fan of this metric. I prefer to look at cash as a proportion of current assets. I think that metric is fairer.

Results for Dell

Dell's cash balance in 2003 is $4,317,000,000 and in 2002 is $4,232,000,000. Again, this ratio won't work for Dell, because you can't have a negative number as either the numerator or the denominator.

Results for Gateway

2003: cash of $349,101,000 / working capital of $664,473,000 = 52.54%

2002: cash of $465,603,000 / working capital of $1,015,023,000 = 45.87%

Conclusions

This shows that Gateway's cash balance is healthy—and we already knew that. No comment on Dell, because of its negative working capital.

CASH TURNOVER RATIO

$$\frac{sales}{cash + marketable\ securities}$$

This asks, "How many times was the investment in cash realized in sales? How hard did your cash work for you in generating sales?" What you will get here is a multiple, such as cash turned over five times or 10 times or 100 times. In other words, the higher the turnover rate or the bigger the multiple, the better: it means your cash is working hard, not just lollygagging around.

Results for Dell

What is Dell's cash turnover ratio is for the last two years?

2004: sales of $41,444,000,000 / cash of $4,317,000,000 + marketable securities of $835,000,000 + $6,770,000,000 = 3.48 times

2003: sales of $35,404,000,000 / cash of $4,232,000,000 + marketable securities of $406,000,000 + $5,267,000,000 = 3.57 times

Results for Gateway

2003: sales of $3,402,364,000 / cash of $349,101,000 + marketable securities of $739,936,000 = 3.12 times

2002: sales of $4,171,325,000 / cash of $465,603,000 + marketable securities of $601,118,000 = 3.9 times

Conclusions

Here we are taking into account both cash and long-term investments—total liquid resources— instead of only current assets or short-term investments and cash. As a result, we have taken out the consideration of investment policy, and Dell and Gateway's numbers look much more alike. Both are in the three-times

range. This ratio, then, is better than the working capital ratio for measuring the ability of these companies to turn their resources into sales.

CASH FLOW RATIO

$$\frac{\text{cash flow from operations}}{\text{current liabilities}}$$

This contrasts not aggregate cash, all cash, but just operating cash to current liabilities. So it is asking if the organization is generating enough cash from selling its products and services to meet current obligations.

Results for Dell

What is Dell's cash flow ratio for some recent periods?:

2004: cash flow from operations of $3,670,000,000 / current liabilities of $10,896,000,000 = .34 to 1

2003: cash flow from operations of $3,538,000,000 / current liabilities of $8,933,000,000 = .40 to 1

Results for Gateway

2003: cash flow from operations of $72,691,000 / current liabilities of $999,004,000 = .0728 to 1

2002: cash flow from operations of -$24,677,000—a negative figure, so we cannot calculate this ratio

Conclusions

Because Gateway's profitability—and hence its cash flow from operations—in the past few years has been weak, this ratio does not look good. Again, Dell comes out on top.

CASH TO CASH DIVIDENDS

$$\frac{\text{operating cash flow} - \text{preferred dividends}}{\text{common stock cash dividends}}$$

This is asking us to determine if the entity has enough cash to meet dividend obligations.

Results for Dell

This metric is not applicable to Dell, as it does not pay dividends—an interesting fact in itself.

Results for Gateway

Gateway pays only preferred dividends, not common stock dividends. According to the notes, Gateway is obligated to pay these dividends every quarter*. If it fails to pay dividends, they accumulate and must be paid later. Gateway paid $8.8 million in dividends in 2003 even though the company suffered a net loss!

What Is the Difference between Common and Preferred Stock?

Generally, preferred shareholders get their dividends first and have special rights that common stockholders don't have, such as conversion rights and extra voting rights. They usually pay a premium for these privileges. The privileges of a preferred stockholder differ per organization and are spelled out in the Articles of Incorporation, the Bylaws, or the preferred stock certificate itself. Many companies have only common stock.

Conclusions

What might have seemed like a good idea to Gateway when it was profitable—to guarantee dividends to its preferred stockholders—must now seem not so good. Maybe the preferred shareholders are the principals of the company and they want to walk away with as much personal money as they can regardless of whether the company is profitable. It's hard to tell from outside the company.

CASH FLOW ADEQUACY RATIO

$$\frac{\text{cash from operations}}{\text{capital investments + inventory additions + dividends + debt uses}}$$

The denominator in this equation is a laundry list of all the desirable ways that a company could spend its cash. This equation asks, "Is cash flow from selling our product or service enough to get us the extra goodies we need to grow and keep our owners happy? Do we have enough cash from operations to buy additional capital equipment, to expand our inventory, to pay dividends to our owners, and to meet additional debt obligations if we decide to take on an expansion loan or a loan for a special project?" This metric is one I would customize for your own situation.

Results for Dell

What is Dell's cash flow adequacy ratio is for the last two years?

2004: cash from operations of $3,670,000,000 / capital investments of $329,000,000 + $636,000,000 (from the cash flow statement) + inventory increase of $11,000,000 (2004 inventory of $327,000,000 – 2003 inventory of $306,000,000, from the balance sheet) = 3.72 times

Note that Dell did not pay off any debt per the cash flow statement nor did it pay any dividends.

2003: cash from operations of $3,538,000,000 / capital investments of $305,000,000 + inventory increase of $28,000,000 (2003 inventory of $306,000,000 – 2002 inventory of $278,000,000) = 10.62 times

Results for Gateway

2003: cash from operations of $72,691,000 / capital investments of $72,798,000 + inventory increase of $25,375,000 + debt payments of 0 + preferred dividend payments of $8,840,000 = .6781 times

2002: cash from operations of -$24,667,000—a negative figure, so we cannot calculate this ratio

Conclusions

So Dell's cash flow adequacy has slowed from 10.62 in 2003 to 3.72 in 2004. This is primarily due to an unusual increase in capital investments due to recognizing $636 million worth of buildings as capital assets instead of as leased facilities. I would expect the ratio to increase back into the double digits in future years. Gateway's cash flow adequacy is improving, mainly because it has operating cash flows this year, unlike last year, when it had negative operating cash flows. (In other words, it was losing cash in selling its products and services!)

MANDATORY CASH FLOWS INDEX

$$\frac{\text{cash used in operations} + (\text{cash used for financing activities} - \text{dividends})}{\text{total sources of cash}}$$

This metric contrasts the cash that the organization is obligated to use on a regular basis with the total cash generated. Cash used in operations to make and sell products or services is a mandatory expenditure, as is cash used to repay loans.

Notice that dividends have been taken out of the cash flow used for financing activities because dividends are not mandatory in many cases. If push came to shove and the organization were in cash flow trouble, it could delay or cancel the dividends.

Results for Dell and Gateway

This is a metric that is hard to get at from outside the company. The two components—cash from operations and cash from financing—are hard to access.

Cash from operations is total cash less rainy-day cash. From the cash flow statement, we cannot derive the cash used in operations. It discloses only the net effect on cash of operations and it is a positive number—termed "cash provided," not "cash used." Because we don't know what rainy-day cash is, we can't get at this number. If you are inside the organization, this could be a great metric to calculate.

DEFENSIVE INTERVAL

$$\frac{\text{current assets} - \text{inventory}}{\text{daily cash operating expenses}}$$

This is a great ratio to calculate if you have the information. It would, in essence, show you how many days you could make it—pay your cash operating expenses—before you would run out of cash. Notice that inventory is taken out of current assets because we might not be able to sell our inventory fast enough to make that daily cash payment.

Results for Dell and Gateway

We have no way to accurately figure daily cash operating expenses for either company.

Conclusions

No calculations are possible, so there are no conclusions.

DIVIDEND PAYOUT OF CASH FROM OPERATIONS

$$\frac{\text{dividends}}{\text{cash from operations}}$$

This metric gives us another perspective on dividend obligations and cash. How able is the organization to generate enough cash from operations to pay dividends?

Results for Dell

This metric is not applicable to Dell since it doesn't pay dividends.

Results for Gateway

2003: dividends of $8,840,000 / cash from operations of $72,691,000 = 12%

2002: dividends of $5,878,000 were paid, although cash from operations was negative

Conclusions

Oh, my! Gateway had negative cash from operations in 2002, yet it was still obligated to pay preferred stockholder dividends. I am sure that at the time these shares were sold, this seemed like a good idea. At this point, I am sure the obligation does not make the managers at Gateway—or the common stockholders—very happy.

DEPRECIATION IMPACT RATIO

$$\frac{\text{depreciation}}{\text{cash from operations}}$$

This ratio helps refine your diagnosis of what might be going amiss in the operating cash index. Depreciation is a noncash expense, so it reduces net income but not cash. This equation might tell you if the difference between cash from operations and net income is largely made up by depreciation expense.

Results for Dell

2004: depreciation of $263,000,000 / cash flow from operations of $3,670,000,000 = 7%

2003: depreciation of $211,000,000 / cash flow from operations of $3,538,000,000 = 6%

Results for Gateway

2003: depreciation of $163,973,000 / cash flow from operations of $72,691,000 = 226%—depreciation exceeds cash flows from operations

2002: depreciation of $159,458,000 / cash flow from operations of -$24,677,000—a negative figure, so we cannot calculate this ratio

Conclusions

The impact of depreciation on cash flows is minimal for Dell. And this makes sense, as we will later find that Dell has very little in the way of fixed assets to depreciate. Its cash balance dwarfs its fixed asset balances.

Gateway's depreciation expense exceeds cash flow from operations. Hmm. Because Gateway is operating at a net loss and, for 2002, with a negative operating cash flow, the way this metric turned out is not surprising.

DEPRECIATION TO TOTAL FIXED ASSETS

$$\frac{\text{accumulated depreciation}}{\text{total fixed assets}}$$

This metric indicates the age of fixed assets.

Results for Dell

2004: accumulated depreciation of $1,133,000,000 / total property, plant, and equipment of $2,650,000,000 = 43%

2003: accumulated depreciation of $749,000,000 / total property, plant, and equipment of $1,662,000,000 = 45%

Note: These numbers for fixed assets come from the notes to the financial statements (Note 9, Supplemental Consolidated Financial Information); the balance sheet does not disclose each individually.

Results for Gateway

2003: accumulated depreciation of $592,586,000 / fixed assets of $923,499,000 = 64.17%

2002: accumulated depreciation of $552,548,000 / fixed assets of $1,033,559,000 = 53.46%

Conclusions

Now this is not at all what I expected. These metrics indicate that half of the useful life of the fixed assets has expired. This means that these assets are pretty old and could indicate that they need to be replaced soon. This item requires further investigation.

For Dell, in looking at the components of fixed assets or of property, plant, and equipment in the notes to the financial statements, I see that in 2004 land and buildings is the largest category of assets, at $1,158,000, followed by com-

puter equipment at $898,000 and machinery and other equipment at $594,000. I would imagine that the computer equipment is totally depreciated because it depreciates so quickly. Does this mean that Dell will have to replace it all soon? I won't be able to tell from the outside.

Gateway's assets seem to be a little older than Dell's.

Per these figures, both Dell and Gateway might need to start investing more of their resources in fixed assets. Because we do not work inside the company, it is hard to tell whether each company is hobbling along with outdated equipment or not. This metric raises a red flag to monitor in the future.

Overall Conclusions about the Cash Positions of Dell and Gateway

Again, Dell comes out looking better than Gateway, although neither is in a crunch cash position at this time. Both have a very nice cash reserve that can more than cover any current obligation and get them through any rough spots. However, unless Gateway's profitability turns around, it might use up their cash reserves to keep operating. This situation bears watching.

Also, we see by looking at depreciation-related ratios that the assets of both companies might be old. This might indicate that they are not making an adequate investment in their fixed assets and might need to spend some of their resources on replacing these assets in the future.

Quiz

1. The cash flow statement divides cash flows into which of the following three categories?
    (a) investing, financing, and asset purchases/disposals
    (b) investing, financing, and operating
    (c) financing, operating, and equity

2. The investing category of the cash flow statement discloses how much the organization has invested in inventory.

T or F

3. The operating category of the cash flow statement discloses how much cash the entity generated in creating and selling its products and services.
T or F

4. When dividends are paid, they are classified in which category of the cash flow statement?
   (a) investing
   (b) financing
   (c) operating

5. When fixed assets are purchased, they are classified in which category of the cash flow statement?
   (a) investing
   (b) financing
   (c) operating

6. The operating cash index contrasts net income to operating cash.
T or F

7. Cash turnover should be expressed as
   (a) a percentage
   (b) a multiple
   (c) a fraction

8. Preferred shareholders usually pay less for their stock than common shareholders.
T or F

9. Common shareholders always receive dividends.
T or F

10. Which ratio helps indicate the age of fixed assets?
   (a) depreciation to total fixed assets
   (b) depreciation impact ratio
   (c) cash to working capital

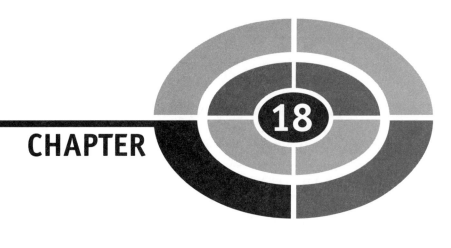

CHAPTER 18

Financing Ratios

There are three ways to finance your organization. You can get a loan, you can sell equity or ownership in your company, or you can generate your own resources by selling your product or service at a profit. Each type of financing has advantages and disadvantages.

Debt

Debt is incurred when you arrange for someone, such as a bank, to give you resources now with the understanding that you will pay them back later, often with a little fee—interest. The lender can require you to conform to a myriad of requirements. If you take the money, you also take on whatever requirements the lender imposes. Examples include being required to keep a certain amount of cash in the bank at all times, keeping inventory levels within an acceptable range, and undergoing quarterly audits. Usually debt financing requires you to make periodic payments and to pay interest.

Debt is not inherently bad. Debt can be a very useful tool. Debt might allow you to take advantage of opportunities that you would otherwise have to pass up. So debt itself is not bad. What is bad is being burdened by such a large amount of debt that all you can do is keep up with the obligation each month.

An advantage of debt financing is that it is often cheaper than equity financing because equity investors often expect a higher return. They expect a higher return because equity holders get paid last in case of liquidation, and they demand a higher return for this risk. Also, the interest on loans is tax-deductible.

Equity

The disadvantage of equity is that you have to answer to the people to whom you sell it. They become owners of the organization and therefore have a say in how the organization is run.

They also expect a return for their investment in the organization, either in terms of an increase in the value of the stock or in terms of distributions or dividends. Either one of these needs can be hard to satiate.

If you are expected to make the value of the stock go up, then you are also expected to earn profits and maintain happy financial metrics. You might have to sacrifice long-term goals for short-term profitability. If you are expected to pay dividends, you must have the cash available every quarter to do so.

The advantage of equity is that you might not be expected to pay dividends and it might be easier to attract investors than to generate a profit. If you are in the early years of building your company, you might not be profitable at all and debt or equity financing are your only sources of money.

Earnings

Ideally, you run on your own steam. You generate enough resources through the sale of your product or service to pay for the things you need to operate and expand. If you generate your own resources through sales, you do not have to answer to either lenders or equity holders. However, making a profit is not that easy. As we have seen from reading earlier chapters, many factors can affect the organization's ability to generate a profit.

I once met a man who was a financial analyst for a venture capitalist. He spent all of his time investigating and analyzing companies to determine if they were worthy of investment. Each quarter, out of the hundreds of companies he evaluated, he recommended that his investors put their money into 10 companies.

He said that out of this 10, five would fail in the first year, two would fail in the first five years, two would generate a decent return for the rest of their existence, and only one would be a star—worth the investment in the other nine. The big companies that we all know and love now—IBM, Microsoft, GM—are all stars. Many a company has failed in their quest to make it to that size.

My point? Generating a profit and staying in business is not as easy as it sounds.

The following ratios help give us a picture of what sort of external financing the company is relying upon. We looked at earnings in Chapter 15 under profitability ratios. Good management of working capital is also a source of resources. Another is prior cash balances.

This chapter looks at how else we finance companies, through either debt or equity financing. I've grouped the ratios into three sets: debt ratios, equity ratios, and fixed asset/capital investment ratios.

Debt Ratios

These ratios tell us if the company is comfortably handling its debt obligations.

DEBT TO EQUITY

$$\frac{\text{total debt}}{\text{total equity}}$$

This is a very straightforward ratio. It asks us to contrast the components of the right side of the balance sheet. The right side of the balance sheet tells us where the organization gets money to operate—through debt, stock, or retained earnings.

So this ratio contrasts debt with the combination of stock and retained earnings. Ideally, because we like retained earnings so much, we would like the bottom to be larger than the top. If the top is larger, we might have hit upon a hint that the organization is overburdened with debt.

Results for Dell

2004: total liabilities of $13,031,000,000 / total equity of $6,280,000,000 = 2.075

2003: total liabilities of $10,597,000,000 / total equity of $4,873,000,000 = 2.175

Results for Gateway

2003: total liabilities of $1,108,700,000 / total equity of $722,018,000 = 1.54

2002: total liabilities of $1,067,467,000 / total equity of $1,246,518,000 = .85

Conclusions

The number for Dell surprised me. I expected equity to be on a par with debt, and I expected Dell to be "better" than Gateway. But there are several factors at play here. For one, Dell stretches its accounts payable out quite a bit. For another, Dell has been buying back its stock and thus decreasing its equity.

I am going to argue that the reason that Gateway's numbers look "better" is because it does not stretch accounts payable as far as Dell. As neither of these companies has long-term debt, this metric might need to be refined—as long-term debt to equity.

But because equity is being affected by Gateway's net loss, it will still be disparaging. Gateway's equity is low because of a reduction in equity because of poor profits. Remember that one of the components of equity is retained earnings. Gateway has experienced a negative retained earnings: compare the total equity figures of $722,018 and $1,246,518—equity is decreasing. That's not good in this case.

So maybe the remaining ratios will give us better, more meaningful results. We need to keep on this track to see what is really going on.

DEBT RATIO

$$\frac{\text{total liabilities}}{\text{total assets}}$$

Here is another way of looking at the debt burden. Instead of contrasting the debt against equity, we contrast it against the total resources we have available to pay off that debt. Obviously, we want the bottom to be larger than the top: this would indicate that the organization has the resources necessary to meet the debt obligation. If we see the top bigger than the bottom, we are likely in serious trouble because that would mean that equity was negative (assets = liabilities + equity).

Results for Dell

2004: total debt of $13,031,000,000 / total assets of $19,311,000,000 = .67 to 1

2003: total debt of $10,597,000,000 / total assets of $15,470,000,000 = .69 to 1

Results for Gateway

2003: total debt of $1,108,700 / total assets of $2,028,438 = .55 to 1

2002: total debt of $1,067,467 / total assets of $2,509,407 = .43 to 1

Conclusions

Neither of these companies is in any hurt as far as debt is concerned. Both are keeping a very low percentage.

CASH TO LONG-TERM DEBT

$$\frac{\text{cash and cash equivalents}}{\text{long-term debt}}$$

I like this ratio because it is getting a little more specific than the first two we looked at. It is looking only at long-term debt. Total debt would include accounts payable and we have seen in previous chapters how both Dell and Gateway are stretching accounts payable.

This contrasts the amount of cash the organization holds to the debt obligation. This gives us an indication of the power of the organization to pay off its debt with the cash it holds.

You might not see the top being bigger than the bottom, because long-term debt might be a huge 30-year obligation and the organization holds only enough cash to meet the currently due portion of that debt plus some to pay current bills. So this might not be as meaningful a ratio as cash to current maturities of long-term debt. Again, you need to choose the ratios that make sense for your particular situation.

Results for Dell

2004: cash and cash equivalents of $4,317,000,000 / long-term debt of $505,000,000 = 8.55 to 1

2003: cash and cash equivalents of $4,232,000,000 / long-term debt of $506,000,000 = 8.36 to 1

Results for Gateway

2003: cash and cash equivalents of $349,101,000 / long-term debt of $109,696,000 = 3.18 to 1

2002: cash and cash equivalents of $465,603,000 / long-term debt of $127,118,000 = 3.66 to 1

Conclusion

Dell is in a stronger cash position and the reasoning for that goes back to our chapter on liquidity.

LONG-TERM DEBT PAYMENT RATIO

$$\frac{\text{cash applied to long-term debt}}{\text{cash supplied by long-term debt}}$$

This is an interesting ratio. It asks us, for the current year, how much cash we got by issuing long-term debt versus how much cash we had to pay out in our obligation on long-term debt. This information comes from the cash flow statement and might not be relevant if the organization did not receive any cash from long-term debt this year.

Results for Dell and Gateway

This metric does not apply to Dell or Gateway because they did not get any cash from long-term debt.

PERCENT OF CASH SOURCES REQUIRED FOR LONG-TERM DEBT

$$\frac{\text{cash applied to long-term debt}}{\text{total sources of cash}}$$

This ratio shows the proportion of cash that is dedicated to paying off debt. Necessarily, this cash will not be available for other uses, so it does not enhance the liquidity or flexibility of the organization.

Results for Dell and Gateway

Dell and Gateway did not apply any cash to long-term debt per their cash flow statements.

SHORT-TERM DEBT TO ALL DEBT RATIO

$$\frac{\text{short-term debt}}{\text{short-term debt + long-term debt}}$$

This ratio separates out short-term debt from long-term debt. Why does this matter? Well, it gives the analyst another piece of information about how the company is financed. Does it prefer to operate on short-term debt—on lines of credit, for example—or on longer obligations?

Which type of debt is more costly to the organization right now? What does this tell us about the operating philosophy of managers? (Do you get the feeling, as I do, that more often than not these ratios raise more questions than they answer? That is the nature of financial analysis.)

Results for Dell and Gateway

Dell and Gateway have no short-term debt other than accounts payables and other accrued liabilities.

LONG-TERM DEBT TO ALL DEBT RATIO

$$\frac{\text{long-term debt}}{\text{short-term debt} + \text{long-term debt}}$$

Here we are getting a sense of the proportion of long-term debt to all debt.

Results for Dell and Gateway

This metric is incalculable, because neither company discloses short-term debt.

CASH TO CURRENT MATURITIES OF LONG-TERM DEBT

$$\frac{\text{cash} + \text{cash equivalents}}{\text{current maturities of long-term debt}}$$

Now here is a specific ratio. It asks how much a company is obligated to pay on its long-term debt right now versus how much cash it has available. This gives us a sense of the organization's ability to pay. To me, this is one of the stronger ratios in this chapter—if you can get the information!

Results for Dell and Gateway

For Dell and Gateway, we cannot tell from the financial statements what portion of the long-term debt is due now. You have to be inside the organization to get this information.

FIXED CHARGE COVERAGE

$$\frac{\text{earnings before interest, taxes, and lease payments}}{\text{interest expense and lease payments}}$$

Interest and lease payments are obligations that an organization can't get out of. Organizations must pay off the interest on a loan or the bank will call the loan. They must pay their lease or they will get kicked out of their facility.

Again, this should be a multiple. Earnings should be able to cover the basic obligations—the fixed charges—of the organization many times over.

This ratio screams for customization. You can add anything you like as a fixed charge and contrast that with the earnings that will be paying the fixed charges.

Results for Dell and Gateway

We can't derive these numbers from outside the company with much accuracy. This one is a good one to calculate if you are internal to the company.

RECEIVABLES TO LONG-TERM DEBT

$$\frac{\text{accounts receivable}}{\text{long-term debt}}$$

This ratio is a little abstract. It is just another indicator of how easily the organization can meet its long-term debt obligation with current resources. Instead of using cash as a current asset, we use accounts receivable. This might make more sense for organizations that prefer to distribute cash earnings to owners and hence have a small cash balance. Accounts receivable will eventually be collected and can be used to pay the long-term debt obligation.

Results for Dell

2004: accounts receivable of $3,635,000,000 / long-term debt of $505,000,000 = 7.20

2003: accounts receivable of $2,586,000,000 / long-term debt of $506,000,000 = 5.11

Results for Gateway

2003: accounts receivable of $210,151,000 / long-term debt of $109,696,000 = 1.92

2002: accounts receivable of $197,817,000 / long-term debt of $127,118,000 = 1.56

Conclusions

Ah, finally a metric regarding debt that we can calculate! For Dell, this metric tells us that it could pay off long-term debt seven times with its current accounts receivable. Gateway could pay it off twice.

Why is this so different? Because, although both have a very small debt— $506 million for Dell and $109 million for Gateway—the relationship of the

debt to total sales is different: sales were $41 billion for Dell and $3.4 billion for Gateway. The debt is small for both, but the proportions are quite different.

So let's calculate the *debt to sales ratio*:

Dell: total debt of $13,031,000,000 / total sales of $41,444,000,000 = 31%

Gateway: total debt of $1,108,700,000 / total sales of $3,402,364,000 = 33%

Wow! Amazingly similar when you factor in accounts payable and long-term debt.

Equity Ratios

These ratios speak to issues that equity holders, shareholders, find of interest. These ratios indicate whether the company distributes its wealth or keeps it.

DIVIDEND PAYOUT

$$\frac{\text{dividends per common share}}{\text{earnings per share}}$$

Once a company starts paying dividends, equity investors come to expect it. This contrasts how much the company earned—on the bottom of the ratio—and how much it distributed to owners. This will tell you that 40 percent of the wealth was distributed and 60 percent retained, for example.

Results for Dell and Gateway

There were no common stock dividends for either Dell or Gateway.

PERCENTAGE OF EARNINGS RETAINED

$$\frac{\text{net income – all dividends}}{\text{net income}}$$

This is another way of looking at what was paid out versus what was retained by the organization.

Results for Dell

All earnings are retained, as Dell does not pay dividends.

Results for Gateway

Gateway pays dividends, but the ratio won't work because Gateway has a negative net income.

EXTERNAL FINANCING INDEX

$$\frac{\text{cash from operations}}{\text{total external financing sources}}$$

We want to generate as much cash on our own as possible, and that is what the cash from operations figure tells us. We contrast this with the cash that we generated from sources other than operations, which would include cash from financing activities and cash from investing activities.

This gives us a sense of whether the company is running on its own steam or running on the steam of external parties. Neither Dell nor Gateway has gone outside for additional financing in the past few years.

Capital Investment Ratios

REINVESTMENT RATIO

$$\frac{\text{capital investments}}{\text{depreciation + sale of assets}}$$

The point of this ratio is to give us an indication of whether the entity is keeping its capital investments fresh. The top of the ratio is what the organization spent this period on new equipment and the bottom of the ratio shows the deterioration of the equipment. Depreciation or the sale of equipment reduces the value of capital investments. This ratio would make a lot of sense to use in a capital-intensive industry, such as an airline or a steel manufacturer.

Results for Dell

I can find no data on whether Dell sold any assets.

2004: capital investment of $329,000,000 + $636,000,000 / depreciation of $263,000,000 = 3.67

2003: capital investment of $305,000,000 / depreciation of $211,000,000 = 1.45

Results for Gateway

I can't tell how much Gateway sold during the year. I see a loss on sale of asset, although I don't know the total asset value. Also, I see a write-down of long-lived assets. Both appear in the operating section of the cash flow statement.

Conclusions

This number leaped out for Dell because it paid $636 million to purchase all of the assets for which it historically had accounted as operating leases. For Gateway, we can tell nothing. So I can't judge Dell's metrics as good or bad in comparison.

CAPITAL INVESTMENT PER DOLLAR OF CASH

$$\frac{\text{capital investments}}{\text{total sources of cash}}$$

This metric is looking at the priority that the organization puts on investing in capital assets. Capital assets often mean the same thing as equipment, but it could mean facilities or software.

So, in contrasting cash and fixed assets (an interchangeable term), does it look like the organization prefers to have its assets in cash or in fixed assets? So this metric is taking two components of assets and contrasting them.

Some might view this ratio as a liquidity ratio. But because investments in fixed assets are often financed or they drive the organization to go and find financing, we are leaving it in the category of financing ratios.

Results for Dell

2004: capital investments of $329,000,000 plus $636,000,000 / total cash of $4,317,000,000 = 22 cents of every dollar

2003: capital investments of $305,000,000 / total cash of $4,232,000,000 = 7 cents of every dollar

Results for Gateway

2003: capital investments of $72,978,000 / total cash of $349,101,000 = 21 cents of every dollar

2002: capital investments of $78,497,000 / total cash of $465,603,000 = 17 cents of every dollar

Conclusions

This result for Dell concerns me—not because of the jump between years, since that is due to a one-time event of recognizing leased buildings as owned buildings, but because Dell is investing only 7 percent of its cash in capital equipment. Gateway invests proportionally more in its capital equipment. Dell might be setting itself up for rough times ahead because of antiquated equipment and facilities. At some point, it might have to increase its investment to replace that old equipment. This theme has come up before, in contrasting depreciation with total fixed assets in Chapter 17.

Conclusions on Financing

What can we conclude by looking at these financing ratios? Neither company is issuing any further debt or equity to operate, although from our profitability metrics, we might expect Gateway to have to get some external help soon. We also see that neither company is overwhelmed by debt. Debt is a small portion of the balance sheet for each.

I am concerned about both companies' capital investments. I am not sure that either company is investing enough back in itself in terms of equipment and fixed assets. Are they being cheap about those investments now to the detriment of profitability and cash flow in the future?

Overall Conclusions for Dell and Gateway

Gateway is not profitable. Its market share is slipping. Its inventory is building. It is required to make preferred dividends even when it's not profitable. So far Gateway has been able to pay its own way, by using cash generated by efficient working capital management and cash savings from prior years.

In the worst-case scenario—and you know we accountants are good at spelling those out!—if Gateway continues running at a loss, it will use up its cash reserves and have to seek external financing. If it is not profitable, debt lenders and equity investors will be reluctant to give it the money, thus costing the company more for financing and further reducing its profitability. It becomes a downward spiral.

Dell is profitable and gaining market share. Its working capital is being managed efficiently. It is able to pay its own way without the help of external financing and has a healthy cash balance. If Dell is able to maintain its profit margins, gain or maintain market share, and continue to wisely manage working capital, it is in good shape.

Both Dell and Gateway are investing minimal amounts in their infrastructure—their capital assets. This might cause them to have to make a major correction or spend quite a bit to improve capital assets in the future. This is something to look out for.

Quiz

1. What are the three ways to finance your organization?
   (a) get a loan
   (b) sell stock or a share of the organization
   (c) earn resources by selling goods or services at a profit
   (d) all of the above

2. What do banks expect in return for doing business with you?
   (a) interest
   (b) follow loan covenants
   (c) make regular, periodic payments
   (d) all of the above

3. Debt financing is often cheaper than equity financing because equity holders expect a higher return for the higher risk they are taking on.
T or F

4. Debt should be avoided at all times.
T or F

5. Equity owners are owners of the organization and have a say in how the organization is run.
T or F

6. Equity holders are rewarded for their investment in the form of
   (a) dividends
   (b) an increase in stock price
   (c) diversification
   (d) long-term strategic initiative
   (e) all of the above
   (f) a and b
   (g) a, b, and c

7. The ratio of cash to long-term debt contrasts current cash balances with all debt.
T or F

8. The ratio of cash to current maturities of long-term debt indicates whether a company has enough cash to cover current debt payments.
T or F

9. The fixed charge coverage ratio should be customized for your situation.
T or F

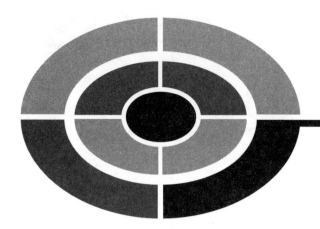

Test: Part Four

1. A company that was deciding on whether to stop offering customer relations training to its telephone sales staff would be affecting which areas of the balance scorecard?
   - (a) the financial component
   - (b) the customer component
   - (c) the learning and growth component
   - (d) all of the above

2. EBIT stands for
   - (a) earnings before interest taken
   - (b) earnings before income taxes
   - (c) earnings before interest and taxes

3. To make IRR increase,
   - (a) invest less on the front end
   - (b) get more cash out later
   - (c) spend more in outer years

4. IRR takes into account the time value of money.
   T or F

5. Ratios should be customized for your particular business.
   T or F

6. Which is a more meaningful ratio for a company that has a large investment in equipment?
   (a) return on assets
   (b) return on fixed assets
   (c) return on working capital

7. Equity tells us how much of the company the owners own through stock and retained earnings.
   T or F

8. Liquidity allows a company to respond to unexpected opportunities or needs.
   T or F

9. Rainy-day cash is
   (a) cash set aside and not used for day-to-day operations
   (b) cash used for day-to-day operations
   (c) cash used to pay long-term debt

10. The quick ratio is the current ratio refined to eliminate inventory from the calculation.
    T or F

11. Days' supply of inventory measures how many days' worth of inventory the company has.
    T or F

12. The longer the cash conversion cycle, the better.
    T or F

13. The defensive interval ratio tells us how long you could operate before running out of cash if all sales and incomes stopped.
    T or F

14. The depreciation impact ratio refines our diagnosis of what is going on in the operating cash index.
    T or F

15. The reinvestment ratio tells us whether the entity is keeping its fixed assets fresh.
    T or F

16. A growing organization will often consume more cash than it earns.
    T or F

17. A growing organization will often have to rely on outside financing—debt or equity—to run.
    T or F

18. A mature organization will be interested in harvesting as much cash as possible from the operation.
    T or F

19. A sustaining organization is looking to improve procedures and increase capacity.
    T or F

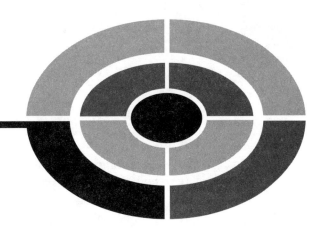

Final Exam

1. Which of the following financial statements is the supersummary of the general ledger?
   (a) the income statement
   (b) the statement of shareholders' equity
   (c) the balance sheet
   (d) the cash flow statement

2. Which of the following statements discloses the total amount of fixed assets held?
   (a) the income statement
   (b) the statement of shareholders' equity
   (c) the balance sheet
   (d) the cash flow statement

3. Which of the following statements contains the proverbial "bottom line"?
   (a) the income statement
   (b) the statement of shareholders' equity
   (c) the balance sheet
   (d) the cash flow statement

4. Which of the following statements was created and required as a result of the savings and loan crisis of the 1980s?
   (a) the income statement
   (b) the statement of shareholders' equity
   (c) the balance sheet
   (d) the cash flow statement

5. Which two statements tell us information about an entity's liquidity?
   (a) the income statement and the statement of shareholders' equity
   (b) the income statement and the balance sheet
   (c) the income statement and the cash flow statement
   (d) the balance sheet and the cash flow statement
   (e) the balance sheet and the statement of shareholders' equity
   (f) the cash flow statement and the statement of shareholders' equity

6. Which of the following statements contains the term "gross profit"?
   (a) the income statement
   (b) the statement of shareholders' equity
   (c) the balance sheet
   (d) the cash flow statement

7. Which of the following statements is divided into three sections—the operating section, the financing section, and the investing section?
   (a) the income statement
   (b) the statement of shareholders' equity
   (c) the balance sheet
   (d) the cash flow statement

8. Which of the following statements discloses the organization's total amount of debt outstanding?
   (a) the income statement
   (b) the statement of shareholders' equity
   (c) the balance sheet
   (d) the cash flow statement

9. Which of the following statements discloses operating expenses?
   (a) the income statement
   (b) the statement of shareholders' equity
   (c) the balance sheet
   (d) the cash flow statement

10. Which of the following statements is refreshed or zeroed out at the beginning of each year?
    (a) the income statement
    (b) the statement of shareholders' equity
    (c) the balance sheet
    (d) the cash flow statement

11. Which of the following statements discloses the ending balance of inventory?
    (a) the income statement
    (b) the statement of shareholders' equity
    (c) the balance sheet
    (d) the cash flow statement

12. The classic accounting equation is
    (a) assets = short-term liabilities plus long-term liabilities
    (b) assets = working capital less equity
    (c) assets = liabilities plus equity

13. To increase an asset account, you record a debit to the account.
    T or F

14. To increase a liability account, you record a credit to the account.
    T or F

15. Banks talk about debits and credits from their perspective, not the perspective of their customers.
    T or F

16. Which of the following is a correct entry when you purchase a desk for $250 cash?
    (a) DR Fixed Assets $250   CR Cash $250
    (b) DR Cash $250   CR Fixed Assets $250
    (c) CR Fixed Assets $250   DR Accounts Payable $250

17. Which of the following is the correct entry when you sell a product on credit for $30?
    (a) DR Products $ 30   CR Cash $30
    (b) DR Accounts receivable $30   CR Finished goods inventory $30
    (c) DR Accounts receivable $30   CR Cash $30

18. Which of the following is the correct entry when you collect on the receivable mentioned in question 17?
    (a) CR Products $30   DR Cash $30
    (b) DR Finished goods inventory $30   CR Accounts receivable $30
    (c) DR Cash $30   CR Accounts receivable $30

19. When you incur an expense, you debit the expense account.
    T or F

20. Net worth, stockholders' equity, and fund balance are all similar concepts.
    T or F

21. Which of the following is the most liquid?
    (a) building
    (b) inventory
    (c) cash
    (d) accounts receivable

22. You should have as large a balance as possible in working capital.
    T or F

23. Which of the following elements of working capital would you prefer to have a large balance?
    (a) inventory
    (b) accounts payable
    (c) accounts receivable

24. Which of the following balance sheet items should be as small as possible?
    (a) inventory
    (b) accounts payable
    (c) fixed assets
    (d) depreciation

25. What is a disadvantage to financing your operation with debt?
    (a) you must pay interest
    (b) you must make periodic payments
    (c) you must comply with bank covenants
    (d) all of the above

26. What is a disadvantage to financing your operation by selling stock?
    (a) you must give up control over key decisions
    (b) you may experience pressure to be profitable in the short term at the sacrifice of long-term goals
    (c) you may be obligated to pay dividends
    (d) all of the above

27. How does the income statement link to the balance sheet?
    (a) through the cash account
    (b) through the retained earnings account
    (c) through the fixed asset account

28. How does the cash flow statement link to the balance sheet?
    (a) through the cash account
    (b) through the retained earnings account
    (c) through the fixed asset account

29. Which financial statement primarily focuses on profitability?
    (a) the income statement
    (b) the balance sheet
    (c) the statement of retained earnings

30. Amortization is the term used to describe the depreciation of intangibles.
    T or F

31. Accumulated depreciation is subtracted from total fixed assets to result in net fixed assets on the balance sheet.
    T or F

32. The proportion of accumulated depreciation to total fixed assets can indicate the age of the fixed assets.
    T or F

33. The book value of fixed assets is always the same as their market value.
    T or F

34. Venture capital must always be paid back to the investor within two years.
    T or F

35. The accrual method of accounting causes cash to equal profit at all times.
    T or F

36. The cash method of accounting is used when you have receivables and payables.
    T or F

37. A budget is
    (a) the translation of the future plans of the entity into financial terms
    (b) operating expenses decreased by 10%
    (c) a listing of all of the expenses of the entity

38. ABC stands for
    (a) action-based communication
    (b) activity-biased costing
    (c) activity-based costing

39. An example of a direct cost is
    (a) advertising
    (b) marketing
    (c) accounting
    (d) electricity
    (e) components

40. A variable cost stays the same no matter how many units you produce.
    T or F

41. Zero-based budgeting is a technique you should use every year.
    T or F

42. Performance-based budgeting links strategic plans with the budget.
    T or F

43. Often, the budget system is kept separately from the general ledger system.
    T or F

44. The frequency and accuracy of financial information will cost you time and money.
    T or F

45. A government should have only one general fund.
    T or F

46. In which of the following fund super-categories should you put a pension trust fund?
    (a) governmental
    (b) proprietary
    (c) fiduciary

47. In which of the following fund super-categories should you put an enterprise fund?
    (a) governmental
    (b) proprietary
    (c) fiduciary

48. In which of the following funds should you put an internal service fund?
    (a) governmental
    (b) proprietary
    (c) fiduciary

49. Which of the following are examples of situations where a government might use a special revenue fund?
    (a) when the government collects tax on gas to fund highway construction
    (b) when the government receives a federal grant
    (c) when the government assesses income tax and uses it for a variety of purposes
    (d) a and b
    (e) b and c

50. What do governments call their income statement?
    (a) an income statement
    (b) a P&L
    (c) a statement of revenues, expenditures, and changes in fund balance

51. The following are aliases for the income statement:
    (a) the profit and loss statement
    (b) the P&L
    (c) the statement of earnings
    (d) the statement of shareholders' equity
    (e) all of the above
    (f) a and d
    (g) a, b, and c

52. Not-for-profits always follow GASB rules.
    T or F

53. FASB stands for
    (a) the Financial Auditing Standards Board
    (b) the Financial Accounting Standards Board
    (c) the Federal Accounting Standards Bureau

54. The SEC was created after the Enron debacle.
T or F

55. The balanced scorecard is a general ledger system.
T or F

56. The balanced scorecard tells us that successful finance is just the result of doing other things right.
T or F

57. One of the four areas of the balanced scorecard is ethics and environment.
T or F

58. The 10-K is a quarterly document submitted by governments to the SEC.
T or F

59. Which of the following sections of the 10-K is a narrative describing the financial results of the organization over the past few years?
    (a) the auditor's opinion
    (b) the notes to the financial statements
    (c) quarterly breakout
    (d) Management's Discussion and Analysis

60. The notes the financial statements are written in simple, lay terms.
T or F

61. The number of shares outstanding appears in the 10-K
    (a) in the notes to the financial statements
    (b) on the cash flow statement
    (c) on the cover

62. The auditor can express which of the following opinions?
    (a) qualified
    (b) adverse
    (c) clean
    (d) all of the above

63. One of the flaws of general ledger information is that it is historic—or a little old—by the time it gets to decision makers.
T or F

64. Common size analysis on an income statement would make which of the following numbers 100% of the total?
    (a) gross profit
    (b) cost of goods
    (c) net profit
    (d) gross sales

65. Horizontal analysis makes every line on the base year 100%.
    T or F

66. Ideally, the company maintains or improves on the proportions or percentages disclosed by doing a common size analysis each year.
    T or F

67. A common size analysis can easily be depicted as a pie chart.
    T or F

68. The three concerns of financial ratios are
    (a) liquidity, profitability, and financing
    (b) liquidity, financing, and debt
    (c) debt, equity, and cash flow

69. The quick ratio is the same which ratio minus inventory?
    (a) the current ratio
    (b) the sales to asset ratio
    (c) the earnings per share ratio

70. Gross profit margin percentage will always be higher than the operating margin percentage.
    T or F

71. Earnings per share is a favorite ratio of investors.
    T or F

72. Working capital is
    (a) current assets minus cash
    (b) current assets minus liabilities
    (c) current assets minus current liabilities

73. DSO stands for
    (a) days sales over
    (b) days supply outstanding
    (c) days sales outstanding

74. DSI is expressed in
    (a) days
    (b) turnover
    (c) percentage
    (d) whole number

75. The cash conversion cycle equation is
    (a) DSO – DSI + DPO
    (b) DSO + DSI – DPO
    (c) DSO – DSI – DPO

76. The shorter the cash conversion cycle the better.
    T or F

77. Which of the following is a liquidity metric?
    (a) DSI
    (b) EPS
    (c) ROIC

78. Which of the following is a liquidity metric?
    (a) current ratio
    (b) quick ratio
    (c) DSO
    (d) all of the above

79. The accounting model is perfect and will never experience a revision.
    T or F

80. When you purchase a fixed asset for cash and capitalize that asset, which of the following financial statements is/are affected on the first day of purchase?
    (a) the balance sheet
    (b) the cash flow statement
    (c) the income statement
    (d) all of the above
    (e) b and c
    (f) a and b

81. When you sell a product on credit, which of the following financial statements is/are affected?
    (a) the balance sheet
    (b) the cash flow statement
    (c) the income statement
    (d) all of the above
    (e) b and c
    (f) a and c

82. LIFO stands for
    (a) last in, first over
    (b) late in, first out
    (c) last in, first out

83. What do accountants call your inventory when you are still manufacturing it?
    (a) finished goods
    (b) raw materials
    (c) work in process
    (d) incomplete
    (e) undone

84. At the end of the year, accountants must adjust the books to
    (a) increase revenues as much as they can
    (b) write off as many expenses as they can
    (c) realize that they owe vendors even though the vendor has not sent a bill

85. Which of the following is a common year-end adjusting entry?
    (a) cash
    (b) long-term debt
    (c) accounts receivable

86. The accrual method of accounting asks us to record expenses that we owe but have not yet paid in cash.
    T or F

87. Before you begin a financial analysis, you should gather which of the following information?
    (a) competitors' financial statements
    (b) historical data on the organization
    (c) market share data
    (d) all of the above

88. The owners of a not-for-profit are the people it serves.
    T or F

89. An encumbrance is when a government spends more than it has.
    T or F

90. The feds love it when you commingle their grant funds with other funds.
    T or F

91. The FASB sets standards for the way financial ratios and metrics should be calculated for public companies.
    T or F

92. EBIT stands for
    (a) everything before income taxes
    (b) earnings before income taxes
    (c) earnings before interest and taxes

93. The sales to fixed asset ratio indicates
    (a) how well the organization is using its fixed assets to generate sales
    (b) how fast sales are created after adding new equipment
    (c) how old fixed assets are

94. R&D stands for
    (a) return and deliver
    (b) return and depreciation
    (c) research and development
    (d) research and depreciation

95. IRR takes into account the time value of money.
    T or F

96. ROI takes into account the time value of money.
    T or F

97. EVA is expressed
   (a) as a percentage
   (b) as a whole number
   (c) in days
   (d) in dollars

98. To get IRR to be higher,
   (a) invest less in the project
   (b) wait until the end of the project to generate a return
   (c) generate less income than cash

99. Debt is inherently bad.
    T or F

100. Which of the following ratios would indicate whether the organization had enough resources to pay its debt?
   (a) gross profit margin
   (b) cash to current maturities of long-term debt
   (c) earnings per share
   (d) return on investment
   (e) DSO

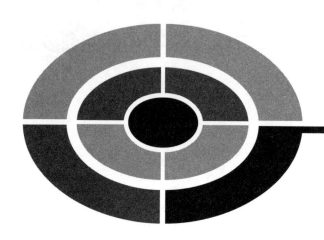

Answers to Quiz, Test, and Exam Questions

CHAPTER 1

1. d	3. F	5. c	7. d	9. d	11. b
2. c	4. b	6. b	8. d	10. a	

CHAPTER 2

1. b	3. c	5. d	7. b	9. b
2. a	4. F	6. F	8. F	10. b

CHAPTER 3

1. d	3. T	5. g	7. c	9. F
2. c	4. c	6. a	8. f	10. b

CHAPTER 4

1. F	3. b	5. a	7. T	9. a
2. F	4. a	6. F	8. g	10. e

CHAPTER 5

1. e	3. c	5. a	7. a	9. e	11. e
2. c	4. c	6. a	8. c	10. g	12. d

TEST, PART ONE

1. b	6. c	11. a	16. a	21. c
2. d	7. b	12. a	17. b	22. c
3. a	8. a	13. a	18. b	23. c
4. c	9. c	14. a	19. c	24. F
5. d	10. a	15. e	20. c	25. T

CHAPTER 6

1. T	3. F	5. T	7. F	9. g
2. F	4. b	6. d	8. c	10. i

CHAPTER 7

1. b	3. T	5. F	7. T	9. T	11. c	13. T
2. F	4. e	6. d	8. F	10. c	12. a	14. T

TEST, PART TWO

1. F	3. c	5. b	7. F	9. T	11. b
2. F	4. F	6. e	8. c	10. F	

CHAPTER 8

1. T	3. e	5. T	7. F	9. F
2. c	4. F	6. F	8. F	10. T

CHAPTER 9

1. T	3. T	5. T	7. T	9. T
2. F	4. T	6. T	8. F	10. T

CHAPTER 10

1. F	3. c	5. F	7. F	9. F
2. F	4. b	6. T	8. F	10. a

CHAPTER 11

1. b	4. c	7. F	10. T	13. T
2. b	5. a	8. T	11. c	14. a
3. c	6. F	9. b	12. F	15. T

CHAPTER 12

1. a	6. c	11. F	16. T	21. F	26. b
2. a	7. F	12. T	17. a	22. T	27. T
3. T	8. T	13. T	18. T	23. F	
4. c	9. c	14. F	19. T	24. T	
5. F	10. a	15. c	20. T	25. F	

TEST, PART THREE

1. f	5. a	9. b	13. T	17. T	21. F
2. F	6. c	10. F	14. T	18. d	
3. g	7. T	11. F	15. F	19. F	
4. f	8. F	12. T	16. T	20. T	

CHAPTER 13

1. F	3. F	5. b	7. F	9. T
2. F	4. T	6. e	8. e	10. T

CHAPTER 14

1. e	5. b	9. f	13. a	17. d
2. T	6. c	10. T	14. T	
3. T	7. e	11. b	15. d	
4. T	8. T	12. T	16. See below	

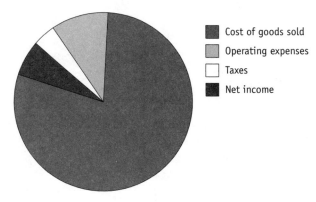

Cost of goods sold
Operating expenses
Taxes
Net income

CHAPTER 15

1. d	3. b	5. b	7. a	9. F
2. c	4. c	6. a	8. d	10. c

CHAPTER 16

1. b	3. T	5. b	7. a	9. a
2. e	4. F	6. a	8. f	10. F

CHAPTER 17

1. b	3. T	5. a	7. b	9. F
2. F	4. b	6. T	8. F	10. a

CHAPTER 18

1. d	3. T	5. T	7. F	9. T
2. d	4. F	6. e	8. T	

TEST, PART FOUR

1. d	5. T	9. a	13. T	17. T
2. c	6. b	10. T	14. T	18. T
3. a	7. T	11. T	15. T	19. T
4. T	8. T	12. F	16. T	

FINAL EXAM

1. c	21. c	41. F	61. c	81. f
2. c	22. F	42. T	62. d	82. c
3. a	23. b	43. T	63. T	83. c
4. d	24. a	44. T	64. d	84. c
5. d	25. d	45. T	65. T	85. c
6. a	26. d	46. c	66. T	86. T
7. d	27. b	47. b	67. T	87. d
8. c	28. a	48. b	68. a	88. F
9. a	29. a	49. d	69. a	89. F
10. a	30. T	50. c	70. T	90. F
11. c	31. T	51. g	71. T	91. F
12. c	32. T	52. F	72. c	92. c
13. T	33. F	53. b	73. c	93. a
14. T	34. F	54. F	74. a	94. c
15. F	35. F	55. F	75. b	95. T
16. a	36. F	56. T	76. T	96. F
17. b	37. a	57. F	77. a	97. d
18. d	38. c	58. F	78. d	98. a
19. F	39. e	59. d	79. F	99. F
20. T	40. F	60. F	80. f	100. b

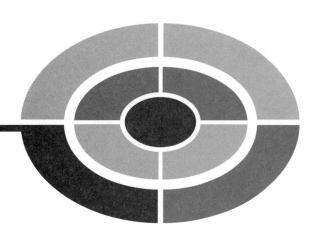

Further Reading

The Balance Sheet Barrier (video), 2nd edition, Video Arts Ltd., London, 1993.

Case, John, *Open Book Management*: *The Coming Business Revolution*, HarperBusiness, New York, 1995.

Hart, Leita, *The Four Principles of Happy Cash Flow™*, FantaSea Press, Austin, TX, 2004.

Harvard Business Review on Measuring Corporate Performance, Harvard Business School Press, Boston, 1998.

Mullis, Darrell, and Judith Orloff, *The Accounting Game: Basic Accounting Fresh from the Lemonade Stand,* Sourcebooks, Inc., Naperville, IL, 1998.

Siegel, Joel G., Jae K. Shim, and Stephen W. Hartman, *Schaum's Quick Guide to Business Formulas: 201 Decision-Making Tools for Business, Finance, and Accounting Students*, McGraw-Hill, New York, 1992.

Stack, Jack, *The Great Game of Business*, edited by Bo Burlingham, Doubleday Currency, New York, 1992.

Tracy, John A., *The Fast Forward MBA in Finance*, 2nd edition, John Wiley & Sons, Inc., New York, 2002.

INDEX

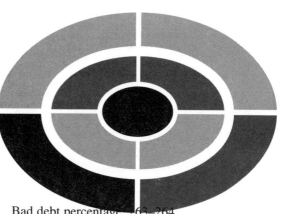

Note: Boldface numbers indicate illustrations.

About the Author

Leita Hart makes finance fun and easy. She is a certified public accountant and a certified government financial manager. She is the author of *The Four Principles of Happy Cash Flow* and *STEP-by-STEP Building a Persuasive Audit Report*. Leita has developed and taught over 20 courses on finance, auditing, balanced scorecard management, and business writing. She writes for two monthly e-zines for auditors and the accounting challenged. To find out more about her and to subscribe to her e-zines, please see her Web sites at www.happycashflow.com, www.leitahart.com, and www.auditskills.com.